W9-BSA-753

American History — British Historians

American history provides superb material for comparative study by British scholars. British Americanists are too introspective. We need a unifying concept into which American history can be fitted, and that is the comparative concept. Comparative studies of American history can be as well done by British Americanists as by any other group of scholars, and they probably can be done better by them in fact.

William R. Brock

The perspective that characterizes the British Americanist is very important and useful, but I do not look upon British Americanists as a race apart. Interchange of ideas and research results between American and British historians is vital, no less so because of the friendships involved.

H. C. Allen

American History—British Historians

A Cross-Cultural Approach to the American Experience

David H. Burton, *editor*

Nelson-Hall, Chicago

For information address Nelson-Hall Inc., Publishers, 325 W. Jackson Blvd., Chicago, Ill. 60606.

Manufactured in the United States of America

LIBRARY OF CONGRESS CATALOGING IN PUBLICATION DATA

Main entry under title:

American history—British historians.
    1. United States—Historiography—Addresses, essays, lectures.   2. United States—History—Addresses, essays, lectures.   I. Burton, David Henry, 1925–
E175.A45   973'.07'2   76-8458
ISBN 0-88229-280-3

To
Lady Arthur

the daughter of Sir Cecil Spring Rice,
both great friends of America

ACKNOWLEDGMENTS

Grateful acknowledgment is made to the following for permission to reprint previously published material:

Denis W. Brogan, "The Character of American Life," *America in the Modern World* (New Brunswick, N.J., 1960), pp. 44–63. Reprinted by permission of Rutgers University Press.

J. R. Pole, "The American Past: Is It Still Usable?" *Journal of American Studies*, vol. I, no. 1, pp. 63–78. Reprinted by permission of Cambridge University Press.

A. E. Campbell, "The Past as Destiny: American History and American Culture," Inaugural Lecture, University of Birmingham, March 1, 1973. (Birmingham, The University Press, 1974). Reprinted by permission.

H. C. Allen, "The Cultural Tie," *Conflict and Concord, The Anglo-American Relationship Since 1783* (New York, 1959), pp. 129–140. Reprinted by permission of St. Martin's Press, New York.

Herbert G. Nicholas, "The Wartime Alliance and After," "The Cold War and After," *Britain and the U.S.A.* (Baltimore, 1963), pp. 32–57. Reprinted with the permission of the author.

Jim Potter, "Some British Reflections on Turner and the Frontier," *Wisconsin Magazine of History*, vol. 53, Winter 1969–1970, pp. 98–107. Reprinted with permission of *Wisconsin Magazine of History*.

John White, "The Novelist as Historian: William Styron and American Negro Slavery," *Journal of American Studies*, vol. IV, no. 2, pp. 233–245. Reprinted with permission of the Cambridge University Press.

William R. Brock, "The Nature of the Crisis," *An American Crisis: Congress and Reconstruction 1865–1867* (London, 1963), pp. 1–14. Reprinted with permission of St. Martin's Press, New York.

J. A. Thompson, "American Progressives Publicists and the First World War, 1914–1917," *The Journal of American History*, LVIII, 2, September, 1971, pp. 364–383. Reprinted with permission.

Esmond Wright, "Lincoln Before His Election," *American Profiles* (Edinburgh and London, 1967), pp. 64–82. Reprinted with permission of the author.

David Nunnerley, "JFK: Assassination, Martyrdom, Impact," *President Kennedy and Britain* (New York, 1972), pp. 219–223; 229–236. Reprinted with permission of the author.

A. E. Campbell, "The Nature of the Rapprochement," *Great Britain and the United States, 1895–1903,* reprinted by permission of the reprint publisher, Greenwood Press, a division of Williamhouse-Regency Inc.

Philip S. Bagwell and G. E. Mingay, "Social Progress 1850–1939," *Britain and America: A Study of Economic Change* (London, 1970), pp. 216–238. Reprinted with permission of the authors.

Contents

ix

Preface

When, in 1907, Theodore Roosevelt, Henry Cabot
Lodge, and Elihu Root joined in presenting a silver loving
cup to Sir George Otto Trevelyan in tribute to the author
of *The American Revolution,* Trevelyan replied: "The cup
is a noble piece, and the simplicity and singular beauty of
proportion struck us much and impressed us with the notion that there must be much artistic feeling among the
silver workers of America." At that point in historiography,
the American Revolutionary War came to an end, though
the spirit of Paul Revere may have suffered some disquiet.
Ever since Trevelyan's famous book an increasing number
and variety of British scholars have been writing knowingly
about America. Yet their work is perhaps insufficiently ap-
preciated. In *American History—British Historians* the findings of a number of representative British authorities have
been brought together as an offsetting factor in this likely
deficiency. Valuable as individual commentaries on different aspects of the American experience, these writings, when
taken in sum, provide an added dimension to the historiography of the United States.

A word or two needs to be said about the choice of the
particular selections used in *American History—British His-*

torians. Rare indeed must be the editor who is able to include the exact selections, as to content and number, which might be thought to serve his purposes ideally. Copyright complications, a ceiling on permissions and general production costs, and a format, sooner or later determined upon, singly or collectively, can prevent the inclusion of certain items which the practiced eye might notice. Such at least has been the experience out of which this collection has grown. Happily, all the selections were among the more than thirty items chosen before the winnowing process began. Unhappily, several important historians are not herein represented, though mention has been made of them and their works in the list of suggested readings. But, hopefully, the chief purposes of this anthology have been served: to alert interested parties to the writings of British authorities, to allow them to sample some examples of these writings, and thus to encourage further exploration of British reflections on the history of the American people.

This collection would not have been possible without the generous cooperation of the historians themselves. In consequence, I am indebted to all of them, an indebtedness I am anxious to acknowledge. This is a good occasion to thank as well The English-Speaking Union of the United States, Philadelphia Branch. Much of my firsthand awareness of the British Americanists on their home ground I gained while an E-SU Churchill Traveling Fellow in 1972. Especially do I want to salute the memory of the late Leslie Woods of the E-SU who, so long as he lived, lent me his ardent support. In addition, Mr. John Russell, a trustee of the Keasbey Foundation, was ever helpful and kind in giving me letters of credence to a number of British scholars. I must also express my appreciation to the Board of Faculty Research, St. Joseph's College, which helped me with timely leaves and useful grants, and to the president of the college, Reverend Terrence Toland, S.J., who concurred in the wisdom of the board's recommendation.

Thanks are due to Fred and Margaret Drew and to Eric and Audrey Matkins; in many ways they helped to make stays in Britain the half holiday which never fails to produce the full day's work. Finally to Antoinette, Monica, and Victoria R., my daughters and to Gerri, my wife, I shall be grateful always for sharing with me "England and all that."

Introduction

One of the frequent criticisms of American historiography is that it has been dominated by American scholars, and in consequence it lacks the leaven of foreign perspectives. Given the growth of the United States over nearly two hundred years as well as its position in the contemporary world, this deficiency is, at first glance at least, a puzzling fact. Few names of non-American historians of the United States come readily to mind, while even the specialist might be hard-pressed to identify more than a handful of foreign authorities on various aspects of our past. Moreover, the condition seems destined to persist, despite the appearance from time to time of new books by non-Americans. Race, rights, and reform offer some attraction to foreign experts in United States history and recent books on slavery, immigration, and women's rights suggest that these topics have an intrinsic appeal to the outside observer. The over-all results are disappointing, however. Though American history books by non-Americans no longer are celebrated by critics as *tours de force*, the relatively meager number of scholarly studies appearing reenforces the impression that non-Americans are unlikely to produce worthwhile treatments of America's past.

The "mystique" of the great American experiment, planted in the soil of the Enlightenment to flower in the next two centuries, undoubtedly has given rise to the view that only Americans themselves, nurtured in a unique tradition, can hope to understand and interpret accurately their national heritage. Consistently enough, it is Americans who are today busy analyzing, discussing, and making judgments about the end of the experiment and the death of the American dream, though such an intriguing proposition is sure to gain some non-American notice as well. In the words of Sigmund Skard, a leading Norwegian authority on America, the "New World always had an air of the strange and fantastic" for Europeans. America was the thing apart, the schoolroom for the world, so that American history has come to occupy an extracomparative place in the historiography of modern times. And just as little insight is to be realized, for example, in treating the politico-economic reform movement in the United States at the turn of the present century by analyzing it with reference to similar movements in other industrial countries, so Europeans in particular and non-Americans generally can make but a negligible contribution to unraveling the threads of the past, to fathoming the depths of American history. Or so the thesis runs. It is not simply that European intellectuals have failed to find American history interesting or the achievement of American historians very significant. There is something in the total American experience which lies beyond the grasp of non-Americans. A young Max Beloff made his confession in 1948 in the preface to his *Thomas Jefferson and American Democracy* when he admitted "for a non-American to attempt to enter the field of American historical writing betrays some degree of timerity."

From a very early time Americans have looked inward upon themselves, the moral counterpart of facing inward upon the continent to conquer and civilize it. This is an important reason why Americans can be especially sensitive to strictures offered by foreigners, and somewhat dubious about studies of their country if done by others. It may very well suggest why Americans who write of their country's past tend to see it exclusively in its own terms. But this does not explain why foreigners, seeking to cast light on American history, constitute so limited a number. Admitting the self-evident proposition that most of the history of a nation will be written by its own citizens, still we are aware of cross-cultural interpretations within and without the European community.

Americans, for that matter, have made valuable contributions to the histories of many countries in Europe and elsewhere in the world, silently bringing American perspectives to much of this work. But why the lack of non-Americans in the United States history field, especially since America and the Americans have such a fascination for the rest of the world when we speak of contemporary events? The answer is bound up with the American myth. One European scholar concluded: "The myth about America which we cultivate in Europe has a psychological reality which is much more important to us than the so-called truth about America." Perhaps, as Skard has observed, the current development of American Studies programs in many European countries is due to "the continued growth of realism and enlightened self-interest toward America in European minds." These programs therefore may produce a generation of scholars for the future. But for the present, American history continues to elude most Europeans and the rest of the world as well. The non-American scholars, in other words, have accepted the basic thesis as operational: only Americans ordinarily possess the appropriate psychological preparation to write the history of their own country.

One exception to the operation of this thesis is British interest in American history. As a genre of historical writing, it is not old, no more than two generations of scholars having arisen. Nor is it overly impressive in the size of its membership, including perhaps a dozen or more historians of wide repute out of the approximately 250 faculty who teach courses in American history at the university level. Yet within the ranks of the British Americanists are some brilliant historians whose writings, when taken together, amount to a collection remarkable for its quality. H. C. Allen, Marcus Cunliffe, Frank Thistlethwaite, Esmond Wright, the late D. W. Brogan, and the late John Hawgood were among the early leaders in the field and their work, along with that of Max Beloff, William Brock, A. E. Campbell, Charlotte Erickson, Maldwyn A. Jones, Herbert G. Nicholas, and J. R. Pole, is widely regarded. More to the point, the writings of such British Americanists offer a substantial source of cross-cultural interpretations of United States history—a much needed leaven in the loaf—and thus the best test of the value of American history written by a single group of non-Americans.

For a long time now, people have spoken of a "special relationship" existing between the United States and Great Britain, not alone because of blood and institutional ties but due also to the shared experience of two great wars. This special relationship however, whether real or imagined, should not be seen as militating against the prospects of a genuine cross-cultural interpretation of American history by British experts. Such factors as language and law, it is true, have worked to create what one early twentieth-century English editor, St. Loe Strachey of *The Spectator*, termed a "sympathy of comprehension." For historians the special relationship has come to mean that Americanists in Britain enjoy, in the phrase of Herbert Nicholas, Rhodes Professor of American History at Oxford, a "natural advantage." Because of the kinship of Britain and the United States, the British historian working in the field of American affairs has a singular perspective on past events in the United States. By his examination of the American record he may understand better the meaning of these events than

selves. William Brock of the University of Glasgow explained his position and outlook as a British Americanist
with an economy of words when he said, "I do not like to
think of myself as a British historian who happens to be
doing American history, but rather as an historian of America who has something to say because he is non-American
and because in addition he is British."

Nevertheless the belief is unanimous among the British
Americanists that the two cultures remain fundamentally
and pervasively distinct, whatever sympathies exist. Unlike
Canada or Australia, for example, where the ties with Britain have been maintained closely at many levels, the United
States has a history and a way of life recognized by British
Americanists as *sui generis*. Thus the question can be posed
in concrete terms: has American historiography been influenced—enriched or redirected—by the cross-cultural interpretations of the British? From this a second question arises
which has wider implications: are there certain ingredients
characteristic of cross-cultural interpretations of history
that can be derived in no other way, evidences of which
are identifiable in the scholarship of the British Americanists? Answers to these questions can be gained by considering
the worth of some of the leading British views of the history of the United States set forth in the pages which follow.

No band of brother British Americanists could be said
to have existed until the close of World War II. Before
then, from time to time, an individual scholar tried his
hand at American history. G. O. Trevelyan wrote a notable
multivolume account of the American Revolution in the
years prior to World War I and its Whiggish outlook lent
fresh perspectives to the Revolutionary Era. In the early
1920s, the well-known Oxford historian, H. E. Egerton,
contributed new slants to the same period in his book, *The
Causes and Character of the American Revolution*, while
budding authorities like D. W. Brogan and John Hawgood

were beginning to make felt a British presence in American history writing just before the outbreak of World War II. After 1945, momentum gathered and within a decade British Americanists had come into their own. By the mid-1950s American history study was planted firmly in British university soil, with books like H. Hale Bellot's *American History and American Historians* helping to show the way. The appointment of H. C. Allen to the Commonwealth Fund Chair for American History in the University of London was something of a milestone, with other chairs provided at Manchester, Birmingham, Hull, Leeds, and Sussex. In his inaugural address at London, Allen offered his own estimate of the surge of interest in United States history: "None of the European powers has anything like the influence over us exerted by America and her history, happily, we can more readily understand because she is truly blood and mind of the West. It does not always seem to me," he went on, "that even yet the full extent of this influence has finally sunk into the British consciousness, but the fact can not be altered by failing to look it in the face." As study of American history continued to grow with the advent of the 1960s, it was also aided by the expansion of the British university system. It seems hardly coincidental that today three of the strongest centers for the study of United States history—Sussex, East Anglia, and Keele—are all post–World War II foundations. As these centers prospered, more American history was written, leading to an increased contribution by British authorities to an understanding of the history of the United States.

The pattern of the writing as it unfolded was a logical one. At first the Anglo-American connection was examined with the intention of telling the story of relations between the two countries and of suggesting influences which one nation had brought to bear on the other. In essence, this amounted to renderings of diplomatic history along conventional lines. Much of this early writing was inspired by a sincere admiration for the United States and something of a determination to foster goodwill between the two academic communities. The research at this stage of growth was thorough and the conclusions illuminating. Allen's book, *Great Britain and the United States: A History of Anglo-American Relations, 1783–1952,* is a good example of this approach. It established a line of inquiry which Americans no less than Britons began to pursue. Among the best of the British studies was *Great Britain and the United States, 1895–1903* by A. E. Campbell. Campbell not only wrote perceptive diplomatic history but foreshadowed later comparativist developments. A variety of seeds had been cast down in fact, which would come to different flower as a younger generation began to come forth.

The maturing of American history writing in Britain witnessed a swing toward investigations of some of the components of that history, especially the periods of Civil War and Reconstruction along with the Progressive Era, all branching into problems of race, rights, and reform. William R. Brock's *An American Crisis: Congress and Reconstruction 1865–1867* is representative of this kind of component history along with Esmond Wright's *The Fabric of Freedom* and *American Immigration* by Maldwyn A. Jones. During the 1960s, the British view continued to flesh out as well as to take on a new dimension, *viz.*, comparative Anglo-American history. In this last phase, the demands placed on the British Americanists were severe. What was required was an intimate knowledge of British and American events and institutions so that a comparative study might be launched with subtlety and restraint so as not to exaggerate the common elements or belabor the conclusions. Nonetheless the growth of this third stage, as it drew on the results of the first two, was inevitable. "It is apparent to some of us, and I believe, will become obvious to all in the next few years," wrote J. E. Morpurgo, an Americanist at the University of Leeds, in 1971, "that the prime emphasis of British-based American study must be on comparison and the consideration of interaction."

This comparative method has come to take an increasing share of the attention of the working British Americanists. Indeed, as such studies grow in number they may come to constitute the truly unique contribution of the British scholars to American historiography. Important new ground was broken in this regard by J. R. Pole's treatment of Anglo-American representative institutions, *Political Representation in England and the Origins of the American Revolution,* published in 1966. Pole's was a major achievement in comparative Anglo-American history by a British authority, demonstrating the immense potential of this species of historical interpretation. Its significance becomes more apparent when it is realized that American historians have themselves somewhat neglected the comparative methodology, though in the area of Anglo-American writing there are some outstanding exceptions like Richard Dunn and Bradford Perkins. Further British efforts in comparative analysis are likely to stimulate more exploration of this fruitful avenue of research.

Throughout the development of a body of historical literature dealing with the American experience, British scholars in essays and in books have endeavored to isolate and identify the main features of "the American character," just as they have sought to come to some accurate and meaningful conception of America in history and in the contemporary world. In summary, writings of the British chiefly fall into four distinguishable categories, usefully summed up as "conceptions," "connection," "components," and "comparative analysis." These categories are linked together by common content and the common concern of the British Americanists for the history of the United States. The most recent writings emanating from Britain continue to emphasize all four approaches, thus containing the potential for shaping our understanding of our own history in those areas where the British Americanists see fit to concentrate.

An Overview

*Sir Denis W. Brogan**

The Character of American Life

No British historian studied the American people longer, gave their history more attention, spent so much time investigating his subject firsthand, or displayed a more kindly attitude in the process than did the late Denis Brogan. He was among the first of his generation to recognize why the history of the United States ought to be studied seriously in Britain. In the essay that follows, conscious comparisons between American and European societies constitute a recurring and valuable theme. No doubt some of what Brogan observed will show the effects of time, as this interpretation was offered originally in 1960. But the reader may be more impressed by how so many of the author's judgments remain entirely appropriate today after one of the most hectic eras in American history. One of these unique and seemingly permanent aspects of the American character is the businessman's mentality. Brogan contended that the rest of the world finds it difficult to comprehend fully the American theory of economic gain, no less than Americans fail to sympathize with this

*Sir Denis W. Brogan (1900–1974) was a Fellow of Peterhouse and Professor of Political Science at the University of Cambridge.

inability to see the American business outlook as integral to what the United States really is. By focusing on the businessman, Brogan reasserted the significance of that peculiarly American species. Was Sir Denis echoing Calvin Coolidge who insisted that "the business of the United States is business"? Or is it that both Coolidge and Brogan agreed on this as a basic fact of the American character?

I am only too conscious of the boldness, the absurdity, of undertaking to say anything of interest or even of minimal good sense on so vast a topic as the character of American life. Despite the boldness of my title, I am more timid or more sensible than may appear and what I propose is to attempt something bold enough in itself and yet more practicable than the vast adventure which my title might suggest.

I shall begin by saying that there are vast areas of American life that I shall ignore. Most of what may be called political economy I shall slip away from. I have no doubt that the economic problems of the farmer are deeply important and reveal something of the character of American life, but I shall do no more than bow at the problem, be silent on the solution, and deal with the farmer only as part of the rapidly changing panorama of American society. There is the role of American women; I shall not ignore it entirely, but again there are many problems concerned with her status, her social and economic role that I shall ignore, both from timidity and from wisdom. For example, I shall not develop my belief that the American woman is to some extent a victim of a confidence trick played by the American man—who is much smarter than the American woman realizes and gives to her more the appearance than the reality of power and equality.

I shall try to say something positive, but I shall try to pick on *some* salient marks of American society, of American life, both for their intrinsic interest and for their relevance to my basic theme—the competitive strength of the United States in the dangerous world in which it now has to live.

That is to say, I shall make some parallels with European society, stressing resemblances as well as differences. And I shall try to weigh some features of American life, if not quite like an observer from outer space at least with the comparative objectivity of a foreigner.

Comparative objectivity, for it would be idle to pretend that I come here as a stranger or a neutral. If I may be permitted some autobiography, I first came to the United States nearly thirty-four years ago when I had just left Oxford, having created some scandal there by insisting on going to America to study the scarcely respectable subject of American history. I have visited America nearly every year since; I even managed to make three visits during the war, and I have sometimes made more than one visit in a year. Altogether I have spent six or seven years in this country and its study has been my chief academic and literary activity since I first came here, an innocent pilgrim, in the golden day of Calvin Coolidge. I come not really as a neutral but as a most friendly observer who has tried hard to understand this country and to pass on what knowledge he has acquired to his often moderately receptive countrymen. Whatever I do, however hard I try to be the stern impartial critic, friendliness and optimism will keep creeping in.

Catholics talk of the "marks" of the Church and I should like to begin by describing some of the marks of American society as I see them. First I shall follow in the footsteps of my great predecessor, Alexis de Tocqueville, and stress the mark of equality. No one not blinded by prejudice, no one knowing Britain or France or Germany, can fail to be struck by the fact that "equality" is as much a distinguishing mark of American society as it was one hundred thirty years ago when Tocqueville made his famous journey.

True, there are apparent differences. There are far more rich people today than there were then; there are many more millions of Americans who can be classified as part of *le peuple*, as Tocqueville's countrymen put it then and now. Economic inequality is more visible now than it was then. Then, if we believe Tocqueville, the rich rather concealed their wealth and if they enjoyed it they enjoyed it in secret. They played it down if they wished to enter politics and an ostentatious display of democratic tastes was called for in candidates for public office. It would be wrong today to deny that candidates profess an enthusiasm that may be genuine for hot dogs and blintzes, for baseball and basketball. But few doubted in 1958 that Governor Harriman or Nelson Rockefeller normally lived on rather more sophisticated diet than what may be called electoral nutriment or that, if they had democratic tastes, they also had tastes whose gratification required very large incomes. There is no cheap, democratic way of collecting French Impressionists, no really democratic way of playing polo; and it is notorious that ex-Governor Harriman and Governor Rockefeller are more than comfortably off and that other governors, many senators, and even a few lesser public figures are at least comfortably off. It may not help them politically (I refuse to speculate) but it does not visibly hurt them. The American voter has got used to economic inequality and no longer resents it in itself. Nor does he resent even the most outrageous display of conspicuous consumption by what is called, I believe, "café society," except possibly when he is paying his modest income tax and wondering what it is like to have a really fat expense account. The popular idols of the screen, the stage, and TV are expected to show appreciation of their good fortune by garish display, and even in contemplating the Texas oil millionaire who can't have a swimming pool because every time he builds one he strikes oil, the American is inclined to say "Nice work if you can get it" rather than "Workers of the world, unite."

My examples of an American attitude have not been chosen quite at random or to provoke easy laughter. Behind them lies an American attitude that Tocqueville did not stress, although I find it hard to believe that it was not visible in his time and it is certainly very visible and worth noting in our time. The United States is a country in which simple jealousy plays a comparatively innocuous and unimportant role in political and social life. Note I do not say in private life. I have read too many powerful novels, too many reports of murder trials when all went black and there on the floor was a dead husband or wife, not to know that Americans are subject to the human if ignoble emotion of jealousy just like other people. But if Americans can endure or even accept with ease a great deal of economic and social inequality in public life, in economic life, in sport and diversion, it is in great part because of the absence of jealousy in the American attitude.

No one who has moved around in England, France, or Germany can doubt that in all these countries jealous, resentful envy is an important source of political animus and of national disunion and weakness. Why is America different?

I shall advance a thesis that is not very novel and not very profound, but has, I think, the advantage of making this important difference appear not simply as an inexplicable difference or even as a proof of American stupidity and gullibility. (If the American common man knew his business as a common man, he would be jealous. So many a European intellectual argues—though perhaps not quite in those words.)

The American political and economic environment has been from the beginning unkind to pretensions that did not have some apparent relation to achievement either in the present or in the recent and what may be called the "usable" past. It is a commonplace of American historiography that all attempts to export feudalism failed. The European entrepreneur who wanted to turn his assets into a political and social superiority that he could leave to his family was making a mistake if he took his capital to British North America. For various reasons that I can do no more than allude to, it proved impossible to set up a hereditary landowning or office-owning class to which admission would be slow, irregular, and not important enough in numbers to flood the existing class structure in each generation to a degree that would destroy its exclusiveness.

I hasten to say that I am not under the illusion that there are no social fences in America, no social barriers that are hard to pass, no cult of exclusiveness. Indeed it could be said that some American social groups are more exclusive than their European counterparts, less willing to admit the promoting power of money. I have lived in Boston and visited Philadelphia!

But even in their great days, the Back Bay and the Main Line were not accepted as their English or French and, still more, German equivalents were, as part of the nature of things. They were picturesque anomalies with, I suspect, more power to bruise than to hurt seriously and less power to give pleasure and comfort than the aspiring climbers hoped. What was and is the use of being admitted to an exclusive society if the vast majority of those excluded don't really care or, what is worse, don't really know that they are being excluded?

The very emphasis on barriers, on clubs, on fraternities, on exclusive schools and pools reveals a social order in which equality is constantly intruding, in which it takes a lot of money and energy and, I should suggest, a high degree of humorlessness, to get men and women to take the trouble to exclude and to include on any grounds but those of social fitness and utility and personal attraction. An English student from Oxford or Cambridge, introduced to the full rigors of the secret society system at Yale, is astounded and amused or horrified, according to temperament and political bias. But if he is a good observer and remembers Oxford or Cambridge when he is at Yale, he will, I think, be forced to conclude that Yale, for all the mystery of Bones, is more democratic than either Oxford or Cambridge, where the barriers are less visible, less stressed but far more difficult to surmount and far more wounding to fail to surmount. I have deliberately chosen an academic example, partly because I know both Oxford and Cambridge well and have seen something of Yale, but partly because it is in the American school system, in its widest sense, that equality and inequality fight a perpetual battle which inequality always loses.

Elsewhere I shall suggest that this is not always a good thing, but it is sufficient for the moment to note that economic inequality in America has, in the main, only economic consequences. As Scott Fitzgerald put it in his celebrated dialogue with Hemingway, "The rich are not like us." "Yes, they have more money," said Hemingway. I would be the last to deny that having more money is important; but having less money is even more important, for the poor suffer from their poverty more than the rich gain from their wealth. Yet in America merely having more money pays less in extra dividends, less in bought servility, less in reverence or its opposite, envious rancor, than it does in any other country known to me.

Because it is assumed (often wrongly) that wealth represents past or present useful service to the economy or, what the average man appreciates quite as much, the democracy of more luck—more luck in striking an oil well, more luck in answering in the dear dead days the $64,000 question—the American takes inequalities in his stride. He may be a victim of an illusion. He probably exaggerates, if not for himself, then for his children their chances of promotion in the economic and social scale. He may neglect the power of the power elite in a naive way. He may even think that his political rights give him in the mass some control over the power elite, and that money and the control of the economy are not everything (in my opinion

he is right in so thinking), but here we are concerned not
with his intelligence, his power of judgment *sub specie
orbis*. A man who feels happy is happy; a man who is contented, by and large, has in that attitude a source of happiness that is not to be neglected or despised. In the pursuit
of happiness the race may be to the swift and the handi-
capping not quite just, but it is an asset for a country that
the race is believed to be so open that nearly everybody
wants to run in it.

This attractiveness of the race accounts for the good
temper with which, in general, its results are accepted as
beneficial, which is a great social asset. If the contentment
of the American were a passive contentment, if it were contentment not with the general system but with his particular place in it, as has often been the meaning of contentment in torpid, tradition-ridden societies, then much could
be said for stirring up discontent, divine or simply human.
But I think it can hardly be denied that one source of American wealth has been the belief in the rewards of economic
virtue and the adequate correspondence of that belief with
the facts.

Turning for a moment to the outside world, it must be
stressed that the role of this competitive spirit, this American theory of the economic game, is not fully understood
anywhere else and over a great part of the world is not
understood at all. Contemplating the American economic
miracle, the European and still more the Asian or the African is not as a rule willing to allow for the role of the businessman or to accept the fact that to get his particular type of
social usefulness he must be willing to ignore formal economic equality or the pretense of it, must be willing to
accept in their role as entrepreneurs some very rough dia-
monds and perhaps some persons who are not even semi-
precious stones. The European, the Asian, the African, in a
descending order of comprehension, find it hard to believe
that the highest virtues and the highest talents can possibly

be observed in a man who devotes the greater part of his life to the accumulation of wealth.

But one will rightly protest, the American businessman as a type does not devote himself to the accumulation of wealth as such; he devotes himself to the production of wealth and his share in it, handsome as it may be, is only a legitimate price for what he gives society in his pursuit of the satisfactions of the business life. This I believe to be true. But at the risk of seeming to lay down general laws that cannot be proved, I shall assert that this acceptance of the business life as one worthy of calling out all the powers of a really able man, giving him the satisfactions of a really worthy lifework, may not be solely American but it is peculiarly American. And it is one of the reasons why America is so wealthy and so comparatively free from the crippling social barriers and social resentments of Europe.

Maurice Zinkin has argued that what India needs is more good businessmen and more respect for good businessmen. I believe this is true also of Britain and even of that businessman's paradise, Western Germany. To be epigrammatic at the risk of seeming foolish, I should say that outside the United States more respect for business achievement is needed and inside the United States one should, without losing one's natural respect for the businessman for what he does well, be more willing to accept the possibility that there are things well worth doing that businessmen cannot do and that cannot be done in a "businesslike way."

Given the American experience, where most successful social enterprises have been run by businessmen for businessmen (and for the economy in general as well), it is natural that this experience should be extended to the outside world. But, in the first place, it is too simple a view of American history to see the growth of the American economy as taking place without political direction, without the state's playing more than a minor or a positively nefarious role. The American businessman owes both the existence of his opportunities and the character of his opportunities to the success of the United States as a body politic. The existence of the Union was necessary in order to create the American market and so was its maintenance. Thus Madison and Hamilton, Lincoln and Grant—none of them, not even Hamilton, a business type—are among the most potent makers of the American market and so of the American economy in which the American businessman has flourished.

I shall dogmatically assert that a Lincoln is not only a more interesting but a much more important figure than a Ford or a Rockefeller. Someone would have invented the equivalent of the Model T or the Standard Oil Company. But Lincolns are scarcer and in 1861 the United States could not have afforded to wait until the turn of the wheel brought up an equivalent of Lincoln and put him into the White House. This is the first important modification of the exalted picture I have honestly painted of the role and the utility of the American businessman. He has played so useful a role and his role has been so handsomely rewarded in cash and credit that he has naturally been tempted to exalt himself even above his merits, which are great, and by implication to denigrate other groups whose essential services to the American experiment have been as great but not so well rewarded as those of the businessman.

The businessman has as a rule taken an ironical view of the politician. He has seen him as a parasite, as a tool, sometimes as a demagogic nuisance who has to be fought or bought off or suffered not in silence but in noisy wrath. He has contrasted the things that business does (and usually does well) with the things the political organizations have done—at every level, city, county, state, nation—and has stressed the things that these political units have done badly—and there are many of them. He has tended to forget that not all businesses have been well run; the bankruptcy courts show that.

The history of American railroads is not an argument for leaving all to the businessman and if some of the energetic men who made great fortunes out of the railroads were national benefactors, some were morally on the level of Jesse James and charged a high price for their services, a high price in money and a higher price in damage to the social and political fabric. I am aware that things have changed, that the days of the robber barons are over or almost over (it is harder to be a robber baron than it used to be; there are more policemen of various kinds). But even if we believe all that business tells us about itself—and I don't believe quite all of it—we have to remember that in many parts of the world the robber barons are still with us and are not, even in the kindest and most generous eyes, as much builders as were some of the most rapacious of the leaders and makers and exploiters of the American economy of the second half of the nineteenth century.

The American businessman, looking abroad and conscious of the services he renders (and charges quite highly for), is liable to ignore important facts about the outside world, facts that alter the picture he paints for himself and imposes on the American government, facts that demand a toleration of "unbusinesslike" methods that shocks the doctrinaires of "free enterprise." If the United States is going to have an economic foreign policy, it will have to deal with societies in which there is no business class or a disastrously rapacious and incompetent business class and in which the only substitute for the absent competent businessman is the state. And the state may be the only competent manager of large-scale enterprise that the country in question either has or can hope to have in the not-unlimited time of competition with the rival Soviet system. This is, I think, the case in India and will continue to be the case in the critical years in which the fate of India—and more than the fate of India—will be decided.

Thus the exaltation of the businessman in the United States, the belief that the standards of the American business economy are easily exported and that there is something sinful in not admitting this fact, is a great handicap to the government of the United States in its economic foreign policy. It may be necessary to strengthen "socialist" economies, to accept irritating political controls, to tolerate what are, objectively, absurdly wasteful ways of doing things simply because the world happens to be like that and most foreign societies have no choice: they have no more right to have an effective business class than they have to have an equivalent of Niagara Falls or of the Grand Canyon.

It is only partly a paradox to suggest that the American businessman (who sets the tone of a great deal of American life though perhaps not quite so much as he thinks and as his predecessors did) is too modest. He underestimates his own uniqueness. And when painful experience teaches him that the business methods of other societies are very different from and very inferior to his, he is less prone to go up to the altar of the temple and thank God that he is not as other men than to think up ways of converting the inferior European or Asian or African model into a 100 percent imitation of the 100 percent American businessman.

This generous ambition is a foolish one. Though the American businessman is less conscious than he should be of his unique character, he is more conscious than he should be of his unique role in making the American way of life that business has so deeply and, on the whole, so beneficially marked. For the American economy is only a part of the American way of life; the American businessman is only one of the makers of the American economy. I have already alluded to the role of the politician in making and preserving the Union. But I would rank as equally important the role of the politician in producing the illusion (which has,

I hold, often been the reality) of a nonbusiness power that could protect the average man both in his interests and in his sentiments. The democratic way of life, American version, has been largely a matter of making—not final, not profound, not revolutionary—adjustments in the way in which the American economy was run, adjustments that for a great part of its formative period, made the necessary harshness of that economy tolerable and did not destroy the faith of the average man in the American way. For there is apparently no way in which an economy can make the take-off, to use Professor W. W. Rostow's admirable metaphor, that does not involve suffering, injustice, flagrantly unequal ways of paying the costs, and the destruction of old and comforting habits.

The histories of Britain and the United States, of the Soviet Union and Communist China alike tell this story. That the story as told in the United States has been one of a continuing faith in the American process is due, as much as to any other group, to the much-maligned politicians who, high as was their price, delivered the goods, the climate of opinion, of generosity, of admiration for achievement in which the American businessman has flourished. And to return to my first theme, the American businessman has been the chief but not the sole maker of the American economic way of life and deserves half the praise he gives himself; and this is, I suspect, about the amount of praise that the American nonbusinessman gives him in his friendly but rather skeptical fashion.

Now, dealing with the marks of American society, it is necessary to say something of the mark that the American politician represents. Earlier I spoke of the special service, the fundamental service that the politician has rendered in creating and preserving the Union and in creating the climate of opinion in which the businessman has been able to work with such success. I now want to describe briefly not only the achievement of the politican but his methods, the peculiar contribution he makes to the American way of doing things and the revelation of the character of American society that this political way provides.

I have alluded to the low ideological content of American party politics and have indicated my doubts as to whether the United States would gain by adopting rigorously doctrinaire systems of party differentiation and organization. Here I shall take it for granted that a political system which organizes democratic choice of persons and, very loosely, controls pressures from one group or another, serves a useful purpose and preserves a higher degree of human values than does the rival and in many ways efficacious system that we call communism. For communism, we must remember, is a *political* solution to the economic problem of the forced-draft progress of a backward agrarian society into the modern technological society. It is the political omnipotence of the Russian Communist party that accounts for Sputnik, as well as for the now visible economic progress to the threshold of abundance that marks the Soviet Union.

The problem in a sense is the same everywhere. How is one to provide the necessary political authority without which the jump over to the more abundant life, to Professor Galbraith's affluent society, cannot be made? Within wide political controls, often intermittent in action, the American method has been to leave the specifically economic problems to a specifically economic class and to leave the organization of consent to this delegation of power and the tempering of its results to a specifically political class. The two classes, naturally, are never in a state of complete harmony or mutually supporting cooperation. There is almost always an imbalance and one can, I think, see two such imbalances in recent American history: in favor of politics under Presidents Roosevelt and Truman; in favor of business under President Eisenhower. Neither imbalance was necessarily wrong, at the time it occurred, and I ostentatiously refrain from asserting that either was necessarily right.

But, given this distribution of functions and this imbalance, what has been the peculiarly American character, the American mark of the American politician? It has not been true all the time that the American politician was not a doctrinaire. Jefferson was one of the most skilled, perhaps the most skilled, of American politicians but he was by temperament a doctrinaire. There was a basic unshakable bias in Lincoln, a bias in favor of human as against legal or property rights, a conviction that some institutions, however respectable by age, however plausible their claims as practical solutions, were wrong. But, like Jefferson, Lincoln was what is called a "practical politician." He worked, and knew he could only work, in the terms given by the American situation. Also, Lincoln was more self-critical than Jefferson and carefully distinguished between his public and his private duties and feelings. Neither was prepared to let the best be the enemy of the good. And in this sense of realities, in this readiness to separate the ideal from the immediately attainable, these two great Americans were representative and serviceable American politicians. They bear the American mark.

At the other end of the scale, we have the moral equivalents of the "robber barons"—the city and state bosses. These, in their scientifically purest form, emptied politics of any trace of ideology that might have been found in it. Their allegiance to one party rather than the other— Democratic in New York, Republican in Philadelphia— was purely formal, purely traditional, and there is no known instance of their sacrificing their own interests and that of their organizations to the remote principles and needs of the national parties. Yet these odious figures played a useful, though expensive, part in the adjustment to the often painful and novel necessities of the American way of life of the millions of immigrants who provided the necessary labor force on whose blood, sweat, and tears the American economy was erected. The bosses may not notably have diminished the blood and sweat, but they did diminish the tears. They made the new society intelligible, tolerable, and gave it a human aspect, including in that aspect the very human attribute of erratic and all the more welcome favor.

That the bosses overcharged for their services is not to be doubted. They were brothers under the skin of the magnates who also overcharged but, like them, did in fact give much in return. And as in the parallel case of the business magnates, the greatest cost was not the cost in dollars, it was the cost in faith in the honest purpose of government, in the rational basis of society. If the average American still finds it difficult to take the purposes and practices of government seriously, or to understand European faith in the potentialities of government, that is part of the price paid for the rule of the bosses and for their utility (which I do not deny was real). And since there are a vast number of things that should be done, even in the United States, and that can be done only by state action, the price is still being paid. If this leads to the postponement of necessary action in the public sector, it may in the world we must live in have a very high price indeed.

But between the great national figures and the mere bosses there lay and still lies a useful and necessary class— the politicians, who are more than mere manipulators of consent though less than statesmen of long and adequately profound views. Because they are not doctrinaire, they are taken more seriously than if they set forth a system of coherent or allegedly coherent doctrines in the European fashion. That the American does not take intellectual coherence seriously enough is a proposition I shall advance in another context. But here I am concerned with a particular fact about American life, a mark of American life. That mark is the readiness of Americans to do things, to try experiments even though total consistency would debar them from trying the experiments, since they are often inconsistent with what is alleged to be the basic and unbreakable principle of American life.

For if principles will not break they will bend, and how adroit the American politician is in bending them! How many Americans appreciate enough the astonishing ingenuity of the primary system? When the late Idaho Republican Senator William Borah laid it down that, even if a candidate advocated the nationalization of the means of production, distribution, and exchange, if he had won in a Republican primary he was a Republican, he turned with great boldness the flank of the unideological party system and made it possible for all doctrines to be advocated without any basic doctrines being called in question —or observed. Needless to say, there is an ugly side to this flexibility.

"You can have fascism in the United States. Only you must call it antifascism." This alleged saying of the late Huey Long has about it an ominous ring of plausibility. Coming from a continent which has pursued consistency to the edge of suicide regarding a rival society that has not yet found a way of escaping from crippling and dangerous dogma, where it is still necessary in fact to find a harmony between the needs of the world of Sputnik and the H-bomb and the systematic intuitions of a man (Karl Marx) who died before the invention of the internal-combustion engine or of an economically effective dynamo, it is hard not to prefer the American way.

If there has been anything to worry about in the state of the American public mind in the past few years, it has been a tendency to react along doctrinaire lines, to be blinded by phrases, by slogans, by the erection of the slogans into systems of political action. Lincoln, Jefferson, Boss Tweed, and Senator Borah would have, in different ways, protested against this bad and new habit, and in our rapidly changing world to react to the doctrines and actions of the adversary merely on a plan of negation and contradiction laid down in advance is to be profoundly anti-American. But I firmly believe that the pragmatic genius of the American people will come to the rescue. So will the boredom of the American people with an attitude that does not pay off quickly and that calls for a degree of doctrinal rigidity which comes hard to the people who have taken the simple political structure of 1789 and have made of it a "more perfect union" than any Hamilton dreamed of.

Now to conclude. I have had to put on one side one of the most visible marks of the American genius, the proliferation of private organizations that strikes even a visitor from England with surprise and strikes a Frenchman or a German with far more surprise. These societies, service clubs, churches, organizations for all conceivable and some barely credible projects have been since Tocqueville's time a mark of American society. And they have, usually in a more respectable way, done much the same kind of service as the political machines. (I say usually, because a body like the Ku Klux Klan is very American. Even the Mafia has taken on an American covering, and what could be less ideological than the higher direction of the Teamsters?)

The societies, secular as well as religious, have mediated between the vast, formal, often apparently inhuman claims of the "American way of life" and the harassed, intimidated, bewildered private citizen. They have also provided a channel for the zeal and energy of countless men and women whom the mere politics of the regular parties repelled or bored. To keep so much zeal from going sour is no small contribution to the commonwealth! And in the endless combinations and permutations of American societal life, the American is made to feel and act as a social and not as a merely economic or political animal. His total role in life has been enriched, even by intrinsically foolish activities.

Even the busybody is better than the type that the Greeks called "the idiot," the citizen who had no interest in the well-being of the commonwealth. To be a member of a society is as much the mark of the American as any I can think of. I can only note the fact and promise to deal with one or two aspects of it at another time.

But as I have expounded my, on the whole, optimistic view of the marks of American society, I have been conscious of some natural skepticism: "Hasn't he read Riesman?" "Hasn't he read *The Organization Man?*" "Doesn't he know that the young today eschew the life of action and its risks and seek, in the womb of Big Business or Big Government, the security that they crave? What is the use of stressing the virtues and even the vices of traditional American polity when it is being changed visibly and at high speed under one's eyes?"

I have read both Mr. Riesman and Mr. Whyte; I have observed some of these phenomena for myself. I think that American society and, notably, American education require a great deal of rethinking in theory and in practice. I am aware that the high degree of mutual toleration that marks the class structure of contemporary America is, for some, simply a proof that the American people can be bought off by a share in the more abundant material life, that this toleration may not survive a serious falling in economic well-being and that, as has been asserted, it is paid for very highly by the universal acceptance of a gadget-and-gimmick civilization. Socrates thought the unexamined life not worth living but the unexamined life is the American life of the current American ideal—if it can be dignified by such a noble name.

So runs the argument of the devil's advocate. I do not deny its plausibility or its important element of truth. But the "organization man" is not the only type of American nor even the only type of American businessman and he is not, as commonly pretended, the whole man of the organization chart. The organization ideal takes less out of a man and uses up less of the whole man than did the simple ferocious life of the businessman in pursuit of "the bitch goddess, Success" a generation ago. And the results of this loss of the full measure of devotion are, on the whole, good.

The United States is now affluent enough, if not to afford all that Professor Galbraith wants, at least to afford far more laziness and consequent opportunity for reflection than any past American generation has known. There may be a falling off in economic drive and productivity, but the competition to which I constantly refer is not only in material well-being but in real or alleged goods of the spirit, of what we loosely call culture. "Things are in the saddle, and ride mankind" was written a century ago. Was Emerson describing his age or prophesying ours? I think he was doing both, and one cure for some current pessimism is to look back at the plausible descriptions and predictions of doom that previous generations have listened to, with half an ear cocked and half a complete dose of faith in the prophets. I have no belief that American productive capacity and genius is in for any serious decline. My fears are of the direction that may be given to that capacity and genius.

If American society preserves, in necessarily modified forms, the marks that I have sought to identify, it will survive its ordeal. I think it can do now without bosses. Business will never again have and never again should have its old immunity from criticism and control. The national government will never be "cut down to size" in face of the political power of the Soviet Union and Communist China. The day (I am ready to say, alas!) is to the strong, the united, the politically dominated. But American society has immense historical as well as physical resources. If it can assess those assets correctly and take corrective action, it will hold its own in the battle that is a battle for mankind's hopes as well as its fears.

If America can hold her own can she fail, in a not-limitlessly remote future, to win? For the "new man the American" represents not only a unique historical experience but an intrinsically attractive type of human possibility. If you (and we in Western Europe are included in that "you") can survive the immediate and terrible crisis that faces all of us we shall find much working for us in men's minds and hearts. If we and you deserve leadership, it will be offered to us. And one of the ways that we can deserve it is for each of the countries of the Western alliance to hold to that which is good in its own traditions. If Americans do that, intelligently, the battle is more than half won and a great part of that half is, to be sure, in our own hearts, that we believe in and trust our way of dealing with the human situation. So far we have no need to fear comparison or competition.

Conceptions
of
American History

*J. R. Pole**

The American Past: Is It Still Usable?

J. R. Pole has been one of the most influential contributors to British interpretations of American history over the past decade. In the article reprinted here, he discusses a major problem of United States history as written by Americans. Pole terms this the need to respect the integrity of the past by avoiding interpretations which assume that specific past issues remain alive and arguable today. This British historian deplores the "instrumentalism" of many American historians. As he points out, much of the difficulty arises from the American tendency to be pragmatic about most things, not excluding scholarship. What good is a study of history if one cannot put that study to immediate, practical use? Pole advises that the past be accepted as it is, or as it was. If there are lessons to be learned, so much the better; but such should not be the avowed or the ulterior purpose of the historian from the outset. He prefers American colonial history as done by Perry Miller to that of Parrington who often used the past to moralize about his own times. Pole concludes his analysis on an unambiguous note: "Time ... is the element with which many

*J. R. Pole is a Reader in American History, Churchill College, University of Cambridge.

American historians have the greatest difficulty in coming to terms." One question which inevitably comes up from considering this essay is whether Americans, as a rule, are able to avoid a resort to instrumentalism as they write the history of their own country.

The past, in the course of its ever recurring encounters with the demands inflicted on it by the present, enjoys one inestimable advantage: it cannot answer, it is not even listening. "We ask and ask, thou smilest and art still," we might almost say, giving to Arnold's ponderous lines a touch of unintended meaning. In spite of appearances to the contrary, even the American past is in the same position. Even after the lapse (the "revolution," as Gibbon would have said) of more than three and a half centuries of continuous settlement, the historian who has been educated entirely in the tradition and the environment of the United States needs rather more than his European contemporary's normal degree of subtlety if he is to free himself from the peculiarly American version of the space-time continuum.

Those Virginians who still talk about Mr. Jefferson as though he might, at any moment, train his telescope on them from Monticello, the distinguished historian of Reconstruction who, emerging from a southern archive and blinking at the day's newspapers, felt a momentary uncertainty as to which century he was actually in or whether any time had passed, the politicians who invoke the ideals of the Founders as though these gentlemen, if alive, would not in fact be over 200 years old and possibly beyond giving a useful opinion, are all inhabitants of this remarkable continuum, this eternal triangle of space, time, and political ideology. It is as though any part of the continent, and any period, could be visited simply by virtue of the efficiency of the tourist trade. Although the people who lived in earlier centuries may, by some accident in the providential design, be technically dead, they remain to a peculiar degree the property of their heirs and successors; what one misses is that sense, inescapable in Europe, of the total, crumbled irrecoverability of the past, of its differentness, of the fact that it is dead.

This situation makes room for, and indeed it partly results from, the persistent force of what may well be called the American extension of the Whig interpretation of history.[1] In its cruder recent forms this attitude has been given by some of its critics the inelegant name of "presentism"; by which is meant that the historian plants his own political values, or those which he thinks belong to his own time, in the minds of the people of the past, and approves of their achievements or judges their shortcomings according to these present-day standards. There are, of course, a number of variants, connected in part with varieties of temperament, and in large part with the prevailing political controversies amid which the historian has found himself; but the Whig interpretation, in American hands, has always taken the view that the United States as a nation was responsible for the preservation and advancement of certain ascertained values, and hence to discover, record, and celebrate these values was the peculiar duty that the historian owed to his country.

It would be impertinent to suggest that the Whigs have had it all their own way. But patriotic history has almost always been identical with Whig history, and these two strands had an early meeting in the work of George Bancroft.[2] Bancroft, it is true, did not succeed in getting the story of America beyond the Federal Convention of 1787, but he was himself a Jacksonian politician and a dedicated Democrat, and it was he who gave the most effective impetus to the idea that American history should be celebrated as the triumph of democratic principles.

It follows that the works of American politicians and others must be evaluated according to their contributions to the advancement of those principles. Those who obstructed, or who saw their problems in some different light, or who sought a path that went over a precipice—these are mere historical curiosities: what defines them is that by the final test, that of democratic success, they are not truly American. It is the fate of the Loyalists, the Federalists, the Confederacy; if some historians of the New Deal have their way it may even prove the fate of the Republicans; even the Antifederalists have only narrowly escaped it.

Before the end of the nineteenth century, the issues of contemporary politics had begun to suggest the need for some redefinition of the actual objects of American democracy; and it was as a consequence of these conflicts that historians who were themselves dedicated to the Progressive movement began to forge American history into an instrument of political action. The immense, almost oppressive veneration for the Constitution, its use by the courts as itself an instrument of capital against labour, and the bitter strife that had grown up as a result of recent economic development—these things make it seem inevitable that social scientists and even historians should have begun to marshal their own resources on the side of reform. They knew what they were about and soon began to get the feeling of the resources at their disposal; certainly they were not driven blindly into this position by the circumstances of their times. The functional application of historical writing was deliberately proposed in 1912 by James Harvey Robinson in the cause of liberal reform;[3] and was carried forward by a giant stride with the appearance, the next year, of Beard's tract on the economic motives of the framers of the Constitution.[4]

This famous tract performed a service of intellectual liberation that was very badly needed, but it did more than that: by virtue of innuendoes whose implications Beard disclaimed, and by the selection of evidence to support a specific conclusion, it inflicted on more than a generation of historians an excessively narrow view of the issues and an almost unavoidable necessity to take sides in a controversy that even now is not fully worked out. Beard, of course, was striking a powerful blow, not at the Constitution of 1787 but at the Constitution in 1913; and this motive gives the clue to the instrumentalist direction that American historiography was to extract from its Whig foundations. Each stage in the argument was proposed, not by a question (in Collingwood's manner) but by an objective: the significance of the whole procedure being that the objective lay in the historian's own contemporary social and political interests rather than in those properly pertaining to the past.

Instrumental historians gained their sense of direction from social conflict. But in the intellectual development of their views of the nature of historical thought they owed a great deal to European as well as to American philosophy. The leading European influence was that of Benedetto Croce, who as a young man in the 1890s turned against the traditions of positivist realism and whose mature philosophy embraced history as a mode of the historian's own thought—a procedure that tied it down as an expression of "present" experience. American instrumentalists saw in this thesis the justification for their own obvious relativism: if their historical thought were relative to their own values and interests, so had been those of all their rivals and predecessors! The reception of Freudian psychology, which began early in the century and had great influence in the 1920s, seemed to those who were inclined to read it in that light to go still further towards justifying a psychology and hence a philosophy of subjective and therefore relativist values. On the American side lay the active influence of the specifically 'instrumentalist' philosophy of John Dewey.[5]

Beard himself had absorbed much of the feeling of the American Populists and had adopted much of the method learnt from Marx. His instrumentalism, however, is characteristic of that of his more orthodox contemporaries in his method of selecting a simple dichotomy of opposed forces. The broad and rough outline of a division, discernible in the later eighteenth century, between mercantile and agrarian interests, became for Beard a precursor of the class war; the immense weight of landed interest that was thrown behind the Constitution could be by-passed as simply irrelevant to his view of what the struggle was all about. In lining up the two sides Beard assumed that the mercantile and moneyed interests, because "capitalist," were conservative, and by inference opposed to the democratic principles of American progress; which meant that the agricultural interest was also the popular and democratic side in the struggle. The fact that the leadership and probably the bulk of the agrarian interests were in important respects profoundly conservative, while the capitalists were, in an economic sense, dynamically progressive, was overlooked because it was irrelevant to the particular conflict on which his attention was riveted.

It was consistent with this method that when Beard came to the Civil War and to Reconstruction he applied a similar analysis, and that he and his disciples discovered in the capitalist North an aggressive business spirit whose interests explained the Radical Republican programme and their victory in the elections of 1866.[6] The Civil War itself was interpreted as a collision between the capitalist North and the agrarian and basically feudal South—an extension of the dualism that Beard had found earlier in American history. It is perhaps odd that Beard, who wrote with great insight about the clash of interests in politics,[7] and who virtually discovered the 10th Federalist, should have yielded his powerful intellect so easily to the idea of a recurring dichotomy that he virtually overlooked the pluralistic nature of American politics.

These remarks are not made here for the sake of reviving controversies or reviewing the now familiar ground on which Beard and his disciples have grappled with their opponents, but to indicate one of the most persistent styles in American historiography. Running through all the grades of this style, a strand that is at once utilitarian and populistic seeks to explain to a sceptical audience that the justification for the study of history is practical; it helps us to understand the present, and can become, in dedicated hands, an instrument of action.

The most extreme statement of this instrumental view of history came, not from the Progressive Movement, but from Conyers Read, in his Presidential address to the American Historical Association in 1949.[8] In a candid and unusual bid to qualify as the Zhdanov of the profession, Read disparaged both the work and the interests of those dedicated historians who take the past seriously for its own sake. "It is the rare bird," he said, "who is interested in the past simply as the past—a world remote, apart, complete, such as Michael Oakeshott has envisaged." Read took the view that the liberal age, "characterized by a plurality of aims and values," was a thing of the past, and that "we must clearly assume a militant attitude if we are to survive." This militant attitude involved the organization of resources and the disciplined interpretation of history towards the propagation of American doctrines. "This sounds," he added, "like the advocacy of one form of social control as against another. In short, it is. But I see no alternative in a divided world." His reassurance that his concept of control meant "no menace to essential freedoms" could hardly have satisfied those whose views and interests might have run the risk of proving inessential.

In a subtler form, the instrumentalist version of the Whig tradition reappeared among certain historians whose early political memories were those of the New Deal. Arthur M. Schlesinger, Jr., whose *Age of Jackson*[9] remains after twenty years a work of extraordinary vitality and intelligence, quoted Franklin D. Roosevelt in his preface and argued explicitly that Roosevelt had carried forward a process which Jackson had inaugurated, but which had subsequently been submerged by other issues. It would not be altogether unfair to Professor Schlesinger (at any rate when he wrote *The Age of Jackson* at twenty-eight) to say that in his view the forces on the other side, the Bank of the United States, or the combinations of monopoly capitalism, represent reaction in much the same sense that the Roman Catholic Church represented reaction to earlier historians of Protestantism; and that the Democratic side, which happily emerges as the winning side, is the more American.

Historians of different temperament have always known that there was an alternative to all this. It begins with a fundamental respect for the integrity of the past in which the instrumental view has no place because its aims are irrelevant. It approaches the subject-matter of history without intense presuppositions and with a mind in which convictions (however strongly held) about right and wrong have been subordinated to a profound curiosity as to what was thought about right and wrong in the period under scrutiny. It places a deep absorption in the substance and detail of history on a higher level of priority than the principles which it expects to discover; it starts, of course, with a hypothesis but this hypothesis is almost invariably modified if not abandoned in the course of the research.

The results often tend to be less spectacular and less susceptible of literary grandiosity than those of the progressive, or reactionary, instrumentalists. Yet they are worth noting, because, if they are properly understood, they not only come nearer the truth but they change the message received at this end of the line. Vernon L. Parrington, a literary historian whose work was an outstanding example of the Progressive school, thought that an early example of political progressiveness was to be discovered in Roger Williams, the founder of Rhode Island. Under this impression, Parrington chose to interpret Williams's

work as being inspired by political interests and the ideals
of democracy. But Professor Alan Simpson, in an article
which should be carefully read for its general as well as
its immediate reflexions, went back to the texts of Roger
Williams' work and showed that his preoccupations were
overwhelmingly religious. If he was a "democrat" it was
by indirection and as a result of the circumstances he was
in.[10]

It would be grossly unjust to suggest that the elders
of the present generation have missed the complexities that
are more clearly apparent to their successors. The difference has always been one rather of temperament and interest than of age. Professor Carl Bridenbaugh has built
up for us a body of information about the early life of
American cities in books that will last longer than many a
fast-selling work of popularization or propaganda; and the
works of those major New England historians, the late
Perry Miller and Samuel Eliot Morison, do more to bring
the past to life than those which have a point to prove about
the present. But there is also, in recent years, an increasing
appreciation of the variety of voices that speak from the
past to those who are willing to listen, "Each generation,"
we are often told, "reinterprets history in the light of its
own interests." But each generation happily contains many
independent minds with a great variety of intelligent interests: so that the arguments for pure historical relativism
lead either towards solipsism or, more fortunately, to can-
celling each other out.

In each of a variety of fields, the last fifteen or twenty
years of American historical scholarship have produced indications of a kind of expertise that tends, not merely to a
revision of the last opinion on the subject, but to the suggestion of new categories of question. The trend is perhaps
nowhere clearer than in those reviews of twentieth-century
foreign policy which have helped to advance our understanding by rejecting the old formalism which dominated

American views of the outside world and which culminated, in the actual conduct of foreign relations, in the reign of John Foster Dulles as Secretary of State. George F. Kennan's trenchant critique of the dominance of moral attitudes in American foreign policy was followed shortly by Professor John M. Blum's unfriendly but cogent analysis of Woodrow Wilson as an agent of moral preconceptions that limited his understanding of political reality.[11] Professor Blum writes from an extraordinary fund of knowledge of recent history and politics, and from a conviction, not perhaps expressed but clearly affecting his method, that the political system he knows so well has enough flexibility to contain and handle the problems that emerge from American society in political form. Meanwhile Professor Ernest R. May[12] has recently opened a searching inquiry into one of the most settled assumptions of American diplomatic historians, the prevailing belief that foreign policy reflects, and, in effect, enacts public opinion on foreign affairs. It is not necessary for one moment to suppose that such writers have said the last word, or even to agree with their individual conclusions, in order to recognize that their style of approach is refreshing in its coolness, its liberation from the favoured American illusions, and its tone of skeptical pragmatism.

The gains to scholarship resulting from this mood can be traced in such widely different fields as the American Revolution, the character of politics in the age of Jackson, and the motives and achievements of the several interests involved in Reconstruction. American historians of the Revolution are conducting the analysis of politics in a manner that owes, and acknowledges, a great debt to Namier; it is an appreciable irony of eighteenth-century studies that this stance of independence of the Whig tradition should in fact owe more to the example of Namier than to the argument of Butterfield. Students of British politics such as Professor C. R. Ritcheson (and Dr. Bernard Donoughue of the London School of Economics) and students of American politics such as Professor Jack P. Greene,[13] together with specialists in a valuable and increasing number of state or local histories, show a relish for facts, for building up the picture as it looked at the time, which gives us a deeper understanding of the kind of choices that were available at that time.

Revisionism does not invariably mean rethinking. It is often possible and sometimes easy to seem wiser than one's predecessors by virtue of some slight change in outlook which renders a new question more attractive. There is no period of American history under a more intense ferment of revision than that of Southern Reconstruction, and none, certainly, in which it is more important to try to distinguish what is the product of new thinking from what is the product of the altering social opinion. An immense amount of research has been put into Reconstruction during a period that corresponds, very roughly perhaps, with the time since the Supreme Court's decision in *Brown* v. *Board of Education*—the school segregation cases of 1954. Most of the results have appeared in articles, and no synthesis of the period in book form has yet appeared to do justice to the full depth of the work. Professor Kenneth M. Stampp's comparatively brief survey, *The Era of Reconstruction* (London, 1965), presents the principal findings of this revision (including of course Professor Stampp's own research) with the cogent persuasiveness of an authority. When Stampp hands down a verdict, he does so in a manner from which there seems little room for appeal. Yet his standpoint is not the only one from which deeper levels of understanding might be attained.

The questions crowd so close upon each other, each entailing the answer to so many others, that any attempt to review the field would require at the least a full-length article to itself. In summary, we risk reducing the subject to a series of paradoxes. When, for example, LaWanda

Cox[14] embarked on a study of the Northern movement to give to the freedmen that fundamentally American form of security, the tenure of freehold land, she clearly expected to find here one of the truly nobler and more redeeming features of the somewhat mixed story of Northern intentions. Her account is scholarly, sound and full of interest: but the interest does not grow any less deep when she arrives, with obvious reluctance, at the discovery that at least some of the congressmen and senators behind this campaign were motivated principally by their anxiety to avert the danger of footloose, freed Negroes flooding into the North. Free land would at least keep the Negroes in the South. To take up the problem of interpretation at another level, the historian who regrets the failure of Radical Reconstruction may put his finger on the antipathy between President Andrew Johnson and the Radical majority in the Congress, and may rightly blame the deadlock on the separation of powers, which emerges as a grave defect in the Constitution itself. But the historian who does not regret the failure of Reconstruction will have equal reason to applaud the wisdom of the Founders, who made it virtually impossible for a temporary majority in Congress to impose so sweeping a policy.

The rewriting of Reconstruction history has produced notable advances in method which have suggested more complex and more interesting categories. The method which depended on imposing the concept of class conflict had the defect of introducing broad, inclusive but basically simple categories. Thus the real force behind the Radical Republicans was held to be that of the Northern business interests that were intent on exploiting the resources of the South, laid open for subjugation by military defeat. But a significant article by Stanley Coben began the work of reconsideration by pointing out that no such unit as that of "Northern business interests" had ever existed, and that in fact the business interests of the Northeast, which were supposed to be prominent in the movement, were not only various in content but divided over Southern policies.[15] Professor Unger's more recent and extensive examination of the social and economic history of the era demonstrates the complexity, the dividedness of the business interests, and renders the old categories obsolete.[16]

> If it is hard to see the consensus in post-bellum America, [Professor Unger observes] it is also difficult to detect a simple Beardian polarity. On the money question there were not two massive contending interests; there were many small ones. If the financial history of Reconstruction reveals nothing else of consequence, it does disclose a complex, pluralistic society in which issues were resolved—when they were not simply brushed aside—by the interaction of many forces.[17]

It can, of course, be argued that the great revision of Reconstruction history is itself a form of instrumentalism.[18] There would be an element of truth in this criticism—an element not to be disregarded because of one's standpoint on civil rights. Yet much of it has been of such value in clearing away cartloads of erroneous information and pernicious mythology—errors about the content of legislation by Southern state assemblies under Radical rule, errors about the actual composition of Reconstruction conventions, myths about the scallawags, to name only a few— that the achievement has been an act of positive liberation.

Yet Southern history, as Vann Woodward has pointed out,[19] has on the whole been by-passed by the more exhilarating winds of the success story that Americans love to tell and to hear. The South, unlike the nation, had suffered a shattering military defeat, and the experience of its white population could never be wholly at one with that which was celebrated in the rest of the Union. The best that could be made of it was a great lost cause, to rank in history with those of the Stuarts or the victims of the French Revolution.

One sign of the critical sophistication about the past which seems to have developed since the Second World War has indeed been a moderate revival of interest in lost causes. The Federalists are now being taken more seriously than they used to be by any except political opponents of the Democrats (though it seems odd that a country that can put up a monument to Robert A. Taft cannot find the heart to commemorate Alexander Hamilton); and recent years have shown a new disposition to study and even to redeem the Loyalists of the Revolution. A most important attribute of this approach, not one confined to lost causes but to the rebuilding of historical knowledge in depth, is the attention which historians are giving to local and state history, and to the examination, in great detail, of the composition of communities. Perceptive monographs about New England towns and about state or provincial politics, amplified by articles based on very extensive use of local records, have appreciably added to our picture of the structure of society and the changes brought in it by the War of Independence; that picture seems to change before our eyes, exposing the frailty of surveys made from the continental centre of politics for the very simple reason that there was no centre.

The most influential single product of this detailed social realism has probably been Professor Lee Benson's book *The Concept of Jacksonian Democracy* (Princeton, 1961). Party divisions, and the ideological claims made by rival parties, have always seemed in the past to present an obvious and a legitimate scheme for organizing the political history of the period, and to lead straight from politics to social structure. But Professor Benson rejects these claims, reconstructing the parties from the social ingredients and finding in their rival policies a reflexion of immediate electoral needs rather than serious differences of opinion or principle. Much the same attitude has influenced Professor Richard P. McCormick's important recent work, *The Second American Party System* (Chapel Hill, 1966). It stands out as an interesting conclusion of this study that by the time of the second American party system, the capturing of the presidency had become the overriding aim of party organization, and that to this end the second American parties, unlike the first, were willing to subordinate almost all considerations of principle. "Between 1824 and 1840, the 'presidential question,' rather than doctrinal disputes, was the axis around which politics revolved."[20] These investigations will undoubtedly lead to further work on the same lines. They represent a brand of toughness, and a skepticism about the proclaimed ideals of party leaders and theorists, that not only appeals to the mood that has succeeded the Cold War, but is obviously producing tangible results.

Yet it would be a pity if this realism, with its useful appreciation of sociological techniques, were allowed to drive out all respect for the values or principles which Americans said they believed in. The history we have to record is that of the United States under Jackson and Van Buren, not under Clay; yet it is permissible to think that the history of that period would have been significantly different if Clay had been elected in 1832, and that such differences would have been due to genuine differences of purpose. The United States without the Bank had a different economy from the United States with the Bank—to name only one divisive issue—and differences on the question certainly turned on matters of substance.

The inevitable attraction of the great controversies has tended to conceal what is in truth another very significant and at times a very subtle division in American historiography. To put the matter with that simplicity that always does injustice to the nuances, it is the division between those who believe in the primacy of mind and those who

believe in the primacy of material fact. The obvious formative and ever-present ingredients of geographical circumstance and economic interest—what may be called the
urgency of the economic problem—in American history have
not prevented the United States from becoming one of the
leading centers of the profession of intellectual history.
Even if we discount the influence, which may indeed be
very important, of the Puritan founders of New England
with their profound sense of mission and their habit of
interpreting human affairs as part of a theocentric order,
we may be justified at least in tracing the practice of giving
a certain primacy to opinions and states of mind back to
John Adams. "The Revolution," he declared in a famous
phrase, "was effected before the war commenced. The Revolution was in the minds and hearts of the people."[21]

Much of what has been styled the "Whig" method in
American historiography has been involved in this process,
because of its intense interest in motive. The search for
the standard-bearers of progress has meant the search for
those who were conscious of their mission; the concept of
commitment to preconceived ideals has always been a part
of the Whig design for the understanding of the past. It
is perfectly legitimate in certain important instances, such
as that of the crusaders against slavery; but it becomes misleading to an equal extent when it generalizes and blurs
the motives of campaigners who were attacking on some
narrow front in the cause of some special interest. And this
kind of commitment is more common, and in general more
effective. Parrington, largely because of the scale of his
achievement, stands out as the leading exponent of this
mode of Whig intellectual history, exemplifying both its
clarity of design and its defects of interpretation. In contrast is the great example of Perry Miller, a historian who
more deeply understood the relation of the minds of earlier
generations to their own past and their own age.

Since their day Richard Hofstadter has emerged as

the most influential of all the historians with a primary interest in states of mind rather than conditions or series of events. In addition to his own impressive and always slightly disturbing studies, he has helped to inspire studies, such as that of Marvin Meyers on the Jacksonians,[22] which may be said to counteract the progressivism of the more conventional Whig thought. Hofstadter, whose extraordinarily trenchant insight—it is almost an instinct—for historical fallacy, has brought about a reorientation in the views of many more conventional judgments over a variety of fields, has seldom been the victim of any undue propensity for optimism—either about the past or the future. In less incisive hands, the method he has developed of recreating past states of mind from the records of published opinions, rather than from archival sources, could easily become cloudy and inconclusive. Oddly enough (considering the feeling he generates that something of value is under attack), it was Hofstadter who proposed the view that American political history should be reconsidered in the light of consensus rather than conflict.[23]

In view of the tremendous emphasis on the conflict of mighty opposites which Parrington and Beard had imposed on their generation, the suggestion that American history owed much to an underlying agreement was a very sensible direction to take. On this view, the successes of the American polity were more important and more enduring than its failures, and those successes were due to the absence of any fundamental divisions in ideology. It would be wrong to attribute the main development of the view to Hofstadter, however. Louis Hartz[24] expounded it in much greater detail on the basis of two principles which he discovered in American history. The first of these was Tocqueville's "equality of conditions"—the absence of feudalism and of all the appurtenances and legacies which feudalism left in Europe. The second was an original "liberal principle." It was not the whole of English society, but what Hartz calls its liberal wing, that settled in America, and being settled it grew without the obstruction of any major contrary power or indeed of any contrary ideal.[25] Hofstadter might agree with Hartz that American development can be explained without recourse to fundamental clashes of ideology, though Hofstadter attaches much more importance to conflicts arising from deep social divisions; it seems that for Hartz the trouble with the Federalists or the Whigs was that they were victims of an intellectual error.

The idea of consensus was a useful direction-finder. It is not an explanation. In a sense it may be called a tautology, for the consensus extends only to the principles about which there is agreement, and deep disagreement may be concealed by different readings of the same sacred texts, when opposing sides affirm their allegiance to the source of these texts. Professor Hartz remarked in his Commonwealth Fund lectures that even the Civil War does not represent a real collapse of the American consensus because the Southern states claimed to have adhered to their own view of the Constitution, which they reproduced, with a few modifications, in that of the Confederacy. At this point consensus may be thought to have lost its usefulness. Might one not as well suggest that the French Wars of Religion do not represent a real religious cleavage because both Catholics and Huguenots avowed their faith in the Christian religion?

To reject the concept of basic ideological conflict is not the same thing as rejecting the influence of ideas, preconceptions, states of mind. In contrast to the entire school of intellectual historians there stands a different tradition, whose exponents emphasize the primacy of material forces. The great progenitor of this line was Turner, who seemed to feel that democracy, and all that was genuinely American about American institutions, rose up like a sort of ground mist from the soil of the continent and entered into the bones of the settlers. It was Turner who really implanted this deep strand of geophysical determinism whose influence has affected so much subsequent historical writing but has aroused such deep resentment—partly, perhaps, because its implicit rejection of the formative influence of ideas seems to be a veiled attack on the commitment of the intellectual life of the historian himself.

The great modern exponent of this style of historical thought, though he has arrived there by his own route and his debt to Turner is indirect, is Daniel J. Boorstin. Professor Boorstin has devoted one book to the thesis that the success of American government, the great ability that Americans have shown in overcoming their practical and political problems, is in fact due to their rejection of preconceived ideological schemes of government. In his major works that have followed, he has extended the same concept to social history in its broadest sense, deliberately extruding ideas or ideals from his terms of reference. As Boorstin shows, in the process of settlement, community came first, government afterwards. Boorstin is not unlike Namier in his hostility to the importation of ideals, ideology, or indeed any form of systematic beliefs—and also, incidentally, in his keen eye for the revealing incident. No contemporary surpasses him in the ability to re-create scenes and situations that bring the past to life; this, we feel, is what it really felt like to be there.[26]

Yet Professor Boorstin's remarkable persuasive powers and the obvious cogency of much of his argument should not conceal two points: First, that it *is* an argument, and as such that it explains the sort of phenomena that primarily interest Professor Boorstin far better than other phenomena that, however, remain significant. The deep and principled convictions that brought about the early political parties, the passions of the antislavery movement, the ratiocinations of Calhoun and other speculative writers are slighted. And, secondly, that the things that interest the author are presented not merely as one aspect of what he calls "the national experience": they *are* the national experience. The rest is worthy only of rejection because, presumably, it is contrary to the true American genius. The rejects of history that fall into this state of gracelessness, because of that failure, can be rather large, and include the second Bank of the United States, which plays no part in the book which covers its lifetime.

Boorstin is far more subtle and complex in his appreciation of American development than Turner was, and his originality and persuasiveness are sure to exert great influence; much, indeed, of what he says is more important than what he chooses to leave out. Like Turner before him he sings the virtue of the land, and might for a text have reversed a line of Robert Frost's to read "We were the land's before the land was ours." It is not the less important on this account to appreciate the extent to which his own ideas form a system.

The deep division of interpretation that has been suggested here is concealed by the fact that Boorstin, Hofstadter, and Hartz join in some measure of belief, shared by such a solid political historian as McCormick, that ideological conflict has not dominated American life; that agreement to work the machinery has been much more important than conflict over principles. But the fact that rival parties agree to work the same machinery does not mean that they intend to work it for the same objects; and the machinery itself sometimes changes shape under the pressure of strong personalities or principles. The machinery of politics is not neutral; it is not "matter," even though it sometimes seems to be treated as though it were of the order of natural or environmental phenomena rather than of those made by man in America.

This division between mind and matter is less dramatic than those in which the participants are to some extent ideological partisans. It results perhaps from a contrast of temperaments rather than ideals. Yet these alternative views cut deep enough to affect any interpretation of specific events or decisions. It may seem strange that American historians should be moved to take sides over the very question of whether there are any sides to take. But an explanation may lie, to some extent, in the actual nature of the theories that have played so dominant a part in the rewriting of American history during the present century. The Populists, the Progressive instrumentalists, and the Marxists asserted the historical primacy of an ideological conflict; and it appears that some historians, anxious to escape this dilemma and convinced of its irrelevance to American development, have in fact been trapped by it. The word "ideology" has itself been given too much work. Ideologies have been thought of as all-embracing, as embodying fundamental views of the state and society, to be wholly accepted or resisted; so that if one rejected "ideological" interpretations one was easily led to deny the relevance, and minimize the intellectual seriousness, of any profound differences of opinion on matters of principle or policy.

But this approach makes too much of the general problem and so, in the end, makes too little of the particular issues. Ideological conflicts may be relatively short-lived, like that between the Federalists and Jeffersonians, and yet intense while they last. Such conflicts, especially when they lead to the adoption of divisive policies, require to be incorporated, not by-passed, in the writing of history. Another of our needs in these matters is to distinguish between the parties who do hold a total view of society and those who are committed to a narrower cause; but it will always be a mistake to trivialize past differences merely because they disappeared with the passage of time.

Time, to come back to the beginning, is the element with which many American historians have had the greatest difficulty in coming to terms; yet they will see into the past, so far as it is given to us to do so, only when they recognize it, in its integrity, as the past. Time is not the enemy of the historian but it is not his friend; it is the prism, the only one, through which we may hope to perceive the dead.

NOTES

1. Herbert Butterfield, *The Whig Interpretation of History* (Cambridge, 1931).

2. George Bancroft: *History of the United States*, 6 vols. (Boston 1879) ; *Formation of the Constitution*, 2 vols. (Boston, 1882).

3. James Harvey Robinson, *The New History* (New York, 1912), pp. 15, 24; Chester McArthur Destler, "Some Observations on Contemporary Historical Theory," *A.H.R.* 55 (April 1950), 503, n.3.

4. Charles A. Beard, *An Economic Interpretation of the Constitution of the United States* (New York, 1913).

5. Destler, "Contemporary Historical Theory," *loc. cit.* pp. 503–6; R. G. Collingwood, *The Idea of History* (Oxford, 1946).

6. Howard K. Beale, *The Critical Year: A Study of Andrew Johnson and Reconstruction* (New York, 1930). Charles and Mary Beard, *The Rise of American Civilization*, revised edition (New York, 1949), chap. xviii.

7. Charles A. Beard, *The Economic Basis of Politics and Related Writings,* William Beard, comp. (New York, 1958).

8. Conyers Read, "The Social Responsibilities of the Historian," *A.H.R.* 55 No. 2 (Jan. 1950).

9. Boston, 1946. In the same connexion see Eric F. Goldman, *Rendezvous with Destiny* (New York, 1952).

10. Vernon Louis Parrington, *Main Currents in American Thought*, 3 vols. (New York, 1927–30) ; Alan Simpson, "How Democratic Was Roger Williams?" *W.M.Q.* (Jan. 1956).

11. George F. Kennan, *American Diplomacy 1900–1950* (Chicago, 1951) ; John M. Blum, *Woodrow Wilson and the Politics of Morality* (Boston, 1956).

12. Ernest R. May, "An American Tradition in Foreign Policy: The Role of Public Opinion," in William H. Nelson, ed, *Theory and Practice in American Politics* (Chicago, 1964).

13. C. R. Ritcheson, *British Politics and the American Revolution, 1763–1783* (Norman, 1954) ; Bernard Donoughue, *British Poli-*

tics and the American Revolution ... *1773-1775* (London, 1964); Jack P. Greene, *The Quest for Power: The Lower Houses of Assembly in the Southern Royal Colonies, 1689-1776* (Chapel Hill, 1963).

14. LaWanda Cox, "The Promise of Land for the Freedmen," *M.V.H.R.* 45 (1958), 413-40.

15. Stanley Coben, "Northeastern Business and Radical Reconstruction: A Re-examination," *M.V.H.R.* 46 (1959).

16. Irwin Unger, *The Greenback Era: A Social and Political History of American Finance, 1865-1878* (Princeton 1964).

17. Ibid., p. 405.

18. For a specific affirmation of these revisionist views (in this case of the abolitionists) as serving an instrumentalist purpose, see Howard Zinn, "Abolitionists, Freedom-Riders and the Tactics of Agitation" in Martin Duberman, ed., *The Antislavery Vanguard: New Essays on the Abolitionists* (Princeton, 1965).

19. C. Vann Woodward, "The Irony of Southern History," *J.S.H.* 19 (1953), reprinted in *The Burden of Southern History,* (New York, 1960).

20. McCormick, *op. cit.* p. 353.

21. Quoted by Clinton Rossiter, *Seedtime of the Republic* (New York, 1953), p. 4.

22. Marvin Meyers, *The Jacksonian Persuasion: Politics and Belief* (New York, 1957).

23. Richard Hofstadter, *The American Political Tradition and the Men Who Made It* (New York, 1951), Introduction.

24. Louis Hartz, *The Liberal Tradition in America* (New York 1955).

25 A view developed in Professor Hartz's Commonwealth Fund lectures at University College, London, in 1962 and in *The Founding of New Societies,* Hartz, ed. (New York, 1964).

26. Daniel J. Boorstin: *The Genius of American Politics* (Chicago, 1953); *The Americas: The Colonial Experience* (New York, 1958); *The National Experience* (New York, 1965).

*A. E. Campbell**

The American Past as Destiny

A. E. Campbell's reflections on American history exhibit a regard both for its place in an overall consideration of history study and for certain of its internal meanings. By placing his views in an intellectual context wide enough to allow elucidation of sensible distinctions between science, social science, and history, he helps lay to rest the criticism that American historians are too often content to operate at the surface, factual level. More significantly, Campbell takes advantage of his own personal externalization respecting America to question "usable history," to remind us that the actuality of change can make a shambles of national objectives and purpose (as he suggests with regard to the Civil War), and to ponder the paradox of rapid change as it combines with a stubborn adherence to tradition, a leading aspect of American folk attitude and belief. In consequence of his assessments of the "past" as America's "destiny," Campbell concludes that America, in the course of its life cycle, has become much like other nations, seeking survival and perhaps achieving some betterment, through adjustment and accom-

*Alexander E. Campbell is Professor of American History at the University of Birmingham.

modation. Yet the impression persists—it remains difficult for Americans themselves to dismiss their past and their ideals. In juxtaposing historical theorizing and realities of the national experience, Campbell succeeds in posing serious questions about the meaning of America while unobtrusively pointing the way to a few answers at least.

From its foundation, many Americans have supposed their country to be more than a nation, and have supposed themselves to be taking part in an experiment, to be leading the advance of mankind. Foreigners too have constantly gone to the United States in the belief that they were going to inspect the future—sometimes political, sometimes social, sometimes merely technological. It was an American, returning long ago from the Soviet Union, who announced with grand simplicity, "I have been over into the future, and it works."[1] But again and again visitors have returned from the United States with the announcement, in effect, that they had been over into the future. It is true that they usually added that they had seen it, and it was perfectly terrible; but then it is also true that those who liked what they saw had the opportunity, and the disposition to stay.

This is not an historical age, for the reason that it is a scientific age. It may seem that there is no special reason why it should not be both. There are, we are often told, more scientists alive and at work today than in the entire previous history of man: possibly there are also more historians. Superb colour printing on every aspect of the past pours from the presses. Yet in the last analysis the attitudes of mind underlying the disciplines of science and of history are quite different. This is not to revive the discredited doctrine of the two cultures: either there is one culture or there are far more than two. There is no reason why the same man should not be both scientist and historian. There is every reason why he cannot be both at once. The pleas heard from time to time that history should become more scientific are simply misguided. The thing cannot be done.

Not very long ago, a well-known historical periodical described itself as "a journal of scientific history." Then the subtitle was quietly dropped. I do not know why. What one can say is that, when it was there, the phrase meant nothing whatever.

Historians need not repine at living in a scientific age. They benefit directly and practically from the dominance of science. Science is, fortunately, very, very expensive. When the governments on whom we all depend have spent their millions on the latest gadgetry, they can hardly in decency refuse the few thousands with which historians can make shift. We are carried onwards, surf-riders on the great wave of science. Moreover, since the past is as various as the present, we can make use of scientific techniques. Few examples are so striking as those from archaeology, where new dating techniques seem to have ruled out some hypotheses and so increased the plausibility of others, but econometricians can apply their techniques to the past and so, I am sorry to tell you, can psychologists. Historians can borrow computers or statistical methods. Yet in essence these make accessible or manageable some sorts of evidence which would otherwise have had to be neglected. The conclusions to be drawn from the evidence remain, as before, a matter for historical judgement.

That judgement is not scientific and cannot be made so. But, because the most obvious links are those between historians and *social* scientists, let me refer briefly to a distinction between the social sciences on the one hand, and the physical sciences on the other, which is perhaps too little noticed. The physical sciences are a cumulative, progressive affair. Scientists do not merely believe in progress. Progress is so much a part of their experience, of their whole way of life, that they give it no thought. Yet scientific progress is of a curious sort, for it is progress only in the sense that one step, one experiment, leads to the next and that work once done does not usually have to be done again. Today's question is identified by yesterday's solution, and today's solution will pose tomorrow's question. There is no goal, no final objective, and there is no suggestion that any is possible. Scientists know that so surely that they can neglect it. They are content with the next step and allow the further future to take care of itself.

This open-ended quality is surely a chief characteristic of the physical sciences. "When a doctor has compounded a new drug," wrote A. E. Housman, "and desires to find out what diseases, if any, it is good for, he has only to give it to his patients all round and notice which die and which recover."[2] Those who know their Housman will realize at once that he was praising doctors. He was saying in his waspish way that doctors behave like rational men in responding to evidence—unlike the textual critics with whom he was contrasting them—but he also thought them fortunate in having evidence to which to respond. Social scientists are less fortunate. When they propound a nostrum and the patient fails to improve, it is always open to them to argue that the prescription was certainly the right one and that what the patient needed was a great deal more of it; or, that ill-intentioned men got at the dose between prescription and administration, so that the patient got only some placebo; or, that the serious disease could not possibly be recognized until something more superficial had first been dealt with.

It is not my purpose to quarrel with social scientists. They must proceed as they proceed. They are bound by the laws of their calling. They are, many of them, stimulated by a keen desire to advance the well-being of mankind, something which, it must be conceded, historians cannot do. But to do that they need a defined goal. Their disciplines do not share the open-ended quality of the physical sciences. For evidence we need only consider the debate which rages, even on the wall of our University Library, over whether the social sciences should be, or indeed can be, nonpolitical. The appeal to science is, of course, in part a device to remove some matter from political controversy. Let me offer a quotation. It is a well-known habit of historians to take an example for proof, but I submit that this is typical:

> ... traditional (and largely unsuccessful) teaching methods were based on the ignorance of old wives' tales. Modern "progressive" educational procedures as they are at present "taught" to student teachers, are based ... on a sound and scientific knowledge of child psychology; a keen awareness of the effects of social background on educability and a rigorous examination of educational aims and procedures.[3]

I do not deny that change takes place in education as in other things, nor even that some of it is progress; but it is progress in the physical scientist's sense that, having changed, it is unlikely that we shall return to where we were before. The conviction, not merely that our forebears were wrong, but that *we* are right or nearly so, sets social scientists apart from physical scientists on one side and from historians on the other. Physical scientists are resigned to being superseded by their successors; and historians know that social scientists will be rejected by theirs. Moreover, the social sciences arouse resistance which the physical sciences do not. We cannot maintain for long the facade of indifference as to what we may discover about ourselves or our society. There are, of course, areas which have been handed over to the technologists; but, either consciously, by claiming them for morals or politics, or unconsciously, by excluding them from serious thought, we save the things we care about from the clutches of the social sciences.

The cumulative quality of the physical sciences, which is the reason for their power and prestige, sets them apart from history and always will. But the open-ended quality of the physical sciences, which sets them apart from the social sciences, does not have a counterpart in history. The historian's subjects, after all, are dead. He can say of them what Yeats's Irish airman said of the Irish poor:

> No likely end could bring them loss
> Or leave them happier than before[4]

and from that fact he gains a similar bleak freedom. His task is that of the artist, though one may hope that the art is representational, and neither abstract nor pop. In a sense the purpose of history is not the advancement of learning at all. Learning there must be, of course, but the final object is, as Professor Trevor-Roper recently put it, to recreate the mind of the past.[5] If our subjects are dead, our task is to restore them to life. It is clearly not easy, but one thing is certain: no amount of learning will suffice to do it. We can surely say of the people we study, with only a touch of metaphor, what Karen Blixen said of the natives on her African farm. "I sometimes thought that what, at the bottom of their hearts, they feared from us was pedantry. In the hands of a pedant they die of grief."[6]

Because they are not scientists, historians, though they may repeat each other, do not advance. Some have deliberately chosen not to study the work of their predecessors: Professor Davis recently gave us the example of Fustel de Coulanges.[7] But whatever his chosen method each can bring only his own judgement to bear on the past. Our experience is that of Kipling's builder:

> When I was a King and a Mason—a Master proven and skilled—/I cleared me ground for a Palace such as a King should build./I decreed and dug down to my levels. Presently, under the silt,/I came on the wreck of a Palace such as a King had built.[8]

If in building our palaces we have a duty other than to satisfy our own sense of design, is is *not* to meet the felt needs of the time. It is not to provide what some today like to call "usable history." On the contrary. Every period,

every society, is in danger—it may even be unavoidable—
of selecting from the past for emphasis those aspects which
it finds appealing or useful. But when people want history,
they commonly want bad history. Even today I suppose
the most familiar examples are taken from the period of
romantic nationalism, when small peoples struggling for
political recognition supposed that it helped their cause
to claim an heroic past. Lacking it, they invented it. Today
patriotic history is out of fashion. Most of us are agreed
that it is poor history to glorify our own nation and denigrate others, and many believe that it is socially harmful
as well. Yet surely it is a similar process which tries to enlarge the past importance of social groups which are now
demanding more consideration. In the area of my own concern, the new emphasis on the history of blacks in the
United States, of the inarticulate poor in the United States,
of women in the United States, is likely to produce more
nonsense, more sheer invention, than anything for a long
time past. The publisher's puff of a recent series claims
to set out "the indelible mark" left by American women on
the history of their country. Well, history—the process, not
the discipline—is pretty tough stuff. In one sense all marks
on it are indelible: it is nothing but marks. In another it
is remarkably resistant. If anyone could make indelible
marks on it, no doubt women could. But it remains perverse to concentrate on the past of underprivileged groups.
History as a subject is the study of change over time and
in the nature of things such groups have less influence on
the course of events than have others. They may, of course,
come to have their day, and then it is time to study them.
If history required justification, it might be found in the
odd fact that so many people feel they cannot have a future
unless they first devise a past, yet if history needs protection, it is against that abuse.

Though the indifference of an age of science does
something to protect it, the historian must play his part.

It is his business to resist that abuse, to restore the empha-
ses that reassert what was once well-known but would now
otherwise be overlooked—to supply what G. M. Trevelyan,
an historian now too much neglected, liked to call "true
bias."[9] It is not an easy thing to do. The easy thing from
every point of view is to fall in with the bias of the moment. Now there are occasions when, by accident, the bias
of the moment is also what Trevelyan called true bias; but
they are few. The prudent historian begins by assuming
that what people want to hear is false. It is not always so,
but that's the way to bet. For, as Peter Laslett recently
remarked,

> It will be a long time . . . before we lose the wish to
> justify what some of us would half like to happen
> in the present by trying to show that it might just
> conceivably have been a half intention of a handful
> of our distant ancestors.[10]

To fulfil that wish is the treason of historians. It is to behave like Kipling's builder—"Taking and leaving at pleasure the gifts of the humble dead."[11]

"The mind of the past" means, of course, the mind
of a small part of the past. It is a rash historian who tries,
in modern history, to identify "the mind" of a period longer
than twenty years. If he limits his scope—say to bankers
or bishops—he can extend his period. To extend both is
to court disaster. Yet even for the most prudent historian
the difficulties remain. In the necessary business of selection and categorization two things happen. First, attitudes
which do not fit his scheme must be thrust aside, rejected
as unimportant or untypical. Second, as a student of process, the historian draws his test of importance from the
future, from some period later than that which he is studying. He likes no phrase better than "a period of transition."
There is, I am sorry to have to tell you, no such thing.
Every period, and therefore none, is transitional. The

phrase implies that the before and the after have some sort of greater cohesion or validity. But they do not. A period of transition is apt to be doubly falsified—by being so dubbed, and by the misinterpretation of the period towards which it is supposed to be in transit.

How are these dilemmas to be resolved? In the full sense, they cannot be resolved. So far as they can be resolved, it is by the usual methods—prudence, caution, and moderation—and by resisting the demand for "usable history." But in the history of few countries are these difficulties so obtrusive as in that of the United States. When it was founded, many supposed that a new and better society, even the ultimate society, might be made there. It had two great advantages which gave it scope—freedom from the entrenched errors and entrenched interests of the Old World, and a land superb in its resources. It was, as Richard Hofstadter put it in a lapidary phrase, "the only country in the world that began with perfection and aspired to progress."[12] The very notion that the American was, in a yet more famous phrase, a "new man,"[13] carried a double implication. First, obviously, that Americans were different from Europeans, but second that this novelty was of no ordinary kind, but something both permanent and unlikely to be repeated. After all, if Americans were merely colonials who would, in the fullness of time, turn into Europeans, why should anyone take much interest in them?

Since those heady days, much has happened. We are, after all, approaching the bicentenary of the Declaration of Independence. American students of American history are energetic, ingenious, ambitious and many. They are forever rewriting the account of those two hundred years, and it is perhaps not surprising that they are able to discover a large number of critical years, of turning points, of revolutions in the American consciousness, from the first Revolution to the Kennedy years. Yet at the same time the notion that there is something innately, indefensibly American—

something imprinted in Americans, so to say—dies very hard. When an American historian reaches a certain eminence and seniority, it is almost obligatory for him to offer some formulation of what he conceives his country to be, some analysis of the American political tradition or the American national character. *The American Mind, The Liberal Tradition in America, Conservatism in America, The Purpose of American Politics, Manifest Destiny and Mission in American History*—the list could be extended almost indefinitely.[14] The past becomes destiny.

Fascinating though these formulations often are, they seem to me misguided. "Fellow-citizens," wrote Abraham Lincoln on a famous occasion, "we cannot escape history." It is true, and it is characteristic that he immediately tried to escape it. That was the paper—his second Annual Message—to Congress—in which he continued almost at once, "We shall nobly save, or meanly lose, the last best hope of earth." Now the issues of the American Civil War were real and great, and Lincoln was here dealing with the greatest of them. In this, perhaps his finest state paper, he was pleading the case for compensated emancipation as the right way to peace, justice, and restored unity. But great though the issues were, they were not as great as that. The fate of the world did not then, and does not now, turn on what happens in the United States. Moreover, we observe in that war, as we observe in all wars, that the war aims of contestants, especially the more powerful, changed as the war continued. While the North may have gained what it was fighting for, it gained much of that in form only, and it gained also a good many things that Northerners would have rejected when the war began. If that was true in wartime, when men are at some pains to formulate their objectives, it is still more true in peacetime. Then men go about their business and, if they last long enough, are surprised to be reminded by historians of the changes which have taken place around them and in which they have had a part. From history in that sense Americans indeed cannot escape.

The story of the United States is, among other things and above all, the great romance of the modern world. We shall get it wrong if we forget that. The transformation of a continent from its primitive colonial state into the mightiest power of a technological age has about it an unequalled scope and grandeur. The story has its full share of brutality, incompetence, narrow-mindedness, folly, and inhumanity; but also its full share of courage, sensitivity, intelligence, generosity, and hope. That last quality is the essential key. When Americans have had faith in their future, they have commonly behaved well in their present; lacking it they have faltered. In the early days belief in the future was absolutely vital. The present, *pace* Richard Hofstadter, was clearly nothing much to boast of. The perfection Americans had was virtue; the light that shone on them was the assurance of future glory. That faith moved West with the settlers; indeed it did more than anything else to take them West. It was often misplaced, in the most literal sense. America is full of small towns which men once believed would become cities. But it also contains the cities which are small towns that made it big.

Yet we should remember that the progress in which these men believed was a short-term affair. They hoped to see it in their lifetimes, or at least in their children's times. Whether they hoped for economic progress, which took place, or cultural progress, which may or may not have taken place, or moral progress, which did not take place, they were thinking of something measurable. A man could cast up his accounts and decide whether he had advanced or not. The degree of advance, not the finishing point, came to be seen as the measure of success. Those men, or some of them, had goals not only for themselves but for their country as well. But the life of a nation differs from the life of a man in this: the point is never reached at which the accounts can be cast. Nations do not make progress because they have no goals. Survival is a condition, not a purpose, but over time it alters purpose. We need only think of our own case. It is not the unfinished business of the past which provides us with our agenda. Rather we spend most of our time and effort on undoing, or on lessening the harm done by, the very achievements in which our fathers took most pride. Men are not so feeble or lacking in invention that when their grievances are redressed they cannot devise new ones. Even the same men can devise new ones. Still more can their successors. Rather than making progress, then, mankind is engaged in what statisticians—I am told—call a "random walk." I do not want to press the analogy too far, because I have also been told, though I have no idea whether it is true, that the longer a random walk continues, the more certain it is to return to its starting point. Be that as it may, we can all borrow the famous slogan of the American depression years and say "We don't know where we're going, but we're on our way."

The consequences for historians is that they can call in national tradition, or the national character which is its present manifestation, only when no other explanation is available. The Spartans at Thermopylae, so the story tells us, stood their ground and died—quite uselessly, as they well knew—because that was the sort of thing Spartans did. It was the Spartan tradition. Anything else would have been un-Spartan. Because they stood and died, they have lived for twenty-five hundred years. But Sparta has not. It is no part of the historian's task to suggest how long the United States will survive. Two hundred years of national existence is not bad in the modern world. Over that time it is hard indeed to think of any course of conduct that has not been followed, or advocated, by some Americans at some time—these are the people who defended slavery and revived polygamy, as well, of course, as attacking both—and it is even harder to find one that has been followed, or advocated, *solely* because it was the American way. The American way has had practical advantages. That is its justification.

At this point, there might well be murmurs of dissent. Again and again, surely, critics inside and outside the United States have caught that great country in some hidebound archaic attitude, reluctant to face facts, unable to adjust, clinging to ancient mores or beliefs now quite out of date. That, I contend, is simply not so. To explore the theme at length would take a whole course of lectures. The Vietnam war, its implications and its aftermath, are perhaps still so recent that an historian may be excused for ducking it. But I must deal, however briefly, with the Civil War to which I have already referred. That, indeed, was a war which broke out because Americans, North and South, took ideological stands—moral stands, if you will. "And the war came."[15] There are circumstances in which that is unavoidable. Some historians would argue that the outbreak of civil war was evidence of a fragile society.[16] I contend rather that we should notice the energy and ingenuity with which Americans tried to avoid taking ideological positions, tried to reduce the moral evil of slavery to a practical and thus a soluble problem. They failed, but that is what they were trying to do. With that exception, they have commonly succeeded. But they have succeeded, of course, not in solving social problems identified by historians later, but only in staggering on past one difficulty to the next.

In dealing with this point, I cannot do better than offer you a myth, in the simplest sense of an expository fable. I choose the myth of the cave—but not Plato's cave; rather a different, more American cave, Tom Sawyer's cave. Some of you may remember the episode in *Tom Sawyer* in which Tom and his childhood girl friend, Becky Thatcher, go with all the other neighbourhood children to visit some notable local limestone caverns. Because Tom was an adventurous lad, they wandered away from the party and became lost, with little food and little light and no assurance of rescue. They spent some time in misery and despair. But what did Tom do? He found in his pocket a kite line, rather a lot, you may think, but he was a nineteenth-century Western boy. He needed a kite line, and he did not have to worry about the fit of his trousers. Anchoring one end of his line to Becky—woman's role—he groped his way down a passage till the line gave out. Finding nothing, he made his way back and began again. Finally, of course, just as he reached the end of his line, he saw a glimmer of light. Both children could make their way towards it and out of the cave. They did not, however, come out where they went in. They came out five miles downstream, and that was so far in Tom's experience that he was out of his ground and had to ask the way. Tom did not much care where he came out. Anywhere would do, but he knew daylight when he saw it. He was inventive and determined. He was, no doubt, changed by the experience. The boy who came out of the cave was not quite the boy who went in. Yet fundamentally, of course, he was the same; and anyway that question could be left to take care of itself. What worried Tom was how to get out of the cave, not how to come out exactly where he went in or how to remain unchanged. Similarly with Americans. The fable applies with special accuracy to the difficult periods of American history—say the Great Depression—but it also applies to the whole.

And similarly with the rest of us. I would not have you think that I am joining in the game of trying to define the American character. Rather I want to argue that the enterprise is fruitless, for Americans as for other peoples. Any point made about national character can be translated, by a sort of topological deformation, into a point about national purpose. By mere survival in a changing world, the United States has lost its claim to national purpose. Now and increasingly, its story is that of a nation state like other nation states, and not that of a great experiment or of the last best hope of earth. In that sense too, fellow citizens, Americans cannot escape history.

I turn now to my final theme of American Studies. On this subject I can speak only as an historian, and I should make it clear that history can claim no primacy in American Studies—seniority perhaps, but not primacy. There are many ways of approaching the subject, and of those who practise it some would not be entirely happy to have historians jogging their elbows. It is not my purpose, however, to discuss academic politics. In this country, the basis of American Studies in cooperation between historians and students of literature is well-established. It is a basis which I myself find valid and attractive, but not exclusively so, and the cooperation is challenging because it requires scholars in both disciplines to question some of their most familiar ideas. At present there is some rivalry between two conceptions of what American Studies might become. One seeks to make it well-defined and tightly-organized, a discipline with its own organizing theories and its own techniques, many no doubt related to those of other disciplines but selected in order to form something both coherent and new. The other is content for American Studies to remain, as it began, interdisciplinary, is content to believe that there are many different ways of approaching the United States—and even more of approaching the Americas—and that anxiety about the intellectual validity of American Studies, if not misplaced, reflects the needs of university organization rather than those of the subject.

I must confess that of these two approaches, the looser seems to me the more promising. A new discipline commonly advances by the elaboration of new techniques, or at least a new conjunction of old ones. In American Studies new techniques may be in the making. We may hope that they are. But they do not, surely, apply specifically or characteristically to a geographical entity, a political entity, a cultural entity—the United States. Rather they inhere in more specific problems which are common to the United States and other countries also. Not a shared discipline but a shared area of interest in what students of America have in common.

It is interesting, though perhaps no more than a paradox, that American Studies should flourish at a time when most Americans are conscious of sharing problems which are world-wide rather than peculiar to themselves. There have been other such periods—the Progressive years before the first world war, for example—just as there have been periods when the United States was seen, by Americans and others, as much more special and distinct. Take those questions which most exercise students of the United States today. The status of blacks. The role of women. The plight of the cities. Pollution and the use of resources. International power. In short, what one scholar likes to call race, rights, and reform. None of these is peculiar to the United States, not even relations between black and white, though that certainly has local form and importance. Each is a subject in which comparison with other societies is fruitful for the understanding of both. Which link is most useful is for the individual scholar to decide, and they need not be exclusive. One of the best-known students of modern urban America has also done work on southern Italy. A prize-winning historian has compared the role of blacks in the United States and in Brazil. And so on and so on.

Equally, it is surely curious that the effort to identify the central core should flourish just at the time when Americans are becoming more and more conscious of variations within the country. The Vietnam War, of course, has done more than anything for long to force introspection on Americans. Is "middle America" to be seen as the real America, with blacks, or Puerto Ricans, or liberated women, or Jewish-Americans or New Yorkers or Californians—the list is endless—seen as variant subcultures, sharing important qualities but deviating from the norm? It is plausible enough to suppose that a nation has a culture, and that there are variations, not fully typical, to be found within it. But the student must be particularly careful when he attempts to formulate or define the essential culture. What he risks is mere invention, temporarily persuasive, quickly irrelevant.

There is indeed something unsatisfactory about attempts to catch the essence of a culture. They all rest, in some measure, on the proposition that a culture is defined by the divergence between reality and the observation of it. And that in turn carries the implication that *our* observation of reality—or that part of it which we are studying—is somehow more accurate or at least more sophisticated than that of our subjects. To pursue this theme, of the relationship of the mind and the "reality" with which it interacts, would raise philosophical problems which would take me too far afield, even if I were more competent to explore them. But self-consciousness, like anything else, should be taken in moderation. We are today all desperately earnest in our efforts not to patronize the poor, the uneducated, the alien, ready to honour any life-style so long as it is not our own. No doubt there is a generous impulse somewhere there, but it is not an aid to comprehension either of the present or of the past. In this determined commitment, we are driven to reject much of the present and most of the past. If others differ from us in their view of Indians or blacks or women or labouring men, we instinctively and at once enquire what it is in their culture that makes them so perverse. Yet realism, like morality, is a quality in which some individuals may make painful progress, of which some may have more than others, but in which the human race advances not at all.

The student of culture, then, like the historian, must begin with the assumption, and probably end with the conclusion, that his subjects are as capable of realistic judgement as he is, and that differences in attitude derive from different circumstances. The point is only valid at a certain level of generalization. We can charge individuals with lack of realism, and while we may be right or wrong the charge is not absurd. Similarly with small eccentric groups—flat-earthers, or the like. At the other extreme some generalizations are so wide as to offer little help. The grand organizing concepts of Toynbee—or even of Marx—are of this kind.

Somewhere between these extremes—tiny splinter groups on the one side, whole civilizations or world classes on the other—lie groups of the scale and cohesion with which we can work, and of which we must suppose that they have reasons for the choices they make. Nations like the United States—or parts of them, whether regions or ethnic groups—are among these. We simply must suppose that most Americans have commonly known what they were about, and still do. Yet if one quality of the United States strikes us more than another, it is the speed of change, felt by many today as oppressive, often in the past felt as opportunity, but always there. The proper response to change is adaptation, and in that Americans have not failed. But how is the student of culture to cope with this? He may not have the historian's professional concern with continuity, but he must try to contend that what he is studying is not so short-lived as to be trivial, and he shares in full measure the historian's problem of deciding what evidence is significant. Bacon put it with his usual neat precision years ago: "Men's thoughts are much according to their inclination, their discourse and speeches according to their learning and infused opinions; but their deeds are after as they have been accustomed."[17]

Some students of culture have tried to argue that the right way to proceed is to distil from the grand rich soup of culture the forming elements, the "sacred values" as they have been termed, to which Americans themselves appeal when they want to test their own performance and which survive while the more superficial aspects of culture change.[18] If one finds a group in the United States—the Red Indians are the obvious example—who do not share those sacred values, then they are an alien culture, not a sub-culture. To the great benefit of Americans, if to the confusion of their students, many of their sacred values have proved highly adaptable. I doubt whether adaptability can properly be described as a value, valuable though it undoubtedly is.

Rapidly and effectively though Americans change, they have never been pushed to the point of abandoning their past. Perhaps no one ever is. "Continuity with the past," as Mr. Justice Holmes once put the point, "is not a duty, it is only a necessity."[19] Continuity in the United States, I suggest, has not been maintained by anything we ordinarily think of as culture. It has been maintained by institutions and by circumstances. To institutions, the more familiar and the more important, I referred to when I began. The institutions of the United States, in the words of Professor H. G. Nicholas,

> are not just an expression of the national spirit; they *are* that spirit. It is not by acquiring the language, or by absorbing the culture of the country, still less by espousing the religious tenets of any sect, that the immigrant becomes a citizen [or, one might add, that the American remains a citizen]. It is by an acceptance and affirmation of a set of political beliefs, codified in a constitution and finding expression in a set of political institutions.[20]

As a recently-arrived historian who arrived, through no fault of his own, just in time to observe his new university engaged in a process of constitution-making which, for meticulous elaboration, would surely have won the respect of the Founding Fathers themselves, it may be appropriate for me to remind my colleagues that constitution-making can become a habit. Part of the strength of Americans is that they resisted temptation and turned instead to the simple homely pleasures of exploration, settlement, and industrial advance. Constitutions gain in value as they survive.

The circumstances, perhaps less familiar, are these. Few things have changed so little in the course of United States history as the nation's international position, and few things, I contend, make a sharper and more rapid change in a nation's culture—in the broadest sense—than a change in international standing. If that is generally true, it is still more true of the standing of the United States in her own hemisphere; and that fact gives an important unity not only to the history of the United States but to that of the hemisphere also. These two elements, political institutions of great adaptability, together with great and continuing international security, have protected Americans from the need for more painful adaptations. Beside them, other aspects of the nation's life are secondary.

The case for American Studies then, rests on grounds something like this. The United States is a nation state which has been for long and still is dominant in a major region. It was settled by a people whose culture was in origin ineluctably Western European, whose political rhetoric will be till the next revolution that of the English enlightenment, who have shown great ingenuity in adjusting their political institutions while claiming to keep them unchanged, and whose geographical position gives them a view of politics, internal as well as external, which is unique. Such a people can surely be used to test wider generalizations about human nature and society. It must be done with great sensitivity and care, and it may even prove to be too difficult for all but a few undergraduates; but it can be done by non-Americans as well as by Americans. If we can do it, we shall resolve the problems of American Studies, intellectual and political, and enlarge our understanding of American history and American culture, of the United States and of the Americas, as we enlarge our understanding of ourselves.

NOTES

1. " 'So you've been over into Russia?' said Bernard Baruch, and I answered very literally, 'I have been over into the future, and it works.' " *The Autobiography of Lincoln Steffens* (New York, 1931) Part IV, Ch. XVIII, 799. Steffens visited Russia as a member of the Bullitt mission of 1919.

2. "The Application of Thought to Textual Criticism," reprinted in John Carter, ed., *A. E. Housman, Selected Prose* (Cambridge, 1962), 137.

3. Letter to *The Guardian*, from members of Goldsmiths College, University of London, 31 January, 1972.

4. "An Irish Airman Foresees his Death." *The Collected Poems of W. B. Yeats* (second edition, London, 1950), 152.

5. "Frances Yates, Historian." *The Listener*, 18 January 1973, 87.

6. *Out of Africa* (London, 1937), 32.

7. R. H. C. Davis, *Good History and Bad* (Birmingham. 1972), 11.

8. "The Palace" (1902). *Rudyard Kipling's Verse*. Definitive Edition (London, 1940), 385.

9. "Bias in History," reprinted in G. M. Trevelyan, *An Autobiography and Other Essays* (London, 1949), 81.

10. "What Happened in Cromwell's England: Doubtful Lessons for a Social Revolution Today." *The Times*, 22 June 1972.

11. Kipling, loc. cit., 386.

12. *The Age of Reform. From Bryan to F.D.R.* (New York, 1955), 36.

13. M.-G. J. de Crevecoeur, *Letters from an American Farmer*, Letter III; Signet Classic edition (New York, 1963), 63. The work was first published, under the name of J. Hector St. John, in 1782.

14. H. S. Commager, *The American Mind* (New Haven, Conn., 1950); Louis Hartz, *The Liberal Tradition in America* (New York, 1955); C. L. Rossiter, *Conservatism in America* (New York, 1955);

H. J. Morgenthau, *The Purpose of American Politics* (New York, 1960) ; Frederick Merk, *Manifest Destiny and Mission in American History* (New York, 1963).

15. The phrase is Lincoln's, from his second Inaugural Address, 4 March 1865.

16. See for example David Donald, *An Excess of Democracy. The American Civil War and the Social Process* (Oxford, 1960).

17. "Of Custom and Education." Francis Bacon, *Essays*, xxxix; World's Classics edition (London, 1937), 163.

18. See for example Stuart Levine, "Art, Values, Institutions and Culture: An Essay in American Studies Methodology and Relevance." *American Quarterly*, XXIV:2, May 1972, 131–165.

19. "Learning and Science," Speech at a dinner of the Harvard Law School Association, 25 June 1895. The piece has often been reprinted, most accessibly perhaps in Max Lerner, ed., *The Mind and Faith of Justice Holmes* (Boston, 1943), 35.

20. H. G. Nicholas, *The American Past and the American Present* (Oxford, 1971), 10.

The
Anglo-American
Connection

*H. C. Allen**

The Cultural Tie

For a great many historians history can be more than past politics. H. C. Allen makes a good case for this position in his discussion of the cultural tie between Great Britain and America. In fact, Allen in his comprehensive book, *Great Britain and the United States: A History of Anglo-American Relations, 1783–1952*, gives a full account of the contacts between the two countries in which he stresses emotional bonds and economic dealings no less than diplomacy. The selection included here is taken from *Conflict and Concord, The Anglo-American Relationship Since 1783*, Allen's reworked version of his larger, general study. His treatment of the cultural tie perhaps best illustrates the subtle yet substantial commonality between the two branches of English-speaking people. The argument begins with a bold enough claim: "The cultural tie has probably been the most important of all the ties binding Great Britain and the United States." Yet Allen is cautious and restrained as he seeks to estimate the cultural flow, westward and eastward, across the Atlantic. By demonstrating that language and its development, for example, are the proper

*H. C. Allen is Professor of American History at the University of East Anglia.

subject of history, the author enables the student to come to some understanding of the role of a common tongue in shaping the more conventional political and economic relations between the two nations.

The cultural tie has probably been the most important of all the ties binding Great Britain to the United States, although its strength is very difficult to assess in any practical manner. Since the proportion of a people which can travel abroad must, even in this age, remain small, it is through the vehicle of culture that knowledge of one nation by another must be acquired. And that mutual knowledge is the only sure way to tolerance: an increase of international knowledge is an essential element in any increase in international understanding. In Anglo-American relations —it is another cliché of profound importance—the common language has made the process of reciprocal comprehension very much easier. We forget all too often how effective a barrier politically lack of a common tongue may be; nations can, like Switzerland, be solidly constructed without a single shared language, but the task is immensely more difficult, because language is the most cohesive national force. It is true that the English language may seem at first, as G. B. Shaw—that addict of the paradox—put it, to separate and not unite the two great peoples; that little of the savour of mutual comment is lost in crossing the Atlantic; and that superficially this makes always for dispute and has in the past made for immense Anglo-American bitterness. More subtly, it may, as Max Beloff has recently pointed out, lead to assumptions that there is an understanding more precise and complete than actually exists. But these are better than the deepest ignorance, and relatively—which is the only valid basis of comparison— the two peoples understand one another much better than peoples who do not possess a common tongue. Unless one takes a deeply gloomy view of human nature, one must believe that in the end he that increaseth knowledge does not increase sorrow; that, in most human relationships, beyond initial mistrust there lies understanding. Certainly the history of Anglo-American relations, with their persistent development of warmth and cordiality as reciprocal information multiplied, appears to be a triumphant vindication of this idea. The instruments of that swelling transmission of knowledge have necessarily been cultural.

Yet a realistic evaluation of the cultural tie is exceedingly hard. Any discussion of "culture"—the very word is suspect—must be conducted with infinite caution, even if it is not primarily concerned with cultural values. There can be no doubt, however, that the culture of the two peoples has, until quite recently, been dominated by England; it is indeed the sphere where the predominance of the British in earlier years was most overwhelming and where it was longest sustained. The air of the United States in the first half of the nineteenth century was filled with lamentations that Americans were

> intellectually the slaves of Britain. The longing for English praise, the submission to English literary judgment, the fear of English censure, and the base humility with which it was received, was dwelt on incessantly in magazines, in newspapers, in addresses, in recollections of distinguished men, and in the prefaces to books. . . . When we examine an American literary production, said the reviewer of a wretched book written in imitation of English models, the first thing we do is to determine whether the author has or has not adopted an English fashionable model. . . . The inevitable consequence . . . is a state of colonization of intellect, of subserviency to the critical opinion of the once mother country.[1]

This dominance was, of course, partly the result of historical events. Though the United States proclaimed her political independence in 1776, she could not assert her cultural independence at once, for the weight of the English tradition was too great and the American lack of it too absolute. Because in 1776 she had in effect no cultural history, America made the previous centuries of English culture her own, as indeed they already were, and with the voices of Chaucer, Shakespeare, Milton, and the rest speaking from over the sea, it is small wonder that America long remained culturally subservient to Britain.

This she would doubtless have been in any case, but it was made doubly sure by the facts of her life. She was in 1783, and was to remain for many years, a frontier society; with prospects of immense riches before them, and only wealthy in the present through the sweat of their brows, Americans were more heavily engaged in pioneering in the wilderness than in the field of letters. When Gouverneur Morris said in 1787 that "The busy haunts of men, not the remote wilderness, was the proper school of political talents,"[2] he was on dangerous ground, but if he had applied his aphorism to culture, he would not have been. There is unquestionably, however difficult it may be to define precisely, a relationship between wealth and culture in society; culture can perhaps only bloom fully after a large economic surplus is attained. As Jefferson said in 1813: "We have no distinct class of literati in this country. Every man is engaged in some industrious pursuit."[3] Not, of course, as the very remark of Morris implies, that America was exclusively a frontier society or that she produced no literature or art. Within half a century of independence a genuine American literature had begun to make its appearance, and Melville, Hawthorne, Emerson, and Longfellow could be matched against much that England could show. But their voices were not the voices of America; indeed to some extent they were voices crying not so much in as to the wilderness, for the function of New England in American life was largely educative. In a curious way she was to the rest of the United States, and particularly the Great West, what England was to her: just as her schoolmarms spread enlightenment towards the frontier, so "The true

Bostonian always knelt in self-abasement before the majesty of English standards: far from concealing it as a weakness, he was proud of it as his strength."[4] But in due time, America's wealth and cultural confidence developed, and the cultural ascendancy of Britain tended to diminish.

But it was considerably slower to disappear than any of her other ascendancies, such as those in commerce and in political power. In fact, it may be open to question whether it has yet disappeared entirely. Certainly if educated Englishmen are asked to point to any aspect of life where they are not yet outweighed by their American rivals and friends, they would be inclined to point to literature, and possibly music and the arts; equally certainly this is a claim which would be bitterly rebutted by many Americans. It is one which it is obviously peculiarly difficult for an Englishman to evaluate justly, while, partisanship apart, questions of this kind have an intrinsic complexity and nebulosity, which make generalization highly dangerous. It does seem possible that cultural bloom tends to follow rather than to precede, or even to accompany, economic maturity—though each of these terms in succession defies exact analysis—and that American native springs of talent have yet to develop their full strength. Indications that English culture can still hold up its head in the presence of American, that it still equals if it no longer surpasses it, are not entirely lacking. Admittedly, the heyday of the American intellectual emigré is over; there will be few more Jameses and Eliots, at least until Britain's economic position becomes a good deal better than it is, and there were, after all, Huxleys moving in the reverse direction, even when England was still, in the nineteen-thirties, quite well off. There are, naturally, many more now. But England can still produce practitioners in the arts to rival any nurtured by America, and it is not without significance that in 1951 Britain, with only a third of the population, produced eighteen thousand book titles to America's ten thousand.

She is still in some degree a cultural Mecca, not merely to the English-speaking peoples of the Commonwealth, but to Americans also.

If this is so, how is it to be explained? It is at least arguable that it is owing to Britain's aristocratic tradition; that it is not only because of the existence of the American frontier, but also of the democracy which it helped to foster. There are some grounds for believing that, in the initial stages of a society's growth, democracy is not the most fertile of soils for the seeds of culture; indeed it remains to be distinctly proven that democracy is ever positively good for the arts. This is obviously a question that bristles with difficulties, and in which it is more than doubtful if proof can ever be forthcoming, but it is a suggestive basis for the analysis of the Anglo-American cultural connexion. No one who has seen Mount Vernon, or Monticello, or even Lee's home at Arlington, can doubt the cultural value of early America's contribution. But those years were in many senses aristocratic years; after them there came, with the triumph of the North in the Civil War, the decadence of the Gilded Age. But a similar decadence can be seen in the architecture, and some of the associated arts, of the Victorian era in the Old World. (Notice in passing as evidence of the strength of the cultural connexion the common American use of the term "Victorian.") And this Old World vulgarity may also be due to the strength of a new social class, if, indeed, it is not simply a product of industrialism. But the effects of this revolution were perhaps less marked in Britain, where tradition dies hard; taste depends in a high degree upon the acceptance of social and artistic authority, and this came more naturally to Britain than the United States. What K. B. Smellie writes of the development of the English Civil Service may be very aptly applied to the realm of taste: "It may be said that it was the very slowness with which in England democratic government was substituted for aristocratic privilege that made possible the success of our Civil Service. It was rescued from private patronage without becoming public spoils."[5]

It may be that this persistence of aristocratic traditions in social life accounts for a division among the English in their reception of American culture, which has been more readily accepted by the common people, and more frequently rejected by the upper classes. It is through the media of mass culture that the power of America has been chiefly exercised, such as the press, popular music, and the cinema. English influence on America remains greatest in the more esoteric cultural realms, for, as Tocqueville would have it, the "permanent inequality" of Europe led men to "the arrogant and sterile researches of abstract truths, whilst the social conditions and institutions of democracy prepare them to seek immediate and useful practical results of the sciences."[6] Pessimistic observers see in this fact a gloomy fulfillment of the destiny of the West hinted at by Toynbee, in which, because the springs of culture remain pure and vigorous and undefiled only in the immediate area of its central wells, the massive powers on the peripheries of civilizations inevitably experience the debasement of culture at the hands of a powerful proletariat. It is from this point of view that criticisms of American materialism become most to the point and most alarming.

For such criticisms reasonable grounds can be found, but they can also be found with nearly equal reason for similar criticisms of the developing pattern of British life. If American culture has points of inferiority to English, they are merely matters of degree; if the Americans are, as Oliver Wendell Holmes said in 1858, "the Romans of the modern world—the great assimilating people,"[7] the English are only to an exceedingly limited degree its Greeks. They are tarred too much with the same brush of pragmatism, democracy, industrialism, and materialism for deep cleavage. Even America is not wholly democratic culturally; there are remarkable enclaves of aristocratic culture in the cosmopolitan and tradition-bound society of the Eastern seaboard, whose members look east towards Europe far more than they look west towards the heartland of Americanism. If any doubts are still felt on the score of America's cultural vigour, a glance at Soviet Russia, whose whole life, including its culture, is in the iron grip of an inflexible materialist dogma, will rapidly dispel them: for the present situation of all her arts, save those most remote from politics, shows clearly the effect of the dead hand of Communism.

But judgments of American culture are more dangerous than even these things suggest, because they are essentially judgments of value. Who shall dare to weigh quality against quantity with infallible certainty? English university teachers are well aware of the fact that the average academic standard of the American student of university age is below that of his English counterpart, and this fact is often loudly proclaimed as a general criticism of the American educational system. The criticism has some validity, but the English superiority is gained at a price; how many of the critics are aware of the *magnitude* of the American educational effort compared with the British? Average American schoolchildren are educated considerably longer than their British counterparts, and a far higher proportion of them (almost certainly much more than twice as many) go to a college than proceed in Britain to university or technical college or their equivalent. There are some qualitative advantages in Britain to offset these facts, but a great deal of English quality is needed to make up for this tremendous American superiority in quantity. Particularly is this so when one of the primary reasons for the economic failure of Britain today is the lack of that abundance of skilled technicians which American universities do so much to produce. Critical Britons might well be reminded that those who live in such a precarious and draughty glasshouse are singularly ill-equipped to cast the first-stone at the super-heated dwellings of their American friends.

If we turn to examine the common language as an index of the extent of Anglo-American cultural intercourse, we are, although not immune from the infection of value judgments, in a much healthier atmosphere, for it provides a fascinating and relatively concrete guide. To explore it fully the reader has only to turn to H. L. Mencken's monumental but absorbing work, *The American Language*. In the first place, however, one must consider to what extent one can truly talk of the common language. It seems that one can more justifiably do so in mid-twentieth century than one could do at any time in the preceding two hundred years, for very soon after the formation of the colonies, the new environment began to produce swift changes in the language of the inhabitants; though, as in other spheres, they were not able to throw off the domination of the mother tongue till after the War of 1812, they did so then with a vengeance. During the succeeding years, the flow of language eastward increased steadily in volume until, despite a sustained British resistance up to World War I, it had virtually conquered by the middle of the twentieth century. This history provides a remarkable illustration of the course of the whole Anglo-American relationship. It not only shows the gradual but insistent restoration of an intimacy unmatched since 1776, despite the ill-feeling of the early nineteenth century, but also the assumption by America of the dominant role in the partnership; the main difference is that America's insensible effort to dominate the language began much earlier than her efforts in other spheres, for the tide of language had begun to turn by the second quarter of the nineteenth century. This swift reaction was due primarily to the stimulating effect of a new environment—the settlers simply had to invent new words to describe new things—and to the tremendous racial admixtures in the new state, but there can be no doubting also the American genius for improvisation, in this as in other branches of human activity, and its swift growth in the climate of freedom, and liberation from tradition, which America offered.

American innovations had begun as early as 1621, with such words as *maize* and *canoe*, and they increased steadily in number. They were derived not only from the Indian, as with *caribou, hickory*, and *warpath*, but also direct from the Spanish, as well as from Spanish adaptations of the Indian, as in the case of *tobacco, tomato*, and *hammock;* some came from the French, such as *portage* and *bogus*; and yet others from the Dutch, such as *dope* and *waffle*. As well as making new words out of old English material, as with *stumped, locate,* and *oppose,* they altered the meaning of old ones, such as to *squat,* and revived English archaisms, such as the *fall, cross purposes, din,* and *offal*. Above all they invented new terms, such as those of politics, to *endorse, affiliate, let slide, high falutin', filibuster,* and *lobbying*.

According to Sir William Craigie, writing in 1927, the tide began to turn about 1820, in the surge of nationalism after the War of 1812, which finally severed America's English moorings. "For some two centuries . . . the passage of new words or senses across the Atlantic was regularly westward; practically the only exceptions were terms which denoted articles or products peculiar to the new country. With the nineteenth century, however, the contrary current begins to set in. . . ."[8] Then, indeed, the swelling flood begins. John Pickering's *Vocabulary or Collection of Words and Phrases which have been supposed to be peculiar to the United States of America,* published in 1816, contained some five hundred terms: a similar glossary by John Russell Bartlett in 1848 contained 412 pages, and another edition of the same work, in 1877, 813 pages. Richard Harwood Thornton's *American Glossary* of 1912 listed 3,700 terms; the University of Chicago's *Dictionary of American English on Historical Principles* of 1944, edited by Sir William Craigie, contained 2,552 large double-columned pages and listed 26,000 terms. Indeed, as one picks at random in this mighty cataract, one is amazed at the words which are in fact Americanisms; *reliable, influential, lengthy, to phone, editorial, filing cabinet, worthwhile, make good, fall for, stand for, placate, antagonize, donate, presidential*—the list could be indefinitely extended. As Alastair Cooke said in 1935: "Every Englishman listening to me now uses thirty or forty Americanisms a day."[9]

Some had a longer struggle for acceptance than others, such as *caucus* and *bunkum* (until it was instantly received as *bunk*); others had a special send-off, such as the *"Indian Summer"* of a *Forsyte* by Galsworthy, and *shyster* in R. L. Stevenson's *The Wrecker*; but mostly they came flooding in, not silently but often unnoticed. Noah Webster was certainly wise when he said in 1827: "[I]t is quite impossible to stop the progress of language—it is like the course of the Mississippi, the motion of which, at times, is scarcely perceptible; yet even then it possesses a momentum quite irresistible."[10] In the twentieth century, with the coming of such instruments of culture for the masses as the cinema, the flood got almost beyond measurement, as the succession of new editions of Mencken's work nicely illustrates, for it was primarily, as Tocqueville had seen a century earlier, in the spoken word that the American impact was felt.

The growth of American power in later years is glaringly illustrated by the paucity of the westward flow of language, for though a few terms like *browned off, good show,* and possibly *char,* may make a very precarious lodgement in the spoken vocabulary of some Americans, most English expressions, such as *shop, maid, nursing home, rotter,* which are for the most part "society" terms, undoubtedly have for Americans—and it is perhaps significant—"a somewhat pansy cast."[11] It is not surprising that the influence

of America is so overpowering; as Brogan pointed out in
1943, "If American could influence English a century ago,
when the predominance of the Mother Country . . . was
secure, and when most educated Americans were reveren-
tially colonial in their attitude to English Culture, how can
it be prevented from influencing English to-day . . . ? . . . Of
the 200 million people speaking English, nearly seven-
tenths live in the United States. . . . As an international language, it is American that the world increasingly learns.
. . ."[12] Certainly it is not artifacts like Basic English, which,
as Roosevelt once pointed out, could do no better "with
five famous words" than "blood, work, eye water and face
water."[13] As an Englishman wrote as early as 1926, "It is
chiefly in America—let us frankly recognize the fact—that
the evolution of our language will now proceed."[14]

This frank recognition has been but reluctantly ex-
torted. Ever since in 1735 Francis Moore set the tone of
English criticism with the words "the bank of the River
(which they in barbarous English call a bluff) ,"[15] the
English have fought a strong delaying action, sometimes,
as in the case of John Witherspoon, who invented the term
"Americanism" in 1781, and Richard Grant White after the
Civil War, aided and abetted by culture-conscious Americans. The reactions of the main body of the American people have been very different. A committee of Congress as
early as 1778 set the tone by talking of "the language of
the United States"; but it was Noah Webster, with his
"American" Dictionary of the English Language of 1828,
who was perhaps the most important single opponent of
subservience to Britain's fiat, declaring that "As an independent nation, our honor requires us to have a system
of our own, in language as well as government."[16] During
the period of the great literary battles of the nineteenth
century, which were exacerbated by the comments of British travellers and the waspishness of certain English periodicals, a ferocious struggle ensued over language; it caused

particular bitterness because it took the form which has always infuriated Americans most, lofty and contemptuous British denunciation. The English assumption of superiority which it implied was resented all the more because it seemed to extend far beyond the cultural sphere and to involve a denigration of democracy; this attack upon the ark of the American covenant still further added to American political rancour against Britain, and fortified the American belief in the fundamental iniquity of the Old World habits and aristocratic institutions of the mother country.

In 1787 a London review of Jefferson's *Notes on the State of Virginia* read: "*Belittle!* What an expression! . . . For shame, Mr. Jefferson! Why, after trampling upon the honour of our Country, and representing it as a little better than a land of barbarism—why, we say, perpetually trample also upon the very grammar of our language, and make that appear as Gothic as, from your description, our manners are rude?" Even more difficult for Americans to take than this forthright sort of attack was the process of damning with faint praise, and assenting with civil leer, which is to be found in such comments as those in 1804 on John Quincy Adams's *Letters on Silesia*: "The style of Mr. Adams is in general very tolerable English, which, for an American composition, is no moderate praise."[17] The apogee of English sarcasm was reached in the works of the—from this point of view—terrible twins, Charles Dickens and Mrs. Trollope. It is necessary only to quote the former's comments on the American use of the word *fix*:

> I asked Mr. Q . . . if breakfast be nearly ready, and he tells me . . . the steward was *fixing* the tables. . . . When we have been writing and I beg him . . . to collect our papers, he answers that he'll *fix* 'em presently. So when a man's dressing he's *fixing* himself, and when you put yourself under a doctor he *fixes* you in no time. T'other night . . . when I had

ordered a bottle of mulled claret . . . the landlord . . . fear'd it wasn't properly *fixed*. And here, on Saturday morning, a Western man . . . at breakfast inquired if he wouldn't take some of "these *fixings*" with his meat.[18]

Henry James was later, it is not surprising to note, to agree with his predecessor, for when his niece said to him: "Uncle Henry, if you will tell me how you like your tea, I will *fix* it for you," he replied, "Pray, my dear young lady, what will you *fix* it with and what will you *fix* it to?"

But if British resentment began to subside in the closing years of the nineteenth century, American counter-resentment did not; indeed it rose to new heights as American power and confidence grew, and only finally died with the passing of the English contempt for Americanisms which had given it birth. Edward Everett carried the battle to the enemy by declaring that "there is no part of America in which the corruption of language has gone so far as in the heart of the English counties," and Walt Whitman proclaimed his wonted faith in the future of America with the words: "The Americans are going to be the most fluent and melodious voiced people in the world—and the most perfect users of words."[19] As the Middle West was the home of isolationism, so it "has always been the chief centre of linguistic chauvinism."[20] And it was there that, in the era of Mayor Thompson of Chicago, a bill was moved in the Illinois Legislature—and passed in a modified form in 1923—in these terms: "*Whereas*, since the creation of the American Republic there have been certain Tory elements in our country who have never become reconciled to our republican institutions and have ever clung to the tradition of King and Empire . . . the . . . official language of the State of Illinois shall be known hereafter as the 'American' language, and not as the 'English' language."[21] Perhaps the official issue to British and American soldiers twenty years later of what were, in fact, little Anglo-American dictionaries, may be deemed to have closed this chapter of Anglo-American history.

For, however loud the British protests, they were steadily drowned out. Take the word *talented* as an instance. In 1832 Coleridge called it "that vile and barbarous vocable"; in 1842 Macaulay designated it a word which it is "proper to avoid"[22]; but in that same year Pusey used it without comment; and fifteen years later it received the imprimatur of Gladstone. The American humorists, such as Petroleum V. Nasby and Artemus Ward, who actually moved to London at the end of his life, did much to break down the barrier, and in 1899, perhaps for the first time, a decided English voice, that of William Archer, was raised in favour of the American influence: "Let the purists who sneer at 'Americanisms' think for one moment how much poorer the English language would be today if North America had become a French or Spanish instead of an English Continent."[23] Soon others were heard, such as Robert Bridges, Wyndham Lewis, and Edward Shanks; and Virginia Woolf wrote: "The Americans are doing what the Elizabethans did—they are coining new words. . . . In England, save for the impetus given by the war, the word-coining power has lapsed. . . . All the expressive, ugly, vigorous slang which creeps into use among us first in talk, later in writing, comes from across the Atlantic."[24] So, as the years passed, the clamour died, until *The Times* could write in 1943: "There is urgent need for surmounting what someone has called the almost insuperable barrier of a common language. It would never do for Great Britain and America to think they understand, yet miss, the point of each other's remarks just now. Both versions of the common language must be correctly understood by both peoples."[25] In fact that great journal was, after a fashion not unknown to it, pontifically shutting the stable door after the horse had escaped, for, broadly speaking, the common people had then been talking American prose all their lives without being aware of it. As Mencken claimed, amongst the younger generation the languages are almost approaching assimilation. There are still many traps, differences, and obstacles; as Churchill pointed out, for example, the phrase "tabling a motion" has exactly opposite meanings in the political life of the two countries. But there is a greater linguistic intimacy, something nearer to a truly common language, than there has been since early colonial days.

NOTES

1. J. B. McMaster, *A History of the People of the United States, from the Revolution to the Civil War* (New York, 1903), V, p. 287.

2. S. E. Morison, *Sources and Documents Illustrating the American Revolution, 1764–1788* (Oxford, 1923), p. 270.

3. H. L. Mencken, *The American Language* (New York, 1946), p. 17.

4. H. B. Adams, *The Education of Henry Adams* (London, 1919), p. 19.

5. J. B. Brebner, *North Atlantic Triangle*. New Haven, 1945.

6. Merle Curti, *The Growth of American Thought*. New York, 1943.

7. Ibid., p. 233.

8. *The American Language*. Supplement One, p. 440.

9. Mencken, p. 232.

10. A. Nevins, *American Social History as Recorded by British Travellers* (New York, 1923), p. 156.

11. J. M. Cain: q. Mencken, p. 264.

12. Ibid., Supp. One, pp. 75–6.

13. Elliott Roosevelt, ed., *F. D. R., His Personal Letters* (New York, 1950), II, p. 1514.

14. Mencken, p. 611.

15. Ibid., p. 3.

16. Ibid., pp. 4, 9–10.

17. Ibid., p. 14.

18. Ibid., p. 26.

19. Ibid., pp. 67, 68, 73.

20. Ibid., p. 81.

21. Ibid., pp. 82–3.

22. Ibid., p. 223.

23. Nevins, p. 446.

24. Mencken, p. 47.

25. Ibid., Supp. One, p. 76.

*Herbert G. Nicholas**

The Wartime Alliance
and After;
The Cold War Alliance

One of the likely elements in cross-cultural interpretations of history is an evident fondness for the subject country on the part of the foreign commentator. Herbert G. Nicholas in his account of the Anglo-American alliance during World War II, and the subsequent Cold War, exhibits this trait unmistakably. The nostalgia of certain passages—"it was civil servants learning that 'restricted' was American for 'confidential'; it was Grosvenor Square turning into Eisenhower Platz; it was G.I.s in the village pub; it was SPAM"—all this speaks for itself. Does this mean that such feelings as Nicholas betrays require that the historian yield criticism to friendship? Nicholas's treatment gives a definite no to the question. He is at pains to show certain differences of opinion and policy between Washington and London, once the war was over in 1945. Indeed, the old war-time alliance was revived only because of the Soviet threat to Europe which introduced the Cold War. Yet once the Allies were in harness again, once SHAEF had been transformed into SHAPE and General Eisenhower was back in his accustomed command position, Nicholas reveals his apparent relief that the alliance had been restored.

* Herbert G. Nicholas is Rhodes Professor of American History at the University of Oxford.

In a notable passage in his *Second World War,* Churchill describes his reaction to the news of Pearl Harbor:

> So we had won after all! Yes, after Dunkirk; after the fall of France; after the horrible episode of Oran; after the threat of invasion, when, apart from the Air and the Navy, we were an almost unarmed people; after the deadly struggle of the U-boat war—the Battle of the Atlantic, gained by a hand's breadth; after seventeen months of lonely fighting and nineteen months of my responsibility in dire stress, we had won the war. England would live; Britain would live; the Commonwealth of Nations and the Empire would live. How long the war would last or in what fashion it would end, no man could tell, nor did I at this moment care. Once again in our long island history we should emerge, however mauled or mutilated, safe and victorious. We should not be wiped out. Our history would not come to an end. We might not even have to die as individuals. Hitler's fate was sealed. Mussolini's fate was sealed. As for the Japanese, they would be ground to powder. All the rest was merely the proper application of overwhelming force. . . . Many disasters, immeasurable cost and tribulation lay ahead, but there was no doubt about the end.[1]

The assurance of American aid embodied in Lend-Lease had perhaps been a guarantee that in this worst of her wars Britain would not be defeated, but only America's actual entry into the fight on Britain's side provided the assurance that Britain would actually win. The awareness, after the fall of France, that victory depended on the U.S.A. sank deep into the consciousness of every Briton and lay behind every major decision that the government took from that time onwards. To secure the closest possible cooperation of the U.S.A. in our war effort became, next to the defeat of Hitler itself, the main objective of British policy.

The realization of this objective was enormously facilitated by the profound mutual respect and strong personal attachment that marked the relations of the two national leaders, Churchill and Roosevelt, but it did not have to rely upon the personalities at the top. A profound identity of thinking about the nature of the struggle and about the ultimate issues involved underlay the policies of both governments at most levels and was itself a reflection of common elements in the habits and beliefs of the two nations. This made possible a wartime alliance which was a real merging of two national wills, two fighting forces and two economies. The partnership in arms worked not through an agreed division of labour so much as through a sharing of burdens and a genuine merging of national identities of which S.H.A.E.F. (Supreme Headquarters Allied Expeditionary Force) was the supreme exemplification. The joint military effort was underpinned by a wholly unprecedented pooling of national resources. This is the phenomenon to which Churchill referred when he spoke of "our affairs . . . becoming rather mixed up." It was exemplified in the development of Lend-Lease into Mutual Aid, it was enshrined in the institution of the Combined Boards, and given perhaps its most explicit expression in the terms of reference of the Combined Production and Resources Board: "The Board shall combine the production programmes of the United States and the United Kingdom into a single integrated programme, adjusted to the strategic requirements of the war."[2] And of course this pooling concept extended into the realm of techniques and ideas, of which radar, atomic energy, military and political intelligence are only the most obvious examples.

The pooling involved in the joint war effort was always a little more real for Britain than for the U.S.A. There were always American leaders who would tolerate no British interference in their theatres, like Admiral King in the Pacific; British generalissimi might be difficult, like Montgomery, but they could never ignore their yoke-fellows. The American economy, rich and sprawling, never came under the same degree of effective government direction and control that the British knew from 1940 onwards; consequently there was never an equivalent degree of conversion from peacetime to wartime requirements. More than this, the U.S.A., who in many fields of services and production supplied Britain's needs as well as her own, had a freedom which Britain lacked to decide which of the elements of her contribution should go into the common pool.

Nevertheless not only did the system genuinely work, to a surprising degree; it was also in Britain's obvious interest, as the weaker and poorer partner, both to preserve the system and, even where it cracked, to maintain belief in it. In Britain it sank deep roots into the national consciousness where it intertwined itself inextricably with the concept of "fair shares" on which increasingly the morale of the British home front came to depend. It made smooth a partnership with a rich and remote ally which had, in the abstract, all the elements that make for fratricidal strife. Personified in Eisenhower, it was immensely popular at all levels, civilian and military. The alliance, so conceived, interpenetrated the national life at every point; it was civil servants learning that "restricted" was the American for "confidential"; it was Grosvenor Square turning into Eisenhower Platz; it was G.I.s in the village pub; it was SPAM. Like the war itself, it was all-pervasive. Its detailed history does not require telling here; it was indeed in large part the history in its later stages of the war itself.

In proportion as the war was total, so the transition to peace, as far as Britain was concerned, was gradual. Too gradual perhaps, but circumstances and a strong demand for social justice combined to make it so. A nation whose life, in all its aspects, had been dedicated to waging war could no more revert at once to peacetime normality than a man whose legs have been tied can walk the moment his cords have been cut. And just as the war persisted in British thinking, so did expectations and habits bred of the alliance.

To preserve the essence of the alliance in the post-war world had become a major British war aim. As the hoped-for intimacy with the U.S.S.R. failed to materialize, as indeed it became obvious that Stalin wanted a European settlement radically different from that which British obligations and interests dictated, so the desire to retain American strength and support in Europe came to dominate British thinking. By 1945 it was abundantly true, as the leading historian of the alliance put it, that "Churchill's greatest fear was that the United States would abandon Europe after the war, leaving Great Britain to face Soviet Russia alone with nothing more than her own resources and whatever Continental allies could be created."[3] To avert such a catastrophe Britain cheerfully waived several of her preferences in the planning of a world organization and accepted at all important points the American design, as well as an American site for the United Nations once it had been created. But the fear of a revived American isolationism did not end with the assurance of United States membership in the United Nations. The premature death of Roosevelt, his legacy of trust in Stalin's good intentions, the alarming indifference of the American military to the political implications of their actions in Central Europe, for example, over the determination of the east-west boundary lines in Germany and Austria—all this kept British anxieties alive. To retain the U.S.A. as a close partner with Britain seemed the only way to avert the perils which post-war Europe seemed to present.

In the U.S.A., unfortunately, very different thinking prevailed about the transition from war to peace and its implications for the alliance. The overwhelming majority of Americans, whether isolationists or not, were agreed on making a clear-cut distinction between war and peace. War was killing, or being killed by, Germans and Japanese. When the fighting was over the war ceased, the troops came back home, and the other abnormalities associated with war came to an end, too. Mr. Truman was only speaking the truth about his fellow-countrymen when he claimed that "no people in history have been known to disengage themselves so quickly from the ways of war."[4] This divergence of attitudes and expectations had immediate implications for the alliance. A week after V-J Day, Mr. Truman announced the ending of Lend-Lease; by the end of the war, as a logical corollary of the bonfire of American domestic controls, the whole structure of Anglo-American economic "pooling" was in ruins; the Combined Food Board alone was left going until December, 1946. The military disintegration was a little less explicit, but no less real. The Combined Chiefs of Staff were not indeed formally wound up; they ceased nonetheless to exist, except for dealing with Trieste and a few other residual side-issues.

For a moment it seemed to the British as if all the firm realities of the bilateral alliance were being washed away in a flood of wishful multilateralism. For the intimate political consultations of F.D.R. and the "Former Naval Person" would be substituted the publicized deadlocks of the Foreign Ministers' Conference; the solid shield of the Anglo-American forces would be replaced by the never-to-be-actualized police functions of the United Nations Security Council; instead of the orderly apparatus of economic pooling and planning there would be a free-for-all, tempered only by the aspirations of an international trade convention and the charity of U.N.R.R.A. To make matters worse, not only did the Americans appear to think that these would be effective substitutes for the alliance; many of them, inside the administration as well as without, had come to regard the alliance as a positive obstacle to the *novus ordo saeclarum*. To think in terms of an Anglo-American alliance was, in the view of a good many, to think in anti-Soviet terms, to be impairing the harmony of American-Soviet relations, on which the real hopes of future peace depended, in order to preserve a fighting partnership whose justification was now ended. Was there not even some support for this view to be constructed out of the fragmentary political testament of the late Franklin Roosevelt himself? Thus when the institutions of the new order failed to function as hoped, there was even a certain disposition to try and remedy this by an ostentatious disavowal of the old alliance. The battles in the infant United Nations in early 1946 over Iran, Indonesia, Greece, Lebanon, and Syria were mainly fought out by Bevin and Molotov with Byrnes often playing the role of mediator and pacifier. Even after President Truman himself had become tired, as he put it, of "babying the Soviets" it was left to his English visitor, Winston Churchill, in his Fulton speech to sound the call for the West to unite and face the full measure of the Soviet threat. Moreover, though the speech received private encouragement and applause from the highest circles in the United States, public official endorsement was still thought inadvisable.

Some of the British alarm of 1945 turned out to be exaggerated. The ending of Lend-Lease turned out in fact to be somewhat less abrupt than Mr. Truman's staccato announcement made it appear. The pipe-line provided time in which to negotiate the economic aid from North America which was embodied in the Anglo-American and the Anglo-Canadian Loan Agreements of December, 1945. Securing this aid was an imperative for Britain hardly less pressing than the maintenance of American co-operation in the political and diplomatic spheres. The war left Britain impoverished and at many points crippled. The sheer physical destruction she had sustained was considerable—£1,500 million on shore in property losses and £700 million at sea in the sinking of one-third of her merchant fleet. Of her overseas investments £1,118 million had been liquidated, while her gold and dollar reserves had dropped from £864 million in 1938 to £453 million in 1945. Meanwhile her external liabilities in the form of debts mainly in the sterling area had risen from £760 million to £3,355 million. In all one could estimate that about one-quarter (£7,300 million) of Britain's pre-war national wealth had been lost in the war. At the same time her export trade was down to thirty percent of its 1938 volume in a world in which the cost of imports had risen by fifty percent. Only America could physically provide the goods and raw materials necessary to keep life going and rebuild the battered industries; only America could provide the economic wherewithal.

Yet here again the tenacious grip of wartime experience and wartime ways of thinking put the British at odds with an America which wanted to treat the war as a closed book, indeed a closed ledger. This was not just the view of the man in the street; it was if anything even more the blinkers in which nearly six years of war had fastened the best minds in Whitehall. It was that restless innovator and fertile genius, Lord Keynes, who wished above all to rest the British proposals for economic aid on the argument of what Britain had suffered in the common cause and what the principle of equality of sacrifice would dictate in a final reckoning. "Since," as he said, "our transitory financial difficulties are largely due to the role we played in the war, and to the costs we incurred before the United States entered the war, we here in London feel . . . that it might not be asking too much of our American friends that they should agree to see us through the transition by financial aid which approximated to a grant."[5] In relation to the wartime concept of "pooling" such an approach could be justified. One major reason for Britain's plight in 1945, was that, though a trading nation, she had, as part of the mutually agreed production plan, switched her export industries to munitions work and also scrupulously abstained from using any Lend-Lease materials for manufacturing export goods. It could be shown, insofar indeed as figures can ever demonstrate such propositions, that, man for man, the British had suffered more in the common struggle than the Americans; it could be argued that much was due in respect of the period before Pearl Harbor when Britain "stood alone."

In line with this kind of reasoning, the Treasury prepared a White Paper setting out what Britain had done and suffered in the common cause and for three days in the Washington negotiations, Keynes expounded the case for an outright grant based upon it. But what seemed obvious and fair in London wore a different appearance in Washington. As Keynes himself put it on his return, justifying the financial agreements before a sceptical House of Lords: "But what a gulf separates us from the climate of Washington; and what a depth of misunderstanding there will be as to what governs relations between even the friendliest and most like-minded nations if we imagine that so free and easy an arrangement could commend itself to the complex politics of Congress or to the immeasurably remote public opinion of the United States. Nevertheless, it was on these lines that we opened our case. For three days the heads of the American delegation heard me expound the material. . . . Nevertheless, it was not very long before the British delegation discovered that a primary emphasis on past services and past sacrifices would not be fruitful. The American Congress and the American people have never accepted any literal principle of equal sacrifice, financial or otherwise, between all the allied participants. . . . We soon discovered, therefore, that it was not our past performance or our present weakness but our future prospects of recovery and our intention to face the world boldly that we had to demonstrate. Our American friends were interested not in our wounds, though incurred in the common cause, but in our convalescence."[6]

The reassuring implications of the final twist of

Keynes's closing epigram were not fully borne out by the
financial settlements which were eventually concluded.
Even Keynes could not disguise his disappointment at the
final form of the Agreements and it was less his advocacy
than inexorable necessity—Britain simply had to have the
dollars—that induced Parliament to ratify them after a
division in which 169 M.P.s abstained from voting, Churchill amongst them. It was not merely that the Agreements
were felt to be ungenerous (this, after all, was an issue on
which the British judgment might reasonably be thought
to be suspect) ; what most worried their critics was their
multilateralism. Here, in the convertibility clauses, in the
links between the loan and the acceptance of the Bretton
Woods institutions, in the whole concept of Britain's problem being just that of negotiating a quick transition to full
multilateralism—in all this there was a very explicit substitution of the new, untried world of international institutions for the familiar and trusted wartime alliance. The
economists had gone even farther than the diplomats and
the politicians in moving Anglo-American relations from
their old moorings. There were many who argued, Keynes
amongst them, that in this open sea lay Britain's truest
safety, that Britain's destiny as a trading nation was ultimately bound up with the maintenance of an international
system of trade and convertibility. They were the counterparts of the positive champions of the United Nations who
saw the organization as the natural expression of the interest in peace and international order which Britain and
the United States had in common. But just as the dry pow-
der school wished to maintain within the United Nations
framework the working mechanism of the diplomatic and
military Atlantic alliance, so even amongst the economic
liberals there was a gloomy conviction that the new international economic institutions could not sustain the weight
that the Anglo-American Financial Agreements imposed on
them. They were right; it was not the Bank and the Fund

which took over the unfinished business of the American loan, but Marshall Aid. At the same time, by a curious paradox, the Financial Agreements did, as it turned out, provide the most striking demonstration that the realities of the Anglo-American alliance had in fact survived.

The passage of the Agreements through the British Parliament was not, of course, sufficient to bring them into operation. To become effective they had to be approved by the body which alone could authorize the expenditure, the American Congress. And in fact their passage through that body was, for different reasons, no less painful and a great deal more prolonged than it had been in Britain. For months throughout the spring and early summer of 1946 while Britain, the proud mendicant, half hoped, half feared that Congress would reject them, the debate dragged on, generating its inevitable accompaniment of mutual resentment and ill-feeling. The arguments of its supporters in the executive branch about the brave new world of multilateralism and free convertibility were poorly received in a chamber whose composition gives the maximum scope to every advocate of economic nationalism—so poorly indeed that it looked as if its prospects would founder. Fortunately, as the months dragged on, economic nationalism was overborne, not by the new liberalism, but by lively fears of what Russia was doing to the Western world on the diplomatic and political fronts. Recognizing the strength of the opposition and the cruciality of the vote, Sam Rayburn, the Speaker of the House, left the chair to make a rare personal intervention. His argument was simple and, as it proved, decisive: "I do not want Western Europe, England, and all the rest pushed toward an ideology that I despise. I fear that if we do not co-operate with this great natural ally of ours that is what will happen . . . If we are not allied with the British democracy, I fear someone will be and God pity us when we have no ally across the Atlantic Ocean and God pity them too."[7]

It could be said at the end of 1946 that the Anglo-American alliance was in an ambiguous condition. On the one hand, its formal structure had disintegrated with the end of the war; on the other hand a good deal of its spirit persisted, exemplified in a resolute British endeavour to keep the U.S. *engagé* and in an American recognition that Britain constituted, for practical purposes, her most reliable friend. What degree of American commitment could be secured and what mutual obligations the friendship would entail were, however, still uncertain. The resolution of these uncertainties was the work of the years 1947, 1948, and 1949.

It is not necessary to re-tell the whole story of the adoption of the Truman Doctrine, the shaping of the Marshall Plan and the evolution of N.A.T.O. But some features of the story are necessary to a full understanding of the relationship which Britain built up with the U.S. in these years. When in late February, 1947, Britain formally notified the U.S.A. that she could no longer continue to be the reservoir of financial-military support for Greece and Turkey, it is doubtful if the full implications of the act were as clearly grasped in Whitehall as in Washington. Superficially it was a matter of $250 million which Britain, in the hard-pressed winter of 1947, could no longer afford. The decision to place the last straw in America's lap seems to have come, like so many fateful British decisions, from the Treasury. The news of the decision initially created relatively little stir in Britain. Indeed it was not until March 5 that news of the British abdication was at all prominently displayed to British readers, and then only in the form of a dispatch from Washington. It was March 17 before a statement was made in the House of Commons. It excited comparatively little comment. What in retrospect may appear a milestone in Anglo-American relations was generally viewed at the time as only a minor adjustment in the load of British post-war commitments. That it would result in a "Truman Doctrine" seems to have been totally unexpected in Britain. Possibly this was because it was only relatively, not absolutely, that it represented a lightening of that load. Only a little more than three months earlier, on November 6, 1946, Mr. Attlee had announced that the rate of demobilization in the services would be slowed down, so that the number of men under arms at the year's end would be 1,427,000 instead of the 1,200,000 originally planned. And on the same day that Mr. Truman spoke to Congress, the British Government published the draft of their bill to perpetuate conscription on the basis of an eighteen-month period of service.

What was happening, of course, was that the Russians were raising the pressure on the British defence line just at a time when *all* economic considerations demanded a cutting of our cloth. Nineteen forty-six had ended with deadlock over Germany and 1947 began with the mockery of "free elections" in Poland. No foreign minister could advise his colleagues that the nation could relax its guard, but in view of the rate at which the American loan was disappearing and the imbalance of payments worsening there had to be a reduction of overseas military expenditure. (Critics pointed out that the £300 million spent on maintaining our overseas responsibilities, mostly in Germany and the Middle East, exactly equalled the gap in the balance of payments.) The solution was not so much to reduce as to shift the burden; to spend, if it must be, more at home, but to unload some of the overseas tasks on to the U.S.A. By one of history's pretty ironies the first burden to be transferred to Uncle Sam's shoulders was the one which, two or three years earlier, John Bull had been most severely censured for assuming—Greece, where Churchill's anti-Communist intervention had won sharp "anti-imperialist" rebukes in the U.S.A. in 1944 and 1945.

One cannot say with confidence how far the government at this moment was working on the assumption that the alliance *à trois* with the U.S.S.R. was dead and that an outright, explicit Anglo-American front should take its place. As late as December 22, 1946, Ernest Bevin had depicted Britain as "midway" between the U.S.A. and the U.S.S.R., "not tying herself to anyone" and, when Stalin alleged that this meant Britain was welshing on the Anglo-Soviet Treaty, Bevin agreed to "reaffirm" the Treaty a month later. But though Bevin undoubtedly did not wish to close the door on a European settlement with the U.S.S.R., his public statements have to be read in the light of his anxiety, as a Labour Foreign Secretary, over maintaining unity in a party with a vociferous left wing. There is no reason to doubt that for all practical purposes the British Government had given up hope of any better relationship with the U.S.S.R. than one of peaceful containment and that since the war's end there had never been any faltering in their desire to have the closest possible relationship with the U.S.A. At the same time it would seem that British official circles were surprised and a little taken aback at the challenging tone of Mr. Truman's message; there is reason to suppose that no one expected the burden which was so quietly dropped to be picked up quite so resoundingly.

Despite the drama of March 12, 1947, what actually happened was very much less than a substitution of *Pax Americana* for *Pax Britannica*. There was no neat and swift switch-over from British to United States responsibility. Far from it. In the first place the United States was by no means in a position to assume such a role. After Mr. Truman's speech there ensued over two months of Congressional debate. Not until May 22 did Mr. Truman sign the Greco-Turkish Aid Bill and when it became law, it merely pledged cash for military and economic aid, while providing for missions, military and naval, of an advisory character. There was no provision for the dispatch of troops. When the Greek situation reached a crisis in June and July, 1947, under pressure from the Yugoslavs, Bulgarians and Albanians, the line had to be held without any United States forces. Indeed the first shiploads of United States military material did not arrive until 14 August. Meanwhile Britain was under steady pressure from the United States administration not to withdraw her forces, first of all on the groups of the anticipated delay in passing the Greco-Turkish Aid Bill, and subsequently in view of the persistently critical situation in Greece. However, the dollar drain accelerated alarmingly in the summer, leading Britain to make renewed announcements of the withdrawal of her forces, announcements which in turn provoked a critical reaction in Washington. Forrestal's diary entry for August 4 indicates how one such communication was received:

> Lunch today with Marshall, Harriman, Snyder. Marshall expressed his deep concern with the implications that might be drawn from the withdrawal of British troops from Greece and Italy. He has wired Bevin in strong language, protesting against the British action in presenting the United States with such decisions as the one of last February advising us that we would have to accept the responsibility for Greece and this most recent one of complete withdrawal from southern Europe. He asked Douglas to inquire of Bevin whether this indicates a fundamental change in British policy. Bevin replied to this in the negative.[8]

In response to pressure such as this, but with great reluctance, Britain left 5,000 men in Greece until well into 1948 and 3,000 or so from then on. The last British troops did not leave Greece until the beginning of 1950.

The fact was that, quite apart from the political difficulty of sending United States troops to Greece, there were hardly the troops available to send. With the expiry of the Selective Service Act on March 31, 1947, Congress allowed the last relics of military conscription to disappear, not to reappear until in June of the following year, 1948, when a fresh Selective Service Act was passed.

Meanwhile, however, the reduction of United Kingdom commitments went on. Although in November, 1946, the government announced their intention to continue conscription from January 1, 1949 (when it was due to expire), in April, 1947, they responded swiftly to pressure from their back-benchers and cut the proposed duration from eighteen months to twelve months. On July 30, 1947, a speed-up in demobilization was ordered and on August 30, 1947, as part of dollar crisis economies, Attlee announced a further cut which would bring the army down to 1,007,000 by March 31, 1948. This was further cut in December, 1947, to 937,000 by the same date, while defence estimates published the following February, 1948, envisaged a further reduction of 220,000 within the next year, and a cut of two-ninths in the defence budget, equivalent to £200 million. The retreat from omnicompetence was on.

Undoubtedly the need to trim commitments also had a good deal to do at about the same time with the decision to wind up the costly and thankless Palestine mandate. The United States' repeated refusals (last in November, 1946), to accept any joint responsibility there led to the British government's decision to hand the problem over to the United Nations. When the United Nations voted for partition in November, 1947, the United States supported it but would not assist in enforcing it. The United Kingdom took the same position, announcing it would withdraw its troops by August 1, 1948. In fact, the first withdrawals occurred on November 16, 1947; in January, 1948, the government announced that Britain would terminate its mandate on May 15, 1948. On March 19, the United States suddenly announced abandonment of support for partition, in favour of United Nations trusteeship. When the question was raised inside the U.S. administration, how far the United States would or could implement this, it turned out that there simply were not any troops available. Forrestal reports a depressing meeting on April 4 with the Joint Chiefs of Staff which ended on an almost pathetic note: "It was suggested that the British might undertake to hold the fort alone pending the augmentation of our forces, following the adoption of Selective Service."[9] But the United Kingdom was not to be turned aside from its course. The mandate ended, the Jewish Agency proclaimed a Jewish State, eleven minutes later, on May 15, Mr. Truman accorded it American recognition, and on June 30, 1948, the last United Kingdom troops left.

From all of which it can be seen that if Anglo-American relations had simply consisted of the United Kingdom passing the sceptre of world responsibility into United States hands, the process would have been attended with a good deal of bitterness and recrimination, and, what is more, the sceptre might well in fact have fallen in the passing. Fortunately this was not what happened. Instead a new basis of United Kingdom-United States collaboration was found in a European, or to be more accurate, North Atlantic and Mediterranean context.

In retrospect the crucial developments of 1947–1948 emerge as logical steps in the evolution of an anti-Russian alliance. And as such indeed they were conceived—all of them by some people, and some of them by all people, but not every one by everybody. Even the Truman Doctrine, though immediately provoked by blatant Communist (even if not overtly Soviet) hostilities against Greece and by Soviet pressure against Turkey, was not approved by the United States Senate until Senator Vandenberg had inserted his proviso that the aid should cease whenever the General Assembly or the Security Council should decide that action taken by the United Nations rendered United States aid unnecessary or undesirable—and that, in a Security Council vote on such an issue, the United States should waive her veto. In both Britain and the U.S.A. there was a body of opinion, not necessarily made up of fellow travellers, which felt uneasy at the too openly anti-Russian tone of the Doctrine and wished to stress its essentially defensive implications. That is not to say that anyone in the government or any but a few far Leftists *disapproved* of the policy; they were merely worried lest it should go too far too roughly. In line with this fear there was a good deal of elaboration of a distinction of which more was to be heard later, between a British policy allegedly aimed at curbing Russian imperialism and an American one which saw the enemy as Communism *per se*.

In this context the Marshall Plan, aired at Harvard on June 5, three months after the Truman Doctrine had been promulgated on March 12, was especially attractive to the United Kingdom. In the first place it was an American initiative and invitation. In the second place it was aid that took an economic, not a military form. "Reconstruction" was its theme. And in the third place it was not overtly anti-Russian: "Any government that is willing to assist in the task of recovery will find full cooperation . . . on the part of the United States Government."[10] The economic emphasis was particularly attractive to Ernest Bevin and though it is very doubtful whether he ever believed the Soviets would join in (except perhaps to wreck it)[11] their inclusion in the invitation undoubtedly helped to solidify Labour support for the plan.

In fact, of course, the Marshall proposals brought not peace but a sword. Invited to confer at Paris, Molotov insisted on individual approaches to the United States and no joint European effort. He warned France and Britain against an action which "could lead to no good." Bevin replied: "My country has faced grave consequences and threats before, and it is not the sort of prospect which will deter us from doing what we consider to be our duty." Thus, ironically, what was a pacific and economic offer came to be a touchstone according to which countries were identified with the American or the Russian camp. Marshall Aid became, under this Russian pressure, a first but quite decisive step towards the unification of Western Europe under British leadership as a pro-American bloc.[12]

This role of British leadership in a European approach to the United States was emphasized when the sixteen nations' conference met at Paris on July 12 by Bevin being in the chair and later by Sir Oliver Franks becoming chairman of the Committee of European Economic Cooperation (C.E.E.C.) which met and produced an outline European recovery programme by September 22.[13]

While the future of the Marshall programme was thus back in the lap of the United States, and more specifically of the American Congress, the Russians were making clear to the world the hostile interpretation they put on it. While Communist Parties in Western Europe were trying to overthrow pro-Marshall governments, the Cominform was formed (announcement on October 5) and the Foreign Ministers' autumn meeting in London, like all its predecessors, stalled under Soviet intransigence. In the middle of December the United States gave interim aid to France, Italy, and Austria and by a new agreement with the United Kingdom relieved her of all dollar expenditure in Germany, as well as assuming seventy-five percent of the cost of both zones.

Thus the division between East and West was becoming more and more explicit. But it was also becoming apparent that if Western Europe was to survive, its collective defence would have to be organized. How far British initiative in this was dove-tailed with American thinking at the very earliest stages we do not know. But by January 13, 1948, Bevin was airing his intentions to the United States in terms which Mr. Truman describes as follows:

> Ernest Bevin, the British Foreign Secretary, had informed Secretary of State Marshall as early as January 13, 1948, that England was planning to approach

France and the so-called Benelux countries (Belgium, Netherlands, Luxembourg) with a proposal for a series of bilateral defence agreements. The pattern he had in mind was that of the Dunkirk Treaty, a postwar agreement by which Great Britain and France had agreed to come to each other's defence in case of renewed German aggression.

General Marshall brought Bevin's message to me. I thought it was a good beginning—a step in the right direction. If the countries of Western Europe were ready to organize for their joint defence, that would be an important contribution to the peace of the world.

Bevin in his message had asked what our attitude would be toward this new alliance. I authorized Marshall to inform the British Foreign Secretary that we agreed with them on the urgent need for concerted measures by the nations of Western Europe. As in the case of the European Recovery Programme, we welcomed European initiative and would give their undertaking our wholehearted sympathy; the United States would do anything it properly could to assist the European nations to bring this or a similar project to fulfillment.

With this backing from the United States, Bevin approached the French and the Benelux countries.[14]

On January 22 Bevin expounded his plan to the House of Commons: "I believe the time is ripe for a consolidation of Western Europe." He talked about "Western Union" and said, vaguely, it "must primarily be a fusion derived from the basic freedoms and ethical principles for which we all stand. . . . It is more of a brotherhood and less of a system." What emerged, in the form of the Brussels Treaty signed on March 17, 1948, was a good deal less than any union. Although the preamble talked about strengthening "the economic, social and cultural ties" of the signatories, the heart of the Treaty was in the pledge to afford "all military and other aid and assistance in their power" to any one of them which might be attacked. It was essentially military; the signatories were the United Kingdom, France, Holland, Belgium, and Luxembourg.

Even before the Treaty was signed there was an ominous development. On February 24 the Communist coup occurred in Prague. On February 26 Britain, the United States, and France launched a joint protest against the U.S.S.R.—a step without precedent. On March 5, General Clay, United States military governor in Germany, warned Washington that tension had reached a point at which war might "come with dramatic suddenness." A few days later (March 12) Bevin made what appears to be the first explicit suggestion of a North Atlantic Pact. Forrestal reports Marshall as having told him that "Bevin makes three proposals: 1. Build around the 51–nation. . . pact; 2. A plan for Atlantic security; 3. A Mediterranean system of security. Bevin suggests a meeting in Washington between British and American representatives early next week."[15] The Brussels Pact, in other words, had in fact already been recognized to be insufficient, in face of a "clear and present danger." Immediately, all the United States could offer was Mr. Truman's call to Congress on March 17 for Universal Military Training and Selective Service and his reference to the Brussels Treaty as "deserving our full support." On April 23, Bevin argued further for his Atlantic Treaty with United States membership on the grounds that only so could the Russians be deterred from war and only so could the French agree to a rebuilding of Germany. "He expressed the opinion that it would be very difficult for the British, or other free nations, to stand up to new acts of aggression unless there was a definitely worked-out arrangement, which included the United States, for collective resistance against aggression."[16]

There was here some juggling for position. Europe (including not least Great Britain) was very anxious not to launch an Atlantic Pact which the U.S.S.R. would regard as hostile before they had the firm promise of 100 percent

United States support; the United States was very anxious (partly for Congressional reasons) to use the European Recovery Programme (ERP) analogy—Europe "to display energy and competence in the perfection of their own plans . . . before we give them any indication of the scope or degree of our support."[17] The argument and the manoeuvring went on throughout the summer, Forrestal recording as late as November 12:

> On the question of an Atlantic Pact, the British [Chiefs of Staff] made it very clear that they considered it essential that the United States should sign a pact to support the Western European powers in the event of "hostilities." "They were asked what the effect would be if the United States failed to sign a pact but made substantial military shipments; they were unanimous in replying that this would be better than nothing but still "totally inadequate.' "[18]

As far as the United Kingdom was concerned two points lay behind all this:

1. Britain's desire as a European power to get the United States as far into a European commitment as possible, because of her conviction that American support was essential for European defence.

2. Her determination as an insular power with wide extra-European responsibilites not to accept any greater commitments on the continent of Europe than the United States would.

How far, in pursuit of the first aim, the United Kingdom would go, was strikingly demonstrated in June–July, 1948, at the height of the Berlin crisis, when the British were sounded out on whether they would accept two squadrons of B-29s stationed in England and the Foreign Office's reaction, "somewhat to the surprise of the Americans," was "prompt and in the affirmative."[19] There was nothing in the British response that should have surprised anyone. Already in the earlier part of 1947 the Royal Air Force and the U.S. Strategic Air Command had agreed on a long-range flight training programme; not surprisingly therefore, agreement on the stationing of the B-29s had already been reached at the operational level before the diplomats and politicians endorsed it. The decision to accept the atomic bombers, crucial though it was, was in fact in direct line with the kind of responsibilities Britain had already assumed and the kind of relationship with the United States which she had all along been seeking.

Though presented publicly as a temporary arrangement, it is doubtful whether anyone really so regarded it or, if they did, that they imagined that this subtracted from the significance of the decision. In August, 1948, another thirty B-29s joined the initial sixty and by the end of the year the number of American air force personnel in Britain had risen to 6,000. When Sir Stafford Cripps, as Chancellor of the Exchequer, visited Washington in October he told Forrestal that "Britain must be regarded as the main base for the deployment of American power and the chief offensive against Russia must be by air."[20] Thus, in advance of agreement on the North Atlantic Treaty, Britain had committed herself to an alliance in arms with the United States and had built her defence strategy around the American atomic deterrent wielded from bases on British soil. Moreover, this was done without any formal treaty agreement; it was an "arrangement," an "understanding" between the political and service chiefs on each side.

The bilateral relationship thus established in air defence was not suitable for application, simply and directly, to the economic problems of Britain and Europe. Yet one may trace elements of the same way of thinking in Britain's attitude to the evolution of the institutions of the Marshall Plan. Thus in the European Recovery Programme (E.R.P.) Britain had thrown her weight in favour of each recipient country negotiating a bilateral treaty with Washington, rather than fusing their negotiating personalities into one and concluding a single multilateral treaty with the United States. On this she got her way. Similarly when the French "Europeanists" had pressed for a strong international secretariat under a powerful chairman for the Organization for European Economic Co-operation (O.E.E.C.) which would develop a vigorous personality of its own and, as such, negotiate directly with member governments —the kind of structure which had served the European Coal Community—Britain opposed it. Instead she advocated the establishment of sixteen national delegations at Paris, served by a small secretariat in a subordinate role— a kind of continuous international conference. Substantially this was what emerged and, fortuitously in fact, but consequentially as it appeared, the eminent British chairman of the C.E.E.C., Sir Oliver Franks, was not made available to its successor organization, O.E.E.C., but instead was dispatched to Washington as British Ambassador. That no slight to the new organization was intended ought to have been apparent by the selection of Sir Edmund Hall-Patch to be chairman of the Executive Committee, who made a signal contribution to the sense of European loyalty that became O.E.E.C.'s hallmark. To the Americans, however, it is doubtful if it appeared that way, especially since Mr. Truman had released his own Secretary of Commerce, Mr. Harriman, to be the American opposite number in Paris. Finally, in line with these restrictions on supranationalism and this determination to keep open direct lines of communication with Washington—indeed to give priority to them—was the British desire to see the crucial question of the allocation of funds handled in Washington and not in Paris. Here Britain's main critics were the Americans themselves, who, pressing for European unification, suddenly insisted on the Europeans doing their own shareout, at least to the extent of making their own recommendations for the division of aid. In fact, the task proved too much for so large a membership and a Committee of "Four Wise Men"[21] were given the task of making recommendations which the council substantially accepted. In fact also O.E.E.C. recommendations were *only* recommendations. The Economic Cooperation Administration, E.C.A., in Washington always retained the legal power to determine the size of aid allotments and when the aid total was cut at the end of the first two years, E.C.A. assumed the major responsibility for fixing the allocation.

As the structure of N.A.T.O. developed, British attitudes towards it could be seen to parallel closely previous attitudes to the Marshall Plan. There was the same aversion to anything suggestive of a supranational secretariat, though a comparable willingness to second an eminent English public servant, in this case Lord Ismay, and to allow him to develop an "international personality." In the matter of the allocation of American aid there was indeed little question of choice between the bilateral and the multilateral approach. When merely economic aid stopped and the new Mutual Defence Assistance Programme, part economic but mainly military, took its place, the United States naturally preferred to decide itself who should have how much. To Britain, reasonably confident of her ability to demonstrate that she was a good risk and no mere crutch-lover, this arrangement was preferable to any round-table haggling. (N.A.T.O. haggling, as in the Annual Review and over the costs of the infrastructure, proved to be arduous indeed.) Similarly, in strategic planning, the structure of N.A.T.O., with its location of the Standing Group in Washington, was highly acceptable.[22] Save for the addition of France, was this not the old Combined Chiefs of Staff Committee of World War II, which also had met in Washington? The resemblance of S.H.A.P.E. to S.H.A.E.F. was even more obvious, while the selection of General Eisenhower as Supreme Commander put the organization of European defence into trusted and familiar hands.

Most important of all perhaps, the essential power structure of N.A.T.O. was (indeed still is) that of an alliance in which two members, the United States and Britain, disposed of a strength different not merely in degree but also in kind from that which the rest could command, namely the nuclear deterrent. The British share in this antedated her development of an independent deterrent of her own (if indeed the V-bomber force can properly be so described); it derived essentially from the facilities which as "the unsinkable aircraft carrier" she afforded to U.S. Strategic Air Command (S.A.C.) at a time when other bases were, in varying degrees, impracticable because they were either liable to be overrun by Soviet ground forces or were only leasable from politically unstable ground landlords. But all along S.A.C. has remained outside N.A.T.O., an arm exclusively and directly under U.S. control. There was thus a paradox at the heart of N.A.T.O. (and still is), that as an alliance it never controlled forces adequate for the defence of its members; owing to the persistent failure in the build-up of its ground troops, N.A.T.O. depended always upon the two air forces which it did not control, S.A.C. and Bomber Command. That this was an element of weakness, and that it occasioned jealousies and anxieties amongst the members is almost certainly true, but from the British point of view, this feature of N.A.T.O. was not the least of its recommendations. A N.A.T.O. which sought to oppose the Soviet millions by an equivalent build-up of ground forces would have drained Britain dry of manpower and left her nothing with which to deal with the "limited" and "brush-fire" wars which might come her way as a worldwide power. It would also have put Britain very much on a par with all the continental European members, with so much of a voice (and no more) as the numbers of her armed forces would have entitled her to. The balance maintained between the conventional forces of N.A.T.O. and the nuclear deterrent was essentially what enabled Britain to continue operating in her dual capacity as a European and an Atlantic power. Moreover, it enabled her to build and maintain the Anglo–American alliance within a structure of Western European collective security, thus by-passing many, if not all, the problems that an exclusively bilateral arrangement would have created, both in Europe and in America. Finally, it put her on a par with the United States in respect of an issue on which she was peculiarly sensitive—her degree of insularity or commitment. Britain was able to hold her contention that as an island power with worldwide obligations she was as good a European as that quasi-island power with worldwide commitments, the United States, and that she would go into Europe as far as America would go (even if that involved greater risks for her than for America, as a more vulnerable and contiguous country) but that she was not under any obligation to go farther.

The testing time for "thus far and no farther" came very soon after the N.A.T.O. structure had been built. When the Korean War made vivid the menace of Communism on the march and at the same time diverted much American strength towards the Pacific, the inadequacy of N.A.T.O.'s forces became glaringly apparent. The demand for the creation of a German army to help in the manning of the European ramparts grew proportionally. It did not indeed grow at an equal pace in Britain and America. Britain, to some extent, had her hand forced by American pressure. Left to herself, she would certainly have preferred to wait rather than demand from a defeated enemy a contribution to an anti-Russian defence force. Britain was more reluctant than the U.S.A. to believe that Germany's "re-education" in democracy and non-aggression was complete at the end of a five-year course. She was also more willing to credit the Soviet argument that once West Germany was re-armed, the reunification of Germany would be out of the question. These differences apart, no one disputed that the revival of a German instrument of war would be only tolerable to her old enemies and victims if it were integrated in a larger whole which it could never hope to dominate. Thus arose the idea of a European army, to which indeed even so robust a British patriot as Winston Churchill gave his endorsement at the Council of Europe in August, 1950. What perhaps his auditors failed to notice was his proviso that such a force should act "in full co-operation with the United States and Canada." Even so, it was a misleading index of Britain's own intentions. The Americans, announcing that they would send more troops to Europe (Mr. Truman on September 5, 1950), began also to step up their pressure for German rearmament. The French, hating the idea of a German national army, hastily devised the Pleven Plan (national contingents integrated at the level of the smallest possible unit under a European Defence Minister, reponsible to the European Assembly with a European budget and Defence Council). But when it came to working out details in the first half of 1951, the United Kingdom made it clear that it would not join the European Army and to the meeting held at Paris to discuss the Plan in February, 1951, Britain sent only an observer. However, when it became apparent later in the year that a direct German contribution to N.A.T.O. would not be acceptable and that the European Defence Community (E.D.C.) was the only alternative, the United Kingdom joined with the United States and France in giving it support. Herbert Morrison, as Foreign Secretary, said we desired to establish "the closest possible association" with it "at all stages of its development." The statement was, however, more indicative of the ambivalence of British pronouncements than of any change of policy.

If, when Mr. Churchill took over from Mr. Attlee in

October, 1951, the Europeans expected the great proponent of a European Army to lead the United Kingdom into E.D.C., they were quickly disillusioned. Despite keen and constant American pressure the response of the British Government was cool. Sir David Maxwell-Fyfe was sent to Strasbourg to say that Britain would "consider" the best way of "associating" herself with a European army—a far cry from integrating her forces in one. In other words, the British government was for a European army—but from outside; Britain was to be a well-wisher, not a participant. We have Sir Anthony Eden's word for it[23] that this policy enjoyed, from November, 1951, onwards, official American support (though he admits even "well-informed" Americans still blamed us for not going in). He does not say what considerations led to this change in the American attitude but to the extent to which it took place it was certainly welcome in Britain. As the E.D.C. negotiations proceeded it became more and more apparent that the British relationship with any such defence community would not be any more intimate than the American. In pursuance of this policy it was a joint and identical assurance that Britain and the U.S.A. gave on the morrow of the signing of the E.D.C. Treaty that

> If any action from whatever quarter threatens the integrity or unity of the Community, the two Governments will regard this as a threat to their own security. They will act in accordance with Article 4 of the North Atlantic Treaty.

In fact, of course, this assurance was not enough to secure the ratification of the E.D.C. Treaty. For nearly two years the E.D.C. debate dragged on inconclusively in France. In face of this, American impatience and irritation mounted. In October, 1953, Dulles as U.S. Secretary of State threatened France with his "agonizing reappraisal" and the threat

that Congress might not continue to support N.A.T.O.
Aimed primarily at France it also had its implications for
Britain. This was the time when Dulles informed Eden
that

> If things went wrong the United States might swing
> over to a policy of Western hemispheric defence,
> with emphasis on the Far East. . . . Mr. Dulles pointed
> out that the consequences of a swing of American
> policy towards hemispheric defence were of obvious
> concern to Great Britain. He hoped therefore that
> they might find an occasion to underline the warn-
> ings which he had issued in his statement and make
> some appeal to France.[24]

In August, 1954, nonetheless, the French Assembly rejected
E.D.C.

The situation thus precipitated was far more critical
than any that had existed before E.D.C. had been thought
of. To resolve this *crise de confiance*, even though in the
strict sense it was none of her making, and to make possible
the only other conceivable solution, the admission of Germany into N.A.T.O., Britain gave a pledge "to maintain on
the mainland of Europe . . . the effective strength of the
United Kingdom forces now assigned to S.A.C.E.U.R.,
four divisions and the Tactical Air Force, or whatever
S.A.C.E.U.R. regards as equivalent fighting capacity" and
not to withdraw them against the wishes of a majority of
the Brussels Powers. For the United States, Dulles also gave
an undertaking but it was in a less explicit form—United
States "to maintain in Europe . . . such units . . . as may be
necessary and appropriate to contribute its fair share of the
forces needed . . . etc." In retrospect the discrepancy between the two commitments may not appear unduly significant; if so, it is because the British Government has not
allowed the Paris Agreements to set a precedent in creating
such discrepancies—indeed, as the British Defence White
Paper of 1957 soon showed, it has not interpreted the Agree-

ments themselves as constituting quite as rigid a commitment as at first appeared.

NOTES

1. *The Second World War,* Vol. III (London, 1959), pp. 539–40 (New York, 1960), pp. 606–7.

2. *Documents on American Foreign Relations, 1941–2,* p. 250.

3. W. H. McNeill, *America, Britain and Russia, 1941–1946* (London, New York, 1953), p. 411.

4. H. S. Truman, *Memoirs,* I (New York, London, 1955), p. 506.

5. H. L. Deb. Vol. 138, col. 779–780, 10 December, 1945.

6. Op. cit. col. 780–782.

7. *92 Congressional Record 9040* (12 July, 1946).

8. *The Forrestal Diaries* (London, 1952), pp. 292–3; (New York, 1951), pp. 301–2.

9. Ibid. (London), pp. 292–3; (New York), pp. 301–2.

10. Mr. Marshall at Harvard. U.S. Dept. of State *Bulletin,* Vol. 16, p. 1159.

11. Though he did say in a speech in London on 13 June that it would "throw a bridge to link East and West."

12. Incidentally the decision to incorporate Western Germany in C.E.E.C.'s plans confirmed the *de facto* position of Germany.

13. Without any overt United States participation, though Clayton, Douglas and Caffery were in the wings to say what Congress would not stand—e.g. to scale down the total from $29 billion over four years to $22.4 (cut by the Harriman Committee to $17 billion) and add pledges to balance budgets.

14. Truman, op. cit., Vol. II (New York, 1956), p. 243; (London, 1956), p. 257.

15. *The Forrestal Diaries* (New York, 1951), pp. 301–2; (London, 1952), pp. 372.

16. Truman, op. cit., Vol. II (New York), p. 245; (London), pp. 258–9.

17. *The Forrestal Diaries* (New York), p. 434; (London), p. 409.

18. Ibid. (New York), p. 525; (London), p. 490.

19. Ibid. (New York), pp. 454–5; (London), pp. 427–8.

20. Ibid. (New York), p. 491; (London), p. 460.

21. From Italy, France, Belgium, and the United Kingdom.

22. The Standing Group's prestige declined from 1953 onwards, when the chairman of the United States Chiefs of Staff ceased to be the day-to-day American representative on the Group; in his place came another senior officer.

23. A. Eden, *Full Circle* (London, Boston, 1960), pp. 32–36.

24. Ibid., pp. 57–58.

Components
of
American History

*Jim Potter**

Some British Reflections on Turner and the Frontier

Whereas most British authorities on United States history keep their assumptions about the possible uniqueness of their conceptions of the American experience subsurface, Jim Potter offers some frank reflections on Frederick Jackson Turner and the frontier. In so doing, he reveals certain characteristics of what is perhaps a basic British approach to the understanding and writing of history in recent years. For example, as Potter clearly indicates, he sees in Turner's thesis about the frontier an exemplification of the British preference for a continuing emphasis on all the social sciences. History supplies but one of the requisite dimensions. Another merit in Potter's critique is that he deliberately poses questions which offer rich possibilities for exploration without setting up counterfactual models. His ear for the contrapuntal notes, such as his stress on the relatively unimportant role assigned to the individual by Turner's frontier thesis, is especially sensitive. In summary, Potter, the non-American Americanist, makes a strong case for the value of a foreign critique of one of the sacred cows of American historical writing.

---

*Jim Potter is a Reader in American Economic History at The London School of Economics.

Once, in Paris, I attended a European Conference on American Studies which consisted of a series of meetings devoted to all kinds of different subjects on American themes. There was one interesting French professor present who managed to get up at the end of every single conference, no matter what the subject—it might have been religion, it might have been immigration, it might have been industry or the frontier or the South or whatever—but regardless of the subject he always arose and made exactly the same two points. Firstly the obvious one, all Frenchmen must say, that America owed her existence to Lafayette and the French army: thus was point one established. Point number two was that it was not Frederick Jackson Turner who really discovered the importance of the frontier and the noble savage: it all came from Jean Jacques Rousseau. So that in both respects these two important factors of the French contribution to American history had always got to be borne in mind.

Such simplicities aside, the fact is that in Europe, perhaps particularly in Britain, Turner is one of the best known, perhaps the best known of all American historians. I do not intend to devote much space here to a discussion of Turner, the historian. That would be out of place; his virtues are too familiar to all; and certainly I do not come simply to praise him. Indeed, it is salutary to reflect that some of his strongest advocates and admirers have done him more disservice than service. Still less, however, do I come to bury Turner. Others have tried and failed. F. A. Shannon thought years ago that he had knocked the final nails into the coffin and buried that coffin under ten feet of prairie soil, but the spirit has shown a most remarkable unwillingness to rest in peace,[1] and the Turner hypothesis still continues as one of the major themes in American history.

Before going on to more general comments, however, I would like to draw attention to two particular aspects of Turner's work. The first one is a reminder of Turner's own caution and reserve in stating the frontier hypothesis. Certainly he mellowed with age and became more reserved as he grew older, but he was perhaps never quite as staunch an advocate of his own theory as were some of his later supporters. An extract from a letter he wrote in 1922 states this caution very clearly:

> When I came back to Wisconsin I started a formal seminary in the library of the State Historical Society of Wisconsin, and began to study, by periods, the social foundations of American history. The Frontier and the Section were aspects of these interests. I recognised them as *parts* of Am. history—*only* parts, but very important ones [italics in original]. However I have not conceived of myself as the student of a region, or of any particularly exclusive "key" to American history. I have tried to make some changes in the perspective, and, as a pioneer, with others, I have found it necessary to talk a good deal upon these aspects; but it is in the *American processes* that I have been interested.[2]

It is very much from this point of view—of having a look at the frontier as one of many aspects of American history—that I approach my own task in this essay.

The second, but associated, feature in Turner which I should like to mention before proceeding is one that appeals especially to the European, and perhaps above all to a historian trained in Britain. One reason why Turner's writings appeal so much to us in Britain—apart from their stylistic elegance and readability—is that they reveal Turner as the prototype of the social scientist who is insisting upon the essential unity of all the social sciences. His approach is highly congenial to a British academic who does not suffer (yet, at any rate) from quite the same degree of compartmentalization and departmentalization which does occur in some American universities (and I hasten to exempt Wisconsin—and not merely as a matter of courtesy, from this particular stricture. It is after all part of Turner's own legacy that the University of Wisconsin has fulfilled his own "dreamful" hopes that "There is an atmosphere of creative activity in the West, . . . and I look for the West to turn its youthful and vigorous enthusiasm and initiative into University lines. . . . Wisconsin University is fitted by nature for a commanding place in this development of culture."[3])

It has at any rate always appealed very strongly to me, in my own approach both to history and to economics, to find throughout Turner's writings a continuing emphasis on the unity of the social sciences. Indeed, this I should regard as one of his leading characteristics. Many citations could be produced in evidence, but let me simply quote from one letter, to his friend and colleague, Max Farrand, in which he was advising on the compilation of a library collection: "It ought to be borne in mind moreover that there is a large area in which American history, economics, politics and literature, overlap, so that books for the one serve also as books for the other."[4]

Let me now proceed to comment more generally about the frontier, as it is seen from a distance of some five or six thousand miles from Wisconsin. We are discussing, of course, what is basically a counterfactual proposition. As the new economic historians have been insisting, we can attribute no causal relationships between phenomena unless we have it at the back of our minds that we are really asking the question: "What would things have been like in different circumstances?" Now I certainly do not propose to set up any counterfactual model based on the assumption of an America of fixed territorial size, defined say, by the frontier of the Proclamation of 1763, and to speculate what the national income would have been in 1968 under the assumption. Indeed, my approach is going to be almost completely devoid of any kind of quantification and I am certainly not going to indulge in that interesting type of analysis.

Nevertheless, we do have to bear in mind the question: What would American society have been like, how would Americans have developed, in the absence of the frontier? There is before our eyes a partial test case for this proposition. Perhaps one of the disservices of excessive concentration on frontier expansion is the extent to which it has focused attention largely on the national period, the period of extensive development, to the neglect of some aspects of the more static life of the Colonial Period. There is always a tendency in American history, I think, greatly to foreshorten that period and to forget that the length of time from the first settlement to the Declaration of Independence is as great as the length of time from the Declaration of Independence to the present day. We too often tend to think of the Colonial Period as just one unified and rather brief period.

My point here is that in some areas in the Colonial Period there was in fact a situation of minimal frontier expansion. For most of the Colonial Period, especially in New England, settlement was territorially contained, and society was confined to a fairly narrow limit. This has been remarked upon recently by Kenneth Lockridge, writing in *Past and Present*. Lockridge discusses some aspects of the relationship between the population and resources in parts of New England, and at one point says of Connecticut: "It was plain to several of these observers that the population, which had grown fourfold from 1715—1756, had become too great for the countryside to support."[5] In other words, there was a situation where expansion was not possible, at least according to Lockridge's argument, and the result was the creation of considerable economic pressures, seen in smaller land units, increasing pauperism, and so on. I am not completely convinced by the evidence that Mr.

Lockridge presents for his case, but at least the proposition is one worth considering. It is worth considering particularly because it was already well understood in the late Colonial Period. Benjamin Franklin himself put almost exactly the same viewpoint in slightly different words in one of his first writings about population, *Poor Richard Improved* of 1750. There, discussing differences between population in England and America, he wrote:

> ... for in old settled Countries, as England for instance, as soon as the Number of People is as great as can be supported by all the Tillage, Manufactures, Trade Manufactures, and Offices of the Country the Overplus must quit the Country, or they will perish by Poverty, Diseases, and want of Necessaries.

You will recognize in this statement coming from Benjamin Franklin an almost exact foretaste of what Malthus was to write some fifty years later. The point to which I am leading is a very simple one. It is obvious to outside observers, I think, that the assumption behind much of the writing about European economic history in the eighteenth and nineteenth centuries (and indeed of earlier centuries) is the Ricardian law of diminishing returns in agriculture, the Ricardian observation that new land is characteristically marginal land and that as the population expands agriculture has to resort to lands of inferior quality in order to meet the demands for food. The first and most obvious effect of the American frontier, or for that matter of any other frontier—the Canadian frontier, the Australian frontier, the Siberian frontier—is that there at least is a possibility that new land brought into cultivation will not be marginal land producing diminishing returns, but that there will at least be the *possibility* that some, if not all of this land, will be of superior quality and will indeed bring increasing rather than decreasing returns. This may seem an extremely obvious observation to make, and yet it does seem to me to be one of the most important ones in distinguishing the study of the economic history of America from that of Britain and indeed of most parts of Western Europe. There the story of agricultural expansion is the story of the intensification of agriculture, the assumption being that new land is going to produce poorer yields. Land is the scarce factor, the one to be economized, whose output is to be maximized by all available means. The whole assumption of American agriculture, at least for so long as the frontier offered possibilities of extension, is that new lands may often be of higher quality than land already under cultivation. I say may be, because quite obviously the notorious heterogeneity of the American soil did not make true the opposite to the Ricardian rule, that all new land was better land. This was certainly not the case and certainly not the case I am trying to make. But land was the abundant factor and the American aim was to increase productivity not per acre, per unit of land, but per unit of labor—the scarce factor.

This is the first and the most simple proposition I am suggesting. One of the most significant economic effects of the American frontier on American economic development was that it did offer the possibility of suspending, as it were, at least for the time being, the Ricardian law of diminishing returns from agriculture during the period of frontier expansion. In passing, let me remind you that agricultural acreage did not cease to expand in 1890, when the census incidentally happened to note in rather an obscure comment that there no longer was a single frontier line. Acreage under improved farms continued to expand until the late 1920s, the peak acreage being reached in 1929; the acreage in improved agriculture is about the same today as it was in 1929.

Obviously, much of British social thought in the nineteenth century proceeds from the Ricardian assumption and the opposite to this American assumption. You will be familiar with all the discussion among the social reformers in the 1830s about "shovelling out the paupers," the assumption being that Britain lacked the resources to maintain her expanding population. Edward Gibbon Wakefield had his colonization schemes for Australia. Even at the end of the century, as a recent article has pointed out, Charles Booth, normally thought of as a writer extremely sympathetic towards the poor, and indeed one of our main sources of information about the poor, nevertheless spoke in rather harsh terms about what could be done to protect the industrial class, the industrious class, against sordidly cheapened labor. These were people who as "social invalids" needed to be dealt with as "in some of the known forms of disciplined colonies . . . and treated with as much consideration as the nature of their case permits."[6] In other words even Booth at the end of the nineteenth century saw an almost insoluble problem of pauperism in Britain and sought some kind of frontier expansion almost in the language of Gibbon Wakefield, with "shovelling out to some colonial area" as the only possible solution available to the economy.[7]

This seems to me to be the first and the most obvious reaction of a European observer to the American frontier and its effect on the American economy. Let me therefore turn from this to other effects, some of which are slightly less tangible. Obviously the least tangible would come under the general heading of the psychological effect of the frontier, and here I am of course on very thin ice indeed. Let me therefore keep as close to Turner as I possibly can in approaching this aspect of the subject. What I feel here is that there is something about Turner's writing that reflects a tone, a general atmosphere, of calm and optimistic inevitability that went with a movement of a population into the empty lands. Personal optimism was certainly part of Turner's individual makeup. Other writers have commented that his own personal optimism led him to promise the publishers a large number of books, hardly any of which he in fact delivered. Certainly there is no lack of op-timism in Turner's own personal life or indeed in his inter-pretation of American history.

But the word I would stress particularly is not so much optimism as inevitability. That is to say that the question that is being asked is essentially the question of *"how?"* not at all the question of "why?" The effort-eroding ques-tions, "Why *should* we do certain things, what is the ob-jective of our society?" were not ones that were character-istically asked on Turner's expanding frontier, where the essential problems were to find ways and means of over-coming known (and sometimes unknown) physical obsta-cles: food had to be grown, and children had to be fed, but these problems were approached, nevertheless, with the same air of optimism that Turner himself generates in his writing. It is interesting, I think, that Professor Bernard Crick has also pointed a similar parallel in American politi-cal life to this view that the question in American economic life and social life is not at all the question of "why"; the only question to be asked was "how."[8] Objectives are taken for granted; first, to exist in the new environment, eventu-ally to subdue it, with as little hardship for oneself and one's family as could be achieved. There are all too many eroding questions of "why" in the stories of Western Euro-pean societies, a great deal more introspection, a great deal more questioning about the ends of society. Once this big debate is started then, to some extent, the problems of "how" unclear and ill-defined objectives are to be reached fall far into the background. My insistence then is that in this choice between "whys" and "hows" (perhaps the only two questions that matter in life anyway), in nineteenth-century America "how" was the question and not "why."

Another aspect of this that we might note in Turner reflects his attitude towards the role of the individual in historical processes. Here, I think, the outside observer is struck by the relative unimportance of the individual. Although characteristically the frontiersman is popularly thought of as the individualist par excellence, in Turner he rather appears as not much more than an item of data in the total environment that he is encountering. I think this has been very well expressed by Professor William Parker of Yale University, speaking of Turner's view of individuals: "they are like water rushing into an empty vessel and assuming the shape of its new container!"[9] This seems to me to express very well Turner's attitude towards the role of the individual in economic and social processes. In other words, there is an obvious element of determinism in Turner's approach to American history. It is a determinism unlike that of Charles Beard to whom individuals, with names and with bodies, not as abstractions, are seen asserting their dominance over the *social* environment, not the *natural* environment as with Turner. This suppression of the role of the individual, I think, is another important factor that strikes the outside observer in looking at Turner's writing.

Let me now proceed to another area of discussion, one that has appealed to me increasingly because of my recent preoccupation and work in American demographic history, i.e., some aspects of the frontier and population. It has, I think, been more instinctive for Europeans to ask the question that Carleton Hayes asked many years ago, "The American frontier, the frontier of what?"[10] In other words Europeans are more inclined, are perhaps more able, to see the American frontier as part of a general pattern of folk-movement; as part of a general situation in which, given nineteenth-century absence of controls between nations, labor as well as capital tended to move, and was able to move, towards areas of greatest profitability. This movement of people was broadly in an east to west direction, and also broadly in a rural to urban direction. Although, for the sake of writing textbooks, American historians have to include a chapter on the frontier as one item and another chapter on immigration as a quite separate item, I prefer myself to look on these subjects *not* as separate chapters in the American story but as having a great deal in common and as part and parcel of that great international phenomenon of the nineteenth century—the unprecedented restlessness of the peoples of the world, leading to the movement of large numbers of people all following similar trends. Particularly this is true when one tries to sort out some of the characteristics of these migratory movements. What are the characteristics of migrants, whether they are immigrants coming from Europe to America, or whether they are New Yorkers moving to Wisconsin and points West? They have, I think, a number of quite definite characteristics.[11] The first that strikes one, of course, is that migration is a selective process. Those who move out from a society are not a representative sample of the total society from which they move. Those who stay put are people who, on the whole, are reasonably content with their circumstances or, if they are not content, they lack the courage, or the drive, to leave. Whether in Old England or in New England those who remain will tend to be the conservative, the satisfied, or merely the passive members of society. By contrast the people who move, the migrants, are in modern parlance the "dropouts" or the "copouts," the impatient ones, the malcontents; at least they are dissatisfied with their lot and consciously and deliberately choose to leave the society they live in. Or, if you prefer it the other way, they are not the misfits but rather the dynamic members of a society, the activists, those who have the drive and initiative to up-sticks-and-away. These are general characteristics of migrants that are as important in examining the impact of foreigners on the American scene as in examining the impact of the east-west migration within the American continent.

Secondly, I suggest that migration is also a continuing process in that once the migrant has made the initial decision to dig up his roots and move to some other area, then the inhibitions against further movement are greatly reduced and he tends to be a highly mobile member of society. Migrants in other words are like rolling stones whether we are considering the movements of New Yorkers by stages across the continent until some of them eventually reach the Pacific, or the similar behavior of the arriving Europeans (especially thinking here of the Old Migration rather than the New, though even the latter retained some of this characteristic of high mobility) . Incidentally in looking at recent figures on mobility I have observed that the 1950 and the 1960 American censuses show a higher percentage of American-born living outside their state of birth than any census in the nineteenth century; in other words, by this measurement mobility continues to be very high and in fact is much higher in the twentieth century than ever it was in the nineteenth.

But more specific, and more interesting from an economic point of view, are the effects of this mobility on the age and sex structures both of the society which is being left behind and the society which the migrant joins. This first, I think, emerged with great clarity in a much neglected document, produced by an acquaintance of Turner's, that is almost contemporaneous with his original frontier essay. This was Henry Gannett's *Atlas of the 1890 Census* which appeared in the late 1890s, putting onto maps most of the census's major findings. Agricultural and industrial data and all the population data that could be conveniently presented either in diagrammatic form or cartographic form were included. This atlas contained one rather famous map, sometimes known as "The Virility of the Frontier," showing the extent to which men between the ages of twenty to forty years were in preponderant numbers in frontier areas in the 1890 census. The mapping of the data demonstrates all too well this notion of frontier "virility."

Here again the general point is that migration is a selective process, that the resultant age and sex structure of the frontier region is eccentric since the migrants were characteristically traveling alone and often between the ages of about twenty and thirty-five. This circumstance gives to the new frontier society a very different age and sex structure from that of the emigration area. One characteristic of the society left behind often is a surplus of women in the population, while in some extreme cases the ratio of men to women at the frontier was as high as 100 to one. Attempts were made, of course, to remedy the situation by all kinds of different measures to bring in womenfolk to the new settlements.

The importance of this is fairly obvious from a social point of view but has not really been fully examined from an economic point of view and does deserve greater investigation. Obviously the most important effect that it has is to create different ratios between producers and dependents in the new society. The new society will characteristically have a very high ratio, in the first place at any rate, of producers to dependents. Before long, however, it will begin to generate its own children and the ratio begins to change. Eventually, forty or fifty years later, there will be an abnormally high proportion of old-aged dependents in the new areas.[12]

Because of the shortage of women it is also found that the frontier has a very high fertility rate. Fertility ratios are almost invariably much higher in the new settlements than in the old. Even at the time of Malthus's first *Essay on Population,* he specifically made the point that "in the back settlements," as he called them, the population was "found to double itself every fifteen years" whereas elsewhere it doubled itself every twenty-five years. Malthus saw the back settlements as providing ideal conditions for extremely rapid population growth.

Throughout the nineteenth century these characteristic differences are to be found in America.[13] The new settlement areas have a very different age and sex structure from the old, but this changes with the passage of time. They also have high fertility ratios, above all because of the shortage of women and the consequent likelihood that all women are likely to be married and liable to produce lots of children. The full economic consequences of this repeating pattern have not been fully worked out. The pattern repeats itself by areas, and it repeats itself over time, since the flow of migrants is uneven. There are, as you well know, periods when migration was particularly intense and other periods when migration was rather slack. The periods of intensity provided a kind of shock wave to the process. Writing about Australia, Mr. Allen Kelly has suggested some rather interesting thoughts along these lines, asking whether the result of these shock waves is a fairly significant pattern of resultant phases in the life cycle. In Australia the shock waves were produced by large arrivals of migrants at one well-defined point of time. Kelly has identified three main phases in this life cycle. At first there is a phase during which the new settlers provide peak participation in the labor force, i.e., while they are between the ages of about twenty to thirty years. Then, somewhat later, the phase in the life cycle is reached when there is the maximum number of heads of household; this phase, Kelly suggests, will produce the maximum demand for residential construction and especially for urban residential construction. The final phase in the process is reached forty years later, perhaps, when the early settlers have reached their peak ability to save. In other words, their propensity to save is at its greatest some decades after the point of peak participation in the labor force and some years after the peak period for household headship. Kelly has worked this out rather neatly for Australia, where there was one single shock wave, that of the 1850s. I have tried to do it for various states within the U.S.A., where the pattern is very much more confused: here there was not a single shock wave but a whole series of recurring waves coming throughout the century. I shall not pursue this line of thought any farther (which is a polite way of saying that I cannot), but the ideas are interesting and fraught with economic significance, not least in their possible relevance to discussions of the Kuznets' or other long cycles.[14]

As you see, I am gradually moving towards the most specifically economic aspects of my reflections on the American frontier. Once again I feel the Turner thesis has great appeal to the British and European observer because it does incorporate so many extremely important elements in American economic life in the nineteenth century. Most interesting I think from the point of view of economic analysis is the way in which one can observe each new settlement reliving virtually the entire economic experience of the whole nation. The problems of the Massachusetts Bay Colony were essentially the same from an economic point of view as the problems faced by each new settlement in the Ohio Valley, in the Mississippi Valley, in the Great Plains, and in the mountains: the problems first of coming to terms with the environment along straight Turnerian lines, the problems of producing a surplus of goods, a salable surplus that could be exchanged for other goods from the outside world, the problems of capital dependence on the outside world—all these problems that can either be considered in general terms so far as the entire American economy is concerned or in specific terms so far as each individual separate settlement is concerned. This is another large subject which I submit as an important and suggestive point of analysis in looking at the frontier. When Turner speaks of the "nationalizing" effect of the frontier, he had a different notion in mind. But I suggest that the frontier had a "nationalizing" effect in that it required this total identification of each settlement with the economic history of the nation, bringing the same problems to each new group of settlers as those the nation had experienced during the process of history. Of course, recalling my earlier citation from Turner, I would certainly not attribute all these effects entirely to the frontier and would acknowledge that many other factors were at work, not the least being immigration, and with it the conscious choice of citizenship made by people arriving in the U.S.A.

The second important economic effect of the frontier is another obvious one, the preoccupation of nineteenth-century America with the conquest of space. (I say nineteenth-century America, but otherwise choose my words with care.) I am referring to the intense preoccupation with transport building in nineteenth-century America, a fact which does not emerge very clearly if you are studying American history alone. Whether you are doing it from the older viewpoint of Professor Jenks or the newer viewpoint of Professor Fogel,[15] it is only when you begin to make some kind of comparisons with other societies that the burden of transport building for the American economy, especially at the beginning of the nineteenth century, begins to emerge with some reality. Per capita railroad mileage in America in all years after 1870 was about five times the per capita railroad mileage in Britain in that same period. Or to illustrate the same point differently, in one decade, and that as early as the 1850s, America built almost as much railroad as Britain did in a whole century of railroad building (just over 20,000 miles in both cases; in the 1880s, the U.S.A. built over four times that mileage). Between 1870 and 1920 the American population trebled while railroad mileage grew eight-fold. However one manipulates these figures it strikes the British observer with great force that this was an incredible capital burden for the economy to undertake. The cost per mile of railroad building was of course less in America because of the cheaper cost of land, but nevertheless the operation imposed an immense bur-

den upon the economy, and indirectly upon each individual member of society. I am certainly not one of those
who adheres to the theory that capital was in any sense
abundant in nineteenth-century America. Both capital and
labor were for the most part in rather short supply, and a
critical choice had to be made in allocating the available
capital to different uses. I do tend to agree with those who
on the whole incline to the view that there was overbuild-
ing of railroads in that period in contrast with all the other
things that might have been done with the scarce capital
that was available.

The third point under this general heading is another
that I see particularly from a European viewpoint. It is
one that is perhaps all too often neglected in America's frequent phases of introspection and of masochism, her frequent phases of self-criticism as in the muckraking period
of the 1900s or in the present period of dissatisfaction of
the late 1960s. What I have in mind here is the fact that
in the process of frontier expansion the settler is always
confronted by a complete absence of social capital. This
was as true of the newly embarked first colonists as it was
of the nineteenth-century frontiersman. He moves into a
vacuum. Cities have to be built from nothing. I am reminded of Charles Dickens' character (wasn't it Martin
Chuzzlewit?) who bought land on the Mississippi and who
went to take up his possession and found he had bought
swamp and nothing else. There was nothing in his previous
experience to prepare him for the complete lack of civic
amenities. He had expected to find paved streets, buildings
already there, a virtual city already in the making. It often
seems to me that one of the greatest contrasts between the
study of European and perhaps particularly British economic history and that of American—one that is rarely discussed—is the difference in inherited social capital in com-
paring the two societies. Britain had a long heritage of city
building before, long before, her Industrial Revolution,

as had most other European societies. Yet already by the end of the eighteenth century, Philadelphia had become almost as large a city as any in the British Isles except London. This city had been built up in a very short space of time and the demands thus imposed upon the construction industry generally, and thus upon the total availability of capital (again referring back to my basic proposition that there was a capital shortage), were immense and intense. The need to provide social capital, the need not merely to improve upon a stock of buildings inherited from previous centuries or at any rate decades, the need to create cities where none existed, was a need Americans always had to overcome. The importance of city building starting from forest or swamp or treeless plain is one that is all too often overlooked in most discussions of the processes of American economic development.

Finally, let me make a basically economic point from a different point of view, namely, the political aspect of the subject, the one of course on which most critics of Turner and most commentators on Turner have tended to concentrate. My interpretation will be slightly different from the traditional ones. Again what strikes the outside observer is the fact that the existence of the public domain, the existence of the land available for settlement, was the one feature, perhaps the only single feature, in American life, in the early national period particularly, that of necessity brought the federal government into the economy. It is rather like the British national debt which meant that the government *had* to raise taxes and *had* to do something about paying off the bondholders. Like it or not, the federal government *had* to do something about the public domain. It therefore had to take conscious decisions about it and in taking these conscious decisions the federal government had to make implicit judgments about the future of American society. People always tend to read history backwards, of course, and assume that no other alternatives were available other than the methods for land disposal that in fact were employed. Yet obviously this is not so. If in 1968 we wanted to make a blueprint for the disposal of the public domain as it existed in the 1780s, I suspect that our proposals would look very different indeed from the actual processes that occurred. Australia found very different solutions in using government rentals rather than government sales as her method of land development. But it seems to me that one most important aspect of the public domain was that the federal government as well as the separate state governments, whether they wanted or not, had to be involved in the nation's economic life. One tends to find in the books merely discussions about the constitutional proprieties of the Louisiana Purchase and then the subject gets lost completely from that point. I do not think it should get lost but should be there the whole time. Even if the government is doing no more than allocate the surpluses that accrued from the sales of public land, it was all the time making decisions that were significant for the nation's economic future. And as the nation moved inexorably closer to Civil War, these decisions also became politically of crucial importance.

The final point in this same general area is that the frontier tended, I think, to obscure the notion of what government was. Nowadays, we tend to have a quite clear vision of what is government and what is not government; these are seen as opposites, quite self-contained departments. This was not self-evident to nineteenth-century British observers of the American scene. Several, for example Harriet Martineau,[16] make the comment that the difference between individuals at the frontier, acting in voluntary co-operation with each other to do certain things, and individuals at the frontier acting as their own established government to do certain things, is a rather narrow one and the distinction between self-help and government action is a very restricted one indeed; so also is the distinction between what local or state governments did and did not do. In other words, I am suggesting that the transitional phases from the characteristic individual action of frontiersmen merge almost imperceptibly into the next stage, that of the community co-operation (which is increasingly emerging as just as important a feature of the frontier as individualism) ; thus neighborly co-operation merges in turn into informal community cooperation, which in turn, is a short step to a rather more formalized type of community cooperation. Once this has become formalized it begins to look rather more like government, and governmental organization may thus develop out of the initial situation of quite separate individual enterprise. This is important as well in establishing certain differences between the notions of government in nineteenth-century Britain and in nineteenth-century America. It has often been rather puzzling to observers to find that many radicals in England in the beginning of the nineteenth century were advocates of something called laissez-faire, i.e., they wanted to minimize government intervention rather than increase it, whereas in America perhaps the opposite tended to be true. Yet the answer is quite obvious on a moment's reflection. If you regarded the ruling class as your enemy and if you assumed that the ruling class had complete control of government, then the first thing you wanted was emancipation from that government; to minimize the influence of that ruling class you tried to reduce the total area of government operations. It seems to me that no such inhibition against the expansion of government activity existed in early nineteenth-century America, particularly in the new settlements. This identification of government with a ruling class did not exist, and no sharp distinction was made between what was done by individuals joined together to form a government on the one hand, and what was done by individuals in their several capacities on the other.

    In conclusion, I realize that I have probably presented

few new messages or new ideas. My purpose, while perhaps discussing only marginally Frederick Jackson Turner, has been to present to American readers my own thoughts about the importance of the frontier in their national history. My intention has been to ask questions rather than to answer them, with the hope that many of the questions raised may be worth reflecting upon.

NOTES

1. F. A. Shannon, "A Post Mortem on the Labor-Safety-Valve Theory," in *Agricultural History*, 19:37 (January, 1945).

2. Quoted in Wilbur R. Jacobs, *The Historical World of Frederick Jackson* (Yale University Press, New Haven, 1968), 60.

3. Ibid., 30.

4. Ibid., 94.

5. Kenneth Lockridge, "Land, Population, and the Evolution of New England Society," in *Past and Present*, 39:69 (April, 1968).

6. John Brown, "Charles Booth and Labour Colonies," in *Economic History Review*, XXI: 349–360 (August, 1968).

7. Ibid., 357.

8. B. Crick, *The American Science of Politics* (London, 1959).

9. W. N. Parker, "American Economic Growth: Its Historiography in the Twentieth Century," in *Ventures* (Fall, 1968), 72.

10. Carleton J. H. Hayes, "The American Frontier—Frontier of What?" in *American Historical Review*, 51:199ff (January, 1946).

11. Of course, whatever generalizations one makes about the migrant, as about the frontier, there will always remain a number of obstinate exceptions which refuse to fit into the neat categories one has established. The historian thus confronts his crucial task, of recognizing what is usual and what is exceptional.

12. Allen C. Kelly, "Demographic Cycles and Economic Growth: The Long Swing Reconsidered." (Unpublished paper presented to the Fourth International Congress of Economic History, Bloomington, Indiana, 1968).

13. To all the foregoing generalizations there are exceptions.

The migrant "drop-outs" from society were sometimes people who could not accommodate themselves to the *changes* that were going on in that society; such people left *because* they were conservative, to seek a new place where old ways could be found again. Similarly, migration to all frontier areas was not identical, depending on various circumstances such as travel conditions. Settlement in Kansas, for example, was much more of a family affair than that in California, and in parts of Kansas the single male was much less characteristic.

14. Simon Kuznets, an American economist, who specializes in and has published extensively on the subject of business cycles, national income, and capital formation.

15. L. H. Jenks, "Railroads as an Economic Force in American Development," in *The Journal of Economic History*, L:1ff. (May, 1944) ; N. W. Fogel, *Railroads and American Economic Growth: Essays in Econometric History* (Baltimore, 1964).

16. Harriet Martineau, *Society in America* (London, 1837.)

John White

The Novelist as Historian: William Styron and American Negro Slavery

John White's evaluation of the historical validity of *The Confessions of Nat Turner* grows naturally out of a British willingness to fuse literature with history to understand better the past through all the means available. This commentary by a non-American has special usefulness because of the intense controversy which the novel occasioned between "white liberals and the new generation of black militants in search of a usable past." (See J. R. Pole's essay concerning the usability of the past.) After noting the main lines of division in the controversy, White proceeds to examine the historical soundness of the novel. He shows that much of the author's description of the Old South draws on the best historical sources and that these sources are fairly and expertly utilized. By concentrating on the operation of the slave system, Styron comes to grips with the central problem: *viz.*, why was the slave so often in appearance a child-man? Did he use his child-man image to mask either fear or hate? Could the slave system produce anything but the extremes of servility or rebellion? If *The Confessions of Nat Turner* is good history, as many

*John White is Lecturer in American Studies at the University of Hull.

authorities claim, it may well be the most accessible way for the student to come to an awareness of what life and labor in the Old South were like.

William Styron's *The Confessions of Nat Turner,* a fictional account of the 1831 Virginia slave revolt, is, in the author's words, "less an 'historical novel' in conventional terms than a meditation on history."[1] It produced an immediate and continuing response from American readers, and was greeted both as "superlative history" and as the distorted creation of a "vile racist imagination." Certainly, no recent American novel has evoked such partisan controversy and made so apparent the already deep but widening emotional and intellectual rift between white liberals and the new generation of black militants in search of a usable past. Nor has any treatment of Negro slavery and the slave personality since the publication of Stanley Elkins's seminal essay been so avidly praised or so bitterly condemned.[2] The question in dispute has been less Styron's treatment of the events of the Turner revolt (Styron incorporates most of Turner's own alleged "Confessions" into the narrative) than the historical accuracy of the author's descriptions of the workings of the slave system, particularly its effects on whites and blacks. A summary of the conflicting responses best indicates the range and impact of Styron's novel and provides also a framework within which to set and evaluate the intentions and achievements of the novelist as historian.

With few exceptions, white historians and literary critics pronounced the *Confessions* a consummate depiction of the *ante-bellum* South, slavery and the most significant slave rebellion. C. Vann Woodward viewed the book as being "informed by a respect for history, a sure feeling for the period, and a deep and precise sense of space and time . . . the most profound fictional treatment of slavery in our literature." Styron, he believed, possessed "a flawless command of dialect, a native instinct for the subtleties and ambivalences of race in the South, and a profound and un-erring sense of place." This is generous praise from one of the most distinguished of Southern historians, and a view shared by others. Thus, to Martin Duberman, the novel provided "the most subtle multi-faceted view of *ante-bellum* Virginia, its institution of slavery, and the effects of that institution on both slaves and masters, available in any single volume." Eugene Genovese, the most prolific recent historian of slave society, similarly pronounced the *Confessions* "historically sound." Styron had, he admitted, taken some "liberties with fact" but, Genovese felt, he had not done "violence to the historical record" of slavery and the Turner episode. From a literary perspective, Philip Rahv believed that Styron was successful in maintaining "throughout his narrative a consistent and highly imagina-tive realism not only on the objective plane (the economics of Virginia in the 1820's, the social relationships, the ideo-logical defence-mechanisms)," but also in "creating the intimate psychology of his characters, the black slaves and the white owners." James Baldwin was reported as simply remarking of his friend's novel, "a very courageous book that attempts to fuse the two points of view, the master's and the slave's. He [Styron] has begun the common his-tory—ours."[3]

The attack on Styron's historical accuracy was led by Herbert Aptheker, himself the author of a short study on the Turner revolt, and one of the severest critics of the new "revisionism" on American Negro slavery. Aptheker saw the novel as reflecting "the author's belief that the views of slavery in the United States, associated with the names of Frank Tannenbaum and Stanley Elkins—which, in sub-stance, are those of Ulrich B. Phillips, the classical apolo-gist for plantation slavery—are valid. The data do not support such views." Aptheker concluded that "Whether 'Sambo' is seen as the creation of racism or the creation of a latter-day socio-psychological environmentalism, the fact is that 'Sambo' is a caricature and not a reality."[4]

A concerned critique of Styron's view of the Negro under slavery appeared with the publication of the symposium *William Styron's Nat Turner: Ten Black Writers Respond*.[5] Its editor, John H. Clarke, asserts of the novel that "no event in recent years has touched and stirred the black intellectual community more than this book." The ten essays which follow singly and collectively (and often slanderously) indict Styron for deliberately falsifying the historical record of Negro slavery and the life and motivation of Nat Turner. On related counts, Styron stands accused of being an unabashed apologist for slavery, of creating a mythical Nat Turner at once homosexual and tormented by lust for white women, and of perpetuating the "Sambo stereotype" of the passive, fawning, infantile, and clowning slave. Thus Lerone Bennett, Jr., senior editor of *Ebony* magazine, in a stinging piece, sees Styron as "playing the 'new history' game of reviving Big Black Sambo," of "trying to prove that U. B. Phillips, the classic apologist for slavery and Stanley Elkins, the sophisticated modern apologist, were right when they projected Sambo—the boot-licking, head-scratching, child-man—as the dominant plantation type." To compound his wilful distortion, Styron, Bennett observes, also "performs the amazing feat of actually putting the Sambo thesis in Nat Turner's mouth." Another contributor, Ernest Kaiser, also criticizes Styron's acceptance of "the fraudulent and untenable thesis of Tannenbaum and Elkins that American slavery was so oppressive, despotic, and emasculating psychologically that revolt was impossible and Negroes could only be Sambos." Repeating the charges of deliberate historical falsification, the novelist John O. Killens notes the absence of any mention of David Walker's incendiary black power *Appeal* of 1829 in Styron's account. He concludes that either Styron was unaware of its existence—Killens suggests vaguely that the real Nat Turner "most probably" had read Walker's pamphlet—or pointedly ignored it to convey the impression that all blacks were docile. John A. Williams sums up for the prosecution with the title of his own essay, "The Manipulation of History and Fact: An Ex-Southerner's Apologist Tract for Slavery and the Life of Nat Turner: or, William Styron's Faked Confessions."

Just as white historians had lauded Styron's novel (which was to receive a Pulitzer prize), so too did they roundly condemn his black detractors who, in turn, launched their own counter-offensive. These published exchanges make for stimulating reading but, one feels, often amount to nothing more or less than the attempted vindication of cherished reputations, with Styron's *Confessions* often mentioned only as a necessary postscript.[6] Thus what Stanley Elkins called the "coerciveness of the debate over slavery" has reappeared in a new guise. Yet, now that the smoke is beginning to lift a little, it is surely appropriate to attempt a more extended and thorough evaluation of the historical accuracy of the novel than either its admirers or detractors have offered.[7]

Even before the appearance of *The Confessions*, Styron had indicated his scholarly and heuristic interests in Negro history. Reviewing a new edition of Herbert Aptheker's impressive but overdrawn account of *Negro Slave Revolts*, first published in 1943, Styron noted significantly his belief that the historiography of the American Negro has "suffered from a career in which genteel apology has been supplanted less by perceptions than by extremist revisionism."[8] Rejecting an "either-or-position" on slavery and slave revolts, and endorsing Elkins's interpretation of the plantation as a "closed system," Styron believed that "to assign a spirit of rebelliousness to human beings under such conditions is to attribute to the Negro super-human qualities which no human being possesses." He added that "among the many humiliations of the American Negro, not

the least burdensome has been the various characterizations
he has had to undergo in the eyes of the white man."
Daniel Boorstin has more recently made a similar point;
surveying the literature on slave insurrections, he notes
that it is generally incomplete or inconclusive. Yet, "there
has been a lamentable tendency to believe that the Negro
must somehow be justified by proving that he did rebel
on every possible occasion."[9] Again, one is aware of the same
coerciveness of the debate on slavery, but a coerciveness
from which Styron has attempted to disengage himself.

In a revealing essay, anticipating his "meditation on
history," Styron reflected on his own Southern childhood,
his feelings toward Negroes and his precocious interest in
slavery and the Turner episode.[10] Surprisingly, Styron
here intimated that his Southern birth, far from aiding his
understanding of such matters, may well have been a decided disadvantage. "My boyhood experience was," he
writes, "the typically ambivalent one of most native Southerners, for whom the Negro is simultaneously taken for
granted and as an object of unending concern. Most im-
portantly, my feelings were completely uninformed by that
intimate knowledge of black people which Southerners
claim as their special patent; indeed, they were based upon
an almost total ignorance." Such a statement stands in
marked contrast to the assertion of the Georgia-born U. B.
Phillips that "a sympathetic understanding of plantation
conditions was my inevitable heritage from my family and
from neighbours, white and black, in the town where I was
born and grew up."[11] For Styron—but not, apparently,
for Phillips—the rigid segregation of Southern society pre-
cluded an intimacy with or any real awareness of Negroes.
The "deadly intimidation" of enforced and sanctioned segregation, Styron believes, later made him suspicious of
"easy generalizations about the South, whether made by
white sociologists or Negro playwrights." But he also felt
strongly the "moral imperative" of coming "to know the

Negro" and, as an undergraduate, immersed himself in the literature of Negro slavery. On the Turner revolt, he read the "only significant sources"—Turner's own "Confessions" and W. S. Drewry's published Ph.D. dissertation *The Southampton Insurrection* (1900) —and later remarked that "any C+ history student can master the offical sources in several days." While writing the *Confessions*, he also re-visited Southampton County, Virginia, "to savour the mood and atmosphere" of the setting of the rebellion. In attempting to retrace the route of Turner's march, Styron believed he discovered the still-surviving house of Mrs. Catharine Whitehead, one of Turner's victims.

Given, then, the polarization of views held by Styron's critics, his own expressed opinions on slavery historiography, and the limitations on understanding imposed by a Southern birth and childhood, how does he, in the novel, treat the debated question of the essential nature and workings of the slave system? To what extent can his observations and fictional portrayals be judged and demonstrated to be convincing?

Regarding the characteristics of the master class, Styron recognizes the operation of the contingent factor: his masters are neither generally benevolent (as portrayed by U. B. Phillips) nor usually harsh (as depicted by Kenneth Stampp).[12] Joseph Travis, Turner's last owner, is described by Nat Turner as being "no task master, being by nature unable to drive his servants unreasonably." He later estimates that his various masters "ranged down from the saintly (Samuel Turner) to the all right (Moore) to the barely tolerable (Reverend Eppes) to a few who were unconditionally monstrous." We have the testimony of such former slaves as Frederick Douglass, William Wells Brown, Solomon Northup, and Josiah Henson that their respective owners fitted into such a spectrum. Harriet Beecher Stowe intelligently accounted for such wide variations in the temperaments of slave owners: "No Southern law requires any test of character from the man to whom the absolute power of master is granted."[13] Again, in portraying the South's indulgence of favoured slaves, Styron is supported by the convincing testimony of travellers in the slave states as to the cause and effect of such permitted intimacies. Styron's Turner recalls that as an intelligent young slave he became "a pet, the darling of Turner's Mill. Pampered, fondled, nudged and pinched, I was the household's spoiled child, witlessly preoccupied with his own ability to charm." He reflects further: "That a white child would not have been so sweetly indulged—that my very blackness was central to the privileges I was given and the familiarity I was allowed—never occurred to me." The observations of Fanny Kemble and Harriet Martineau are, perhaps, the direct sources of Styron's invented description. Recording her experiences on her husband's Georgia plantations, Kemble asserted that:

> Southerners are fond of exhibiting the degree of license to which they capriciously permit their favourite slaves occasionally to carry their familiarity. Servants whose claims to respect are properly understood by themselves and their employers, are made pets, playthings, jesters, or companions of, and it is only the degradation of the many that admits this favouritism to the few—a system which, as it is perfectly consistent with the profoundest contempt and injustice, degrades the object of it quite as much, though it oppresses him less, than the cruelty practiced upon his fellows.[14]

In similar vein, Martineau remembered that: "I was frequently told of the "endearing relation" subsisting between masters and slaves, but, at the best, it appeared to me the same "endearing relation" which subsists between a man and his horse, a lady and her dog."[15] Styron has Turner say of Miss Sarah: "I do not wish to malign her by declaring that the affection she bore toward me resembled the

warm impulsive tenderness which might be lavished carelessly upon a dog." Again, in the novel, the boy Putnam,
Hark's tormentor, represents the effects of slavery on children of the master class; both Kemble and Martineau comment on the warping of young minds exposed to the ethic
of slavery. Thus, Martineau believed that "The children
suffer, perhaps most fatally of all, under the slave system."
She asked:

> what can be expected from little boys who are
> brought up to consider physical courage the highest
> attribute of manhood; pride of section and of caste
> its loftiest grace; the slavery of a part of society es-
> sential to the freedom of the rest; justice of less ac-
> count than generosity; and humiliation in the eyes
> of men the most intolerable of evils? What is to be
> expected of little girls who boast of having a negro
> flogged for being impertinent to them?[16]

Fanny Kemble was horrified to see that her eldest child
soon demanded and received immediate attention from
one of the house slaves on her husband's plantation and
confided in her diary: "think of learning to rule despotic-
ally your fellow creatures before the first lesson of self-
government has been well spelt over!" Again, Tocqueville
remarked that Southerners early acquired the expectation
of absolute obedience and deference from all Negroes.

Styron is particularly effective in his treatment of the
Southern pro-slavery argument. Lawyer Gray recites a version of the ethnological justification of slavery, of the Negro
as "a biologically inferior species." In a thinly veiled par-
ody of Samuel Cartwright's essay of 1857 on the "Natural
History of the Prognathous Species of Mankind," Gray dis-
courses on the salient features of the "nigger head" with
its "deeply receding jaw, measurable by the gnathic index;
the sloping beetle-browed cranium with its lack of vertical
lobal areas that in the other species allow for the development of the most upwards-reaching moral and spiritual

aspirations." These and other characteristics, Gray concludes ponderously, "demonstrate that the Negro occupies at best but a middling position amongst all the species, possessing a relationship which is not cousin-german to the other human races but one which is far closer to the skulking baboon of that dark continent from which he springs." Styron also distils the essence of the South's scriptural and historical defence of slavery when Gray invokes the finding of two professors at the University of Georgia who had "demonstrated from a theological standpoint, the innate and inbred, the predestined deficiency of the Negro in the areas of moral choice and Christian ethics." Accordingly, Richard Whitehead delivers the authorized version of religious instruction for slaves, constantly stressing the earthly duties of slaves towards their masters. He warns his black congregation that "what faults you are guilty of towards your masters and mistresses are faults done against God Himself, who has set your masters and mistresses over you in His own stead." Frederick Douglass scathingly recalled the brutality of one of his former masters to a young female slave—"and in justification of the bloody deed, he would quote this passage of Scripture—'He that knoweth his master's will and doeth it not, shall be beaten with many stripes.' "[17] Fanny Kemble soon became aware of the highly selected version of Christian doctrine imparted to slaves in Georgia, remarking tartly that most Southerners "jump the present life in their charities to the slaves, and go on to furnish them with all requisite conveniences for the next." Margaret Whitehead, humane and perceptive, calls such clerical entreaties "folderol for the darkies." Styron's Turner observes that such exhortations were not original, "having been composed by the Methodist Bishop of Virginia, for annual dispensation by his ministers, to make the Negroes stand in mortal fear."

The depiction of the Negro as a (conscious or unconscious) role-playing "Sambo" has been the most contentious question debated by historians and social psychologists.[18] Styron clearly accepts the credibility of Sambo and, while not all of his fictional slaves appear in this role, many do—notably Hark, Nat Turner's confidant and lieutenant, whose voice "when the desire to play the obsequious coon came over him became so plump and sweet that it was downright unctuous." Styron has Turner himself deliver a thoughtful description of the Negro as a *conscious* role-playing Sambo.

> Certain Negroes [Turner remarks], in exploiting their own particular niggerness, tell dumb jokes on themselves, learn to shuffle and scrape for their owners, wallowing in the dust at the slightest provocation, midriffs clutched in idiot laughter. Others reverse this procedure entirely and in *their* niggerness are able to outdo many white people at presenting to the world a grotesque swagger, becoming a black driver who would rather flog a fellow Negro than eat Smithfield ham, or at the most tolerable limit becoming a tyrannical, fussy, disdainful old kitchen mammy or butler whose very security depends upon maintaining without stint—safely this side of insolence—an aspect of nasty and arrogant dominion.

In a remarkable passage in *Democracy in America*, Tocqueville suggests that the Negro "was reduced to slavery by violence, and the habit of servitude has given him the thoughts and ambition of a slave; he admires his tyrants even more than he hates them and finds his joy and pride in a servile imitation of his oppressors." The Negro, constantly reminded "that his race is inferior to the white man," comes to believe it and "holds himself in contempt."[19] In effect, Tocqueville offered a "Sambo thesis" anticipating that of Stanley Elkins. John Hope Franklin has warned students of slavery that some manifestations of the slave's behaviour "were superficial and were for the purpose of misleading his owner regarding his true feeling. Any understanding of his reaction to the slave status must be approached with the realization that the Negro at times was possessed of a dual personality."[20] Styron, in creating conscious Sambo figures, recognizes this possibility, but unlike Phillips, has arrived at a non-racial interpretation of slave personality. Yet, as Genovese has recently remarked, Phillips's views of the Negro under slavery "present a firmer basis for Elkins's social-psychological analysis" of slave personality (from which Styron has obviously borrowed) than the depiction of the slave as a constantly "troublesome property" drawn by Kenneth Stampp. Styron, while "putting the Sambo thesis in Nat Turner's mouth," also has Turner declare of his time with the Reverend Eppes that although he (Turner) appeared as "a paragon of rectitude, of alacrity, of lively industriousness, of sweet equanimity and uncomplaining obedience . . . never a day went by when I was not conscious of the weird unnaturalness of this *adopted role*" (my italics) . Yet this "Sambo" was plotting not only an escape from slavery but a terrible vengeance upon his white oppressors. Frederick Douglass remembered that he deliberately appeared at his most docile and compliant while actually plotting his escape; Lunsford Lane, another fugitive slave, noted that, while considering flight, he "had never appeared to be so intelligent as I really was"; and Southern slaveowners frequently expressed themselves baffled at the unexpected escape of a seemingly contented slave. Whatever his motivation, Sambo existed, and Styron's treatment of a complex subject is lucid and penetrating.

Moreover, Styron also speculates on other possible patterns of slave behaviour. Nat Turner reflects that: "A Negro's most cherished possession is the drab, neutral cloak of anonymity he can manage to gather around himself—allowing him to merge faceless and nameless with the common swarm." Above all, the Negro has "constantly to interpret the *tone*" of anything addressed to him by a white person since "motiveless nigger-needling is a common sport." The comments of contemporary observers substantiate both points. Frederick Law Olmsted remembered riding through the lines of a large force of field hands, "often coming upon them suddenly, without producing the smallest change in the dogged action of the labourers, or causing them to lift an eye from the ground . . . considering that I was a stranger, and that strangers could but very rarely visit the plantation, it amazed me very much."[21] Fanny Kemble recalled suddenly confronting an intelligent and normally voluble slave with the question of whether he would like to be free. "A gleam of light absolutely shot over his whole countenance, he stammered, hesitated, became excessively confused, and at length replied: 'Free missis! what for me wish to be free? Oh no . . . me no wish to be free, me work till me die for missis and massa!' " Kemble concluded that: "The fear of offending by uttering that forbidden wish—the dread of admitting, by its expression —the slightest discontent with his present situation—the desire to conciliate my favour, even at the expense of strangling the intense natural longing that absolutely glowed in his every feature—it was a sad spectacle, and I repented my question."[22] Slaves, then, regarded every white questioner as a possible spy or *agent provocateur* and shaped their responses accordingly. Frederick Douglass reported that, for this reason, most slaves "when inquired of as to their condition and the character of their masters, almost universally say that they are contented, and that their masters are kind." In his conversation with the drunken Jeremiah Cobb, Nat Turner displays this necessary caution, in his desperate attempt to give the responses expected of a compliant slave. Elsewhere, Styron skilfully delineates the major characteristics of slave society. He correctly emphasizes the small size of most slaveholdings, the recalcitrance of slave labour, the anomalous position of free Negroes, the ambivalence of Southern slave codes which recognized the slave, for limited purposes, as both property and as a person, and the hierarchy of colour among slaves themselves. As a boy, Nat Turner shares his mother's belief that: "Us folks in de house is quality!"—and admits his "disdain for the black riffraff which dwells beyond the close perimeter of the big house." F. L. Olmsted discovered that, generally, house slaves were well-dressed and intelligent, and those "slaves brought up to house work dread to be employed at field labor; those accustomed to the comparatively unconstrained life of the Negro settlement, detest the close control and careful movements required of the house-servants." Styron depicts the frontier and uncertain conditions of the South and the remoteness and monotony of plantation life, also remarked on by Olmsted. Not all of Styron's Southerners are convinced as to the economic profitability of plantation slavery. Samuel Turner (like Hinton Rowan Helper[23]), views slavery as politically, economically, and socially ruinous for the South—but (unlike Helper) opposes immediate emancipation. His brother, Benjamin, sees slavery as being economically ordained, believing that despite its admitted inefficiency and unreliability, slave labour alone can meet the South's productive and domestic requirements. Jeremiah Cobb delivers a passionate denunciation of intensive staple crop agriculture, declaring that in Virginia he sees: "The soil wrecked and ravaged on every hand, turned to useless dust by that abominable weed." He adds that the state has consequently become "a nursery for Mississippi, Alabama, Arkansas. A monstrous breeding farm to gratify the maw of Eli Whitney's infernal machine." The Virginia legislature debates of 1832, prompted by an agricultural crisis, a fast-growing Negro population and the Turner rebellion, considering a plan of gradual emancipation of the state's slave population, revealed a fundamental division of opinion, similar to that expressed by Styron's characters. Samuel Turner also voices the South's traditional indictment of the slave trader: "It is the traders who are an abomination.

They are unscrupulous and would think nothing of separating a mother from her only child." In his definitive treatment of the subject, Frederic Bancroft advised his readers: "Imagine a compound of an unscrupulous horse-trader, a familiar old-time tavern keeper, a superficially complaisant and artful, hard-drinking gambler and an ignorant, garrulous, low politician, and you will get a conception that resembles the Southern *ante-bellum* notion of the 'nigger trader.' "[24]

Although little is actually known about the historical Nat Turner, his background and early life, Styron believes that this paucity of material "is not disadvantageous to the novelist, since it allows him to speculate—with a freedom not accorded the historian—upon all the intermingled miseries, ambitions, frustrations, hopes, rages, and desires which caused this extraordinary blackman to rise up out of those early mists of our history"[25] to lead the most sustained and bloody American Negro slave revolt. Yet, to many critics, the least satisfactory part of the novel is Styron's interpretation of Turner's compelling motivation. The original "Confessions," taken down by lawyer Gray, reveal Nat Turner as being moved to violence in 1831 by the mystical experiences of his childhood and later years. Thus the "real" Nat Turner stated that:

> Having arrived to man's estate I had a vision—and I saw white spirits and black spirits engaged in battle, and the sun was darkened—the thunder rolled in the Heavens, and blood flowed in streams . . . and shortly afterwards, while labouring in the field, I discovered drops of blood on the corn . . . and then I found on the leaves in the woods hieroglyphic characters and numbers, with the forms of men in different attitudes, portrayed in blood.

These and other signs convinced Turner that "I should arise and prepare myself, and slay my enemies with their own weapons." Styron modifies and incorporates this ex-

tract from the "Confessions" into his narrative and portrays Nat Turner as an intensely religious character. But
Styron also, as his black critics charge, imputes a psycho-
sexual motive behind Turner's revolutionary impulses. Indeed, Styron makes Turner's ambivalent relationship with
Margaret Whitehead—one of unfulfilled but reciprocated
sexual feeling, culminating in murder—the mainspring
of Turner's actions. We have the recent testimony of El-
drige Cleaver that Negroes continually discuss the sexuality
of white women,[26] but to make Nat Turner's erotic fan-
tasies the trigger for his later actions conflicts with the
theme of religious inspiration, of Turner as the personifica-
tion of Old Testament vengeance. As Alan Holder has observed:

> Styron's novel appears to be poised between taking
> Nat's religious sensibility seriously, working out its
> theme in religious terms, and reducing Nat's behav-
> iour to psychosexual terms which function to explain
> *away* his religious notions. The book wants to be in-
> side Nat's religious frame of reference, and to view
> it with a cold, secular gaze. The two impulses pull
> the novel apart.[27]

One might add that nowhere in the novel does Styron develop an interesting point he made elsewhere concerning
the nature of the Turner episode: "That the insurrection
was not purely racial, but perhaps obscurely pre-Marxist,
may be seen in the fact that a number of dwellings belonging to poor white people were pointedly passed by."[28]

With these qualifications, and viewed as an historical
monograph, Styron's book provides a provocative, mas-
sively informed (one involuntarily looks for the footnotes)
and comprehensive synthesis of the Southern slave system.
He draws on the lexicon of slavery scholarship, incorporating the various conclusions of such acknowledged authorities as U. B. Phillips, Stanley Elkins, Kenneth Stampp,
E. D. Genovese, John Hope Franklin, Clement Eaton,

Lewis Gray, and others.[29] Moreover, all of Styron's comments on the interrelationships of masters and slaves can be documented from an impressive and often neglected collection of primary sources. As an overview of American slavery, these *Confessions* are essential reading for all students of the Negro experience—whatever their historiographical persuasion or complexion.

NOTES

1. William Styron, *The Confessions of Nat Turner* (New York, 1967; London, 1968; paperback edition, London, 1970).

2. S. M. Elkins, *Slavery: A Problem in American Institutional and Intellectual Life* (Chicago, 1959, 1968).

3. C. Vann Woodward, *New Republic* (7 Oct. 1967); Martin Duberman, *New York Times Book Review* (11 Aug. 1967); E. D. Genovese, *New York Review of Books* (12 Sept. 1968); Philip Rahv, *New York Review of Books* (26 Oct. 1967); James Baldwin, *Newsweek* (16 Oct. 1967).

4. Herbert Aptheker, "A Note on History," *Nation* (16 Oct. 1967). See also, Aptheker, "Styron–Turner and Nat Turner: Myth and Truth," *Political Affairs*, 46 (Oct. 1969), 40–50. Aptheker, *Nat Turner's Slave Rebellion* (New York, 1966) contains the full text of the original "Confessions." Frank Tannenbaum, *Slave and Citizen: The Negro in the Americas* (New York, 1946). U. B. Philips, *American Negro Slavery* (New York, 1918, Baton Rouge, 1966); *Life and Labor in the Old South* (New York, 1929).

5. John H. Clarke, ed., *William Styron's Nat Turner: Ten Black Writers Respond* (Boston, 1968).

6. Marcus Cunliffe makes a similar point about the "Styron Imbroglio" in "Black Culture and White America," *Encounter*, 34 (Jan. 1970), 22–35. "It has been one of those controversies much taken up with displays of credentials and refusals of accreditation" (p. 30). On the Styron controversy see especially E. D. Genovese, "The Nat Turner Case" (review of *Ten Black Writers*), *New York Review of Books* (7 Nov. 1968); Michael Thelwel and Robert Coles, "The Turner Thesis," *Partisan Review*, 25 (Summer, 1968), 403–14; Alan Holder, "Styron's Slave: The Confessions of Nat Turner," and R. F. Durden, "William Styron and his Black Critics," *South Atlantic Quarterly*, 48 (1969), 167–87.

7. Two recent essays question Styron's historical accuracy. See W. E. Aiken, "Toward an Impressionistic History: Pitfalls and Possibilities in William Styron's Meditation on History," *American Quarterly,* 21 (Winter 1969), 805–12, and H. I. Tragle, "Styron and His Sources," *Massachusetts Review,* 11 (Winter 1970), 135–53. Aiken asserts: "Styron's book . . . may be the most profound treatment of slavery in our literature because it portrays the black slavery experience in its essential schizophrenia and inhumanity in a fashion that no other study matches," but argues, I think unconvincingly, that Styron's depiction of Nat Turner makes "severe alterations of the known facts." Tragle's concern is with the existing records of the Turner trial and the personalities of those involved in the revolt. Neither article, however, considers Styron's wider depiction of the slave system.

8. Review of Aptheker, *Negro Slave Revolts,* in *New York Review of Books* (26 Sept. 1963).

9. D. J. Boorstin, *The Americans: The National Experience* (New York, 1965, 1967), p. 467.

10. William Styron, "This Quiet Dust," *Harpers' Magazine* (Apr. 1965), pp. 135–46.

11. Quoted in Harvey Wish, "U. B. Phillips and the Image of the Old South," in *The American Historian: A Social Intellectual History of the Writing of the American Past* (New York, 1960), p. 240.

12. K. M. Stampp, *The Peculiar Institution: Slavery in the Ante-Bellum South* (New York, 1956, 1964).

13. Harriet Beecher Stowe, *The Key to Uncle Tom's Cabin* (London, 1853), p. 86.

14. F. A. Kemble, *Journal of a Residence on a Georgian Plantation in 1838–1839,* edited with an introduction by John A. Scott (London, 1961), p. 102.

15. Harriet Martineau, *Society in America* (1837), edited, abridged, and with an introductory essay by Seymour M. Lipset (New York, 1962), pp. 207–8.

16. Martineau, *Society in America, loc. cit.* p. 232.

17. *Narrative of the Life of Frederick Douglass an American Slave* (1845), B. Quarles, ed., (Cambridge, Mass., 1960), pp. 85–6.

18. See Elkins, *Slavery,* pp. 82–6, 131–3, 227–8. For discussions by historians of the "Elkins Sambo Thesis" see: Mary A. Lewis, "Slavery and Personality: A Further Comment," *American Quarterly,* 19

(1967), 114–21, and E. D. Genovese, "Rebelliousness and Docility in the Negro Slave: A Critique of the Elkins Thesis," *Civil War History*, 13 (1967), 293–314.

19. De Tocqueville, *Democracy in America*, vol. 1 (1835), p. 393. The quotation is taken from the edition edited by Max Lerner and J. P. Meyer, with a new translation by George Lawrence (London, 1968).

20. J. H. Franklin, *From Slavery to Freedom: A History of Negro Americans* (New York, 1967), p. 206. Similarly, the Negro novelist Richard Wright observes: "The steady impact of the plantation system ... created new types of behaviour and new types of psychological reaction. Even when a white man asked us an innocent question, some unconscious part of us would listen closely, not only to the obvious words, but also to the intonations of the voice that indicated what kind of answer he wanted ... we would answer not in terms of objective truth, but in terms of what the white man expected to hear" (R. Wright, *Twelve Million Black Voices: A Folk History of the Negro in the U.S.A.* (London, 1947), p. 41).

21. F. L. Olmsted, *The Cotton Kingdom: A Traveller's Observations on Cotton and Slavery in the American Slave States* (1861), A. M. Schlesinger, ed., (New York, 1953, 1962), p. 542.

22. Kemble, *Journal, loc. cit.* p. 84.

23. Hinton Rowan Helper (1829–1909), born in North Carolina, was a non-slaveholder and radical critic of slavery. His book *The Impending Crisis of the South: How to Meet It* (1857), was a documented (and sensational) attack on slavery as the cause of the South's economic backwardness. Accordingly, Helper announced himself "an abolitionist in the fullest sense of the term."

24. Frederic Bancroft, *Slave Trading in the Old South* (Baltimore, 1931), p. 368.

25. Styron, "This Quiet Dust," *loc. cit.* p. 139.

26. Eldridge Cleaver, *Soul on Ice* (London, 1969). One of Cleaver's companions remarks: "Every time I embrace a black woman I'm embracing slavery, and when I put my arms around a white woman, well, I'm hugging freedom ... when I mount a nigger bitch, I close my eyes and concentrate real hard, and pretty soon get to believing that I'm riding one of them bucking blondes" (p. 109). In his perceptive essay, *Sex and Racism in America* (New York, 1965; London, 1970), Calvin C. Hernton (a Negro) suggests: "To the black man who is sexually sick, the white woman represents an ob-

ject for symbolic mutilation as well as an escape from a despised self through the act of sexual intercourse. To the depraved Negro, every white woman is the living embodiment of the forces that have oppressed and crippled him" (p. 78). Under slavery, such feelings were obviously frustrated and generated a potential for violence. Genovese concludes, therefore, that "for the best of reasons [Styron] has Nat Turner attracted to an upper-class white girl whom he must personally kill" (E. D. Genovese, *The World the Slaveholders Made: Two Essays in Interpretation* (New York, 1969; London, 1970), p. 7).

27. Holder, "Styron's Slave," *loc. cit.* p. 178.

28. Styron, "This Quiet Dust," *loc. cit.* p. 140.

29. For a recent critical survey of slavery historiography and literary images of the Negro see John White and Ralph Willett, *Slavery in the American South* (London, 1970).

*William R. Brock**

The Nature of the Reconstruction Crisis

Past crises which have a way of perpetrating themselves in United States history are likely to profit our understanding when examined by non-American scholars. Because the inheritance of Reconstruction continues its long and controversial life today, the detached observations of an authority like William R. Brock are to be the more valued. To Brock, the Reconstruction crisis was "an ideological struggle, and the crisis must be understood in emotional terms and not merely as a record of personal rivalries, conflicting interests, and political manoeuvers." He argues that after 1861 nothing could remain the same—North or South—even should the Union be preserved. For one thing, the war involved the deepest feelings of all Americans. For another, freeing the slaves meant that the future status of the Negro "stood at the heart of the whole Reconstruction problem. . . ." Finally, the changes in America amounted to a "new concept of national existence [which] demanded a new construction of the Union." In offering his statement of the nature of the crisis, Brock draws on British sources, which helps to break down the ex-

*William R. Brock is Professor of American History at the University of Glasgow.

clusivity of American history. By likening the Republican party to the Gladstonian Liberals in their common quest for moral and material progress, the Reconstruction crisis in Brock's analysis, becomes "a part of the worldwide crisis of the nineteenth–century liberal tradition."

Reconstruction presented the United States with a probing challenge to their institutions and political beliefs, and it cannot be understood at the superficial level of recrimination and apologetics. It followed upon the greatest failure in American history, and it is intimately bound up with the subsequent failure to solve the problems of a bi-racial society or to produce real harmony between the North and the South. It has been tempting to find scapegoats to bear the responsibility for failure and there has been a tendency to blame individuals and groups rather than to appreciate the character of the Reconstruction crisis. Books have been written upon the assumption that a little good-will and a little good sense could have combined reconciliation with justice to all, while ignoring the fact that after April 1861 nothing could ever be the same again. When war broke out, the argument over constitutional obligations, the rights of States, or the extension of slavery, ceased; thereafter the question was simply which side would father enough force and show sufficient pertinacity to win. When the South surrendered, the Northern force remained in command of the situation, and with the power to act went the necessity of decision. Whatever happened in the South—whether it were a resumption of the old life or a revolutionary departure—must be the result of Northern decision. Responsibility lay with the power which had won the military victory, and it could not be avoided by pretending that the page could be turned back to 1861. My purpose is to examine the nature of that responsibility, the interpretations placed upon it by those who had to act, and the arguments which produced the decision reached by the Northern people through their elected representatives.

It is a great error to suppose that the ideals enunciated by people during war are insincere and that their force evaporates when the fighting ends. The catastrophe of war had cut deeply into the emotions and forced men to decide for themselves why, how, and with what objectives it was necessary to fight. Ideas which had been dimly perceived before the war emerged as clear-cut propositions, and views which had been held by small minorities suddenly became great national convictions. It was a war to preserve the Union, and a good many men hoped that it need be no more than that; but the political and material ascendancy of the Union was too cold a cause to sustain the will and enthusiasm of a people trained in idealistic modes of thought. Two years after the end of the war a sober Northern journal, catering for educated opinion, could assert editorially that "if there be anything which the press, the pulpit, the prayers, the hymns, the conversations of the North have been emphatic in affirming during the last six years, it is that the late war was not merely a contest for empire, as Earl Russell called it, not merely a struggle to settle a political difference, but a struggle between moral right and moral wrong. . . . We took a far higher than political ground. We said that the rebellion was an immoral enterprise, conceived and carried out not by mistaken men, but by bad and unscrupulous men, animated by corrupt and selfish motives, and determined to gain their ends at whatever cost or suffering to others."[1] It is impossible to understand the crisis of Reconstruction unless one also understands the depth, extent, and sincerity of feelings such as these; and whether they were justified or unjustified, it is an idle hypothesis to suppose that people who had fought through a soul-searing war would calmly abandon ideals which had been so loudly proclaimed. The war had been started to preserve the Union, but for the majority in the victorious North it had become a war to create a more perfect Union.

In July 1861 Lincoln had described the war as "essentially a people's contest" to preserve that form of government "whose aim was the betterment of mankind."[2] The idea of defending a form of government was easily translated into the need to eradicate those elements in American society which had threatened American government with failure. At the end of the war there might be malice towards none, but in the meantime Northern propaganda had sown deep in the Northern mind a picture of all the evils propagated and preserved by the leaders of the South. It was not only a political clique but a whole system of society which fell under the axe of condemnation; the South had to be fought not only because it had broken the Union but because "aristocracy" and forced labour were incompatible with American aims. It was not only necessary to defeat the South but also to democratize it, and of all needs the first was the abolition of slavery. In a famous letter, Lincoln told Horace Greeley that his sole object was to save the Union, and that if he could save it without touching slavery he would do so; but when this letter was written Lincoln had already drafted the Emancipation Proclamation and was waiting only for an expedient opportunity to issue it.[3] The process by which the character of the war changed was described in oversimplified but illuminating terms by Senator Stewart of Nevada: "We commenced to force the Southern people to obey the Constitution. We said they had no right to secede. That was the first proposition. In the progress of the war it was ascertained that the negro had become an element of strength to the South . . . and President Lincoln, patriotically and properly, thank God, had the boldness to issue his proclamation and strike a blow at the war power. We then declared, and the nation's honour was pledged, that we would maintain for the negro his freedom. Then the issue became the Union and the freedom of the negro."[4] Indeed the end of slavery came to assume ever greater significance in Northern eyes; if the passions of war looked less happy as enthusiasm cooled, if the "democratization" of the South was too elusive and too much in conflict with treasured notions of local self-government, the abolition of slavery stood forth as a single, simple, and essential contribution to the betterment of mankind. But was the achievement a simple one? If the Negro was not a slave, what was he? And who would decide?

Leslie Stephen once attacked the London *Times* for its attitude towards the Civil War by saying that "a foreigner looking on at a cricket match is apt to think the evolutions of the players mysterious; and they will be enveloped in a sevenfold mystery if he has a firmly preconceived prejudice that the ball has nothing to do with the game. At every new movement he must invent a new theory to show that the apparent eagerness to pick up the ball is a mere pretext; that no one really wants to hit it, or to catch it, or to throw it at the wickets: and that its constant appearance is due to a mere accident. He will be lucky if some of his theories do not upset each other. As, in my opinion, the root of all the errors of *The Times* may be found in its views about slavery, which lay, as is now evident, at the bottom of the whole quarrel."[5] Stephen's interpretation of the Civil War is one upon which Americans will never agree amongst themselves, but his remarks can be applied to those historians who have written about Reconstruction with the firmly preconceived prejudice that the question of race had nothing to do with the game and that any concern for the civil rights of Negroes must be ignored or explained away. In fact Negro status stood at the heart of the whole Reconstruction problem and presented a devastating challenge to American civilization. In October, 1867 *The Nation* summed it up by saying that "We boast of having gone beyond others in social and political science, but we have at last come to a place where the claim is to be most solemnly tested. This question of race is put before us as stone of stumbling, or a rock of exaltation. It is for the rising or falling of our Israel. . . . Over and over again, in every form but one, have we set forth the principle of human equality before the law. We have boasted of our land as the free home of all races. We have insulted other nations with the vehemence of our declamation. And now we are brought face to face with a question that will test it all. . . . Is the Negro a man? Say what we will, this is the real issue in the controversy respecting him."[6]

If one preoccupation of Reconstruction was with the poorest in the land, the other was with the men who were to fill the highest offices and provide government for the people. The Confederate leaders were the avowed enemies of the Union and countless Northerners held them personally responsible for the war and all its losses. It was a perfectly proper question to ask whether these men could be allowed to continue to rule in their States and to resume their old power in the national government. Yet side by side with this problem was the indubitable fact that the war had been fought to force the Southern states to remain as states in the Union and, if states in the Union were to be denied the right to place in office those whom their people chose, a traditional bastion of American federal government would have fallen. Many Northern Americans believed that states' rights had been the cause of the war, but few emerged from the war with any clear idea of the way in which the rights of states could or ought to be modified. Were the states to be denied the right to do wrong, to elect the wrong people, or to commit whatever folly the local majority might sanction? Again it was idle to suppose that these questions could be ignored, or answered by reference back to the Constitution as it was in 1861. The words of the precious document might remain unaltered but the people for whom it provided had changed.

To Charles Sumner "the problem of reconstruction did not appear perplexing at all."[7] He believed that the Declaration of Independence was the charter document incorporating the American nation and that the Constitution must be interpreted in the light of its assertion of self-evident equality and inalienable rights. On the other side, Democrats became frantic when confronted with the suggestion that the work of their great Founding Fathers could be invoked to justify an attack upon the rights of states.[8] The right to amend was, of course, a part of the Constitution, and the principles of the Declaration could well be added in this way, but it might be argued that the Constitution could not be amended without the participation of all the states. Many Republicans were inclined to agree that there was no power in the Declaration to control interpretation of the Constitution, and were troubled by the thought that an amendment made only by the loyal states might be legally invalid. Yet everyone knew that any proposed amendments must affect adversely the Southern states and that once in Congress they would have power to block them for ever. It might have been simplest to do what Thaddeus Stevens wished: to regard the Constitution as suspended, to alter it as might be necessary to guarantee the results of the war, and to present the amended document as the Constitution to which "rebels" must swear allegiance. But in a world governed by lawyers the idea of suspending the Constitution seemed to offer far more difficulties than remedies, and the majority of Republicans preferred to get the illogical best of both worlds by excluding the Southern states from participating in the making of amendments, but by asking them to ratify, and then making ratification an explicit or implicit condition for re-admission to Congress. This constitutional tangle, and the other means by which the Republican majority sought to keep within the Constitution while breaking it, has been made a standing reproach by those who wish to discredit Congressional Reconstruction. It might be fairer to ask whether the Constitution itself was not responsible for many of the difficulties and whether an instrument of government which had failed deserved the veneration which a subsequent generation bestowed upon it.

Within the national government the problems of Reconstruction imposed a severe strain upon the system of checks and balances. The outstanding political novelty of the crisis was the solidarity of the Republican party. At no other period did an American party stand together with such consistency. The Fourteenth and Fifteenth Amendments both obtained the necessary two-thirds in both Houses of Congress. Of President Johnson's seven vetoes of major Reconstruction bills only the first failed—by one vote in the Senate—to win re-passage by the requisite two-thirds. In addition the Republicans won a resounding electoral victory in 1866 half-way through the Reconstruction controversy. It has sometimes been customary to dismiss this record with a sneering reference to "strict party votes" though it is never explained how the party whip was applied or why party loyalty should be regarded as discreditable. In fact the Republicans could hardly fail to be conscious of the weight of opinion behind them, and it was not unexpected that they should have spoken of themselves as national representatives of the national will, and regarded a president who had been repudiated and a Supreme Court which represented no one and still contained members who had concurred in the notorious Dred Scott decision as their inferiors in the scales of popular government. Legislative supremacy looked more logical, more desirable, and more just than executive encroachments or judicial usurpations. If this view was challenged, as Johnson challenged it, by stating that a Congress which excluded eleven states was no Congress, it could be claimed that a Congress which had had authority to fight the war must have equal authority to decide the conditions of peace. Indeed the president's argument seemed so absurd and so insulting that it added weight to the theory of legislative supremacy and helped to reduce the presidency to a point at which its power to initiate disappeared and its power to check survived as mere obstruction. The Supreme Court, having made a major raid upon the preserves of the legislature in *ex parte Milligan,* was tied by restraints upon its appelate jurisdiction, threatened with major changes in its right to review congressional statutes, and saved its power only by a timely retreat. It is easy to see these conflicts in an unfavourable light, and most historians of Reconstruction have been ready to add unconstitutional behaviour to the long list of indictments against the Republicans; but what was at stake was not the reputation of individuals but the ability of a government of separate powers to deal with a crisis. As on other occasions the American system of government helped to confuse policy, to foster harmful delays, and to prevent anyone from making an effective decision.

The political controversies over Reconstruction took place at a significant moment in American economic history. The war had distorted and in some cases retarded the development of the Northern economy and it had ruined the economy of the South but, as it ended, the United States was on the threshold of a great age of expansion. The first benefits of growth were enjoyed by the economy of the Northeast, the Middle Atlantic, and the Midwestern States; the less-developed regions of the South and West were certain to feel the impact of this vigorous society mesmerized by the benefits to be gained from entrepreneurial activity. In a sense, political Reconstruction reflected the economic tension between developed and under-developed societies, but it would be an error to oversimplify the relationship between economic and political aims. The great political upheaval which lay behind Congressional Reconstruction is not to be explained by the aims of comparatively small business groups. The Republican party was predominantly the party of the small entrepreneur—both in farming and in manufacturing—and of the small towns. Its heartland was the Midwestern rural region where everyone was interested in economic betterment and small towns were established with amazing rapidity as commercial, marketing, and manufacturing centres. On specific economic issues there was, however, little agreement within the party. Leading Radicals professed currency heresies which were equally shocking to old Jacksonian hard-money men and to banker adherents of the gold standard. The tariff tended to divide Eastern from Western Republicans, and among the Easterners there was often a sharp difference of opinion upon what should be protected. Many Republicans carried on the old anti-monopoly theme which was most unpleasing to railway promoters and operators, and some Radicals were beginning to interest themselves in labour causes such as the eight-hour day. Disagreement upon these ecomonic questions was muted because men felt that the political questions of Reconstruction were more urgent and more important. It was the crisis of Reconstruction which gave solidarity to the Republican party, not the economic aspirations of business.

At a more profound level, it is possible to seek a reconciliation between political and economic aims of the Northern and Midwestern society. If men differed about the incidence of economic policy, they agreed upon the great benefits to be expected from economic enterprise, and the South had a long record of obstruction to railway land grants, homestead laws, internal improvements, and tariffs. The Northern and Midwestern society was not united in its opposition to the Southern economic policy, but almost every part of it had reason to regard the former policy of the South as having been, at some point, harmful and obstructive. The picture of the South as the enemy of economic progress completed the picture of the South as opposed to that government whose object was the betterment of mankind. Like their English contemporaries, the Gladstonian Liberals, the Republicans saw moral and material progress as two aspects of the same great movement, and the crisis of Reconstruction was a part of the worldwide crisis of the nineteenth-century liberal tradition.

To the majority of Northern people, the problems of Reconstruction took their place in an historic process which had been unfolding since the origin of the American nation. The immediate past assumed a forbidding aspect as the shadow of the slave power was seen in retrospect with ever greater intensity. Thaddeus Stevens reminded Congressmen of the days when "the mighty Toombs, with his shaggy locks, headed a gang who, with shouts of defiance on this floor, rendered this a hell of legislation. . . . It was but six years ago when they were here, just before they went out to join the armies of Catiline, just before they left this hall. Those of you who were here then will remember the scene when every Southern member, encouraged by their allies, came forth in one yelling body, because a speech for freedom was being made here: when weapons were drawn, and Barksdale's bowie knife gleamed before our eyes."[9] Elihu B. Washburn recalled in milder terms the time "when the slaveholders, in the pride and insolence of their power, undertook to crush out in the Senate every aspiration for liberty and every noble and elevated sentiment for freedom; when treason upheld by a perfidious and treacherous executive, stalked through the Senate Hall with brazen impudence, and when the galleries roared their applause of traitors."[10] In this dark past the anti-slavery men had held aloft the lamp of reason and humanity; they had been "the little band of cou-

rageous and patriotic men who resisted with unsurpassed
ability and eloquence the repeal of the Missouri compromise";[11] they had been the despised prophets of the new
age, and now with honour at last in their own country
they were held up as shining examples to their fellow
countrymen.

If the past had been fearful, the old abolitionists felt
that they were now riding the crest of the wave of history.
"For nearly ten years past," exclaimed Ben Wade, "no
man has won any considerable promotion unless he has
won it at the hands of those who are called radicals. The
radical men are the men of principle; they are men who
feel what they contend for. They are not your slippery
politicians who can jigger this way, or that, or construe
a thing any way to suit the present occasion. They are the
men who go deeply down for principle, and have fixed
their eyes upon a great principle connected with the liberty of mankind or the welfare of the people and are not
to be detached by any of your higgling. The sternness of
their purpose has regenerated as it were this whole continent, has revolutionized it, at any rate."[12] Henry Wilson
of Massachusetts took Radical history back to the original
settlers who "ran away from conservatism and became
radicals in America," and then to the Revolution, the Declaration of Independence, and the Constitution ("made
by those same radicals who carried us through the fire and
blood of the Revolution and founded a nation!"). The
task was now to "accept the living truths of the present,
and . . . incorporate into the fundamental law of the land
what is necessary to make the country what its founders
intended it should be."[13] What was never quite clear was
the relationship between this epic struggle for principle
and the democratic processes of American government. In
1869 Henry Wilson resisted the suggestion that the Fifteenth Amendment, enacting Negro suffrage, should be submitted to the people in the form of a referendum and not

for ratification to the state legislatures. He explained that
"The struggle of the last eight years to give freedom to four
and a half millions of men who were held in slavery, to
make them citizens of the United States, to clothe them
with the right of suffrage, to give them the privilege of
being voted for, to make them in all respects equal to the
white citizens of the United States, has cost the party with
which I act a quarter of a million votes. There is today
not a square mile in the United States where the advocacy
of the equal rights and privileges of those coloured men
has not been in the past and is not now unpopular."[14]
This gave Radicalism a curiously uncertain attitude
towards popular government; at one time they would be
speaking of the will of the people as the supreme and
sovereign authority, at another they spoke of the need to
enshrine their policy in constitutional amendments beyond the reach of the people, and they could never for
long remain unconscious of the threatened Democratic
majority of the future.

The political interpretation of the past as a contest
between the darkness of slavery and the light of anti-
slavery was reinforced by an apocalyptic view of the war.
A people trained in the language and imagery of the Bible
turned naturally to think of the war as the vengeance of
God and one did not have to seek far to discover the sins
which had incurred His displeasure. "Struggle and long
agony were needful to this nation," wrote one Northerner,
"Frivolous, worldly, imitating other nations; nourishing
in the very bosom of the Republic the serpent of a barbarous despotism; in our heedlessness and hurry giving
no ear to the cries of the oppressed; we needed the baptism
of blood and the awful lessons of loss to bring us back to
sanity and soberness."[15] The war had been the wage of
sin, but with the shedding of blood came the promise of
remission. It was not military prowess or industrial might
but repentance and retribution which had turned away

the wrath of God, and men remarked that the turn of the
tide for Northern arms had come with the Emancipation
Proclamation and that the final collapse of the South followed immediately upon the passage of the Thirteenth
Amendment.[16] This religious interpretation of the war was
particularly obnoxious to Democrats who strove to confine
the war to its first objective—the preservation of the
Union—and looked forward to political alliance with a
restored South. Writing upon Lincoln's second inaugural,
the *World* remarked that "instead of God as the author
or abettor of this horrible war, it would seem more consistent with humility, at least, to ascribe it to the unhal-
lowed sectional passions and the accursed personal ambitions which were the visible agencies in bringing it on."[17]
It was a politicians' war insisted one Democratic Congressman "and of politicians who were faithless to the obligations of the Constitution of their country,"[18] and another
did not "believe that this war is an instrument of God for
the purpose of working out His design with reference to
the institution of slavery. I do not believe that God writes
His decrees in the blood of brother shed by brother."[19]
Rational though these protests might be, the apocalyptic
vision had caught firmly hold of many Northern minds
and reinforced their determination not to restore the past.

The sense of moving with the great tide of history
was a lively one. A Republican Senator asked those who
argued that the objects of the war had been achieved if
they were "utterly oblivious to the grand results of four
years of war? Are we not in the midst of a civil and political
revolution which has changed the fundamental principles
of our government in some respects?"[20] "Each hour has
its duties," declared Sumner in 1867, "and this hour has
duties as few others in our history have ever presented. Is
there anyone who can question it? Are we not in the midst
of a crisis? It is sometimes said we are in the midst of a

revolution. Call it if you will simply a crisis. It is a critical hour having its own peculiar responsibilities."[21] As men looked to the future they could see the same demands for present action. "History is not repeating itself," declared William D. Kelley in a striking speech, "we are unfolding a new page in national life. The past has gone forever. There is no abiding present; it flies while we name it; and as it flies it is our duty to provide for the thick coming future. . . . We are to shape the future. We cannot escape the duty; and 'conciliation, compromise, and concession' are not the methods we are to use."[22] A few Radical Republicans saw the antislavery movement merging into a wider struggle for human rights. G. W. Julian of Indiana saw abolition as "simply the introduction and prelude to the emancipation of all races from all forms of servitude. . . . The rights of men are sacred, whether trampled down by Southern slave-drivers, the monopolists of the soil, the grinding power of corporate wealth, the legalized robbery of a protective tariff, or the power of concentrated capital in alliance with labor-saving machinery."[23] Wendell Phillips transferred his whole enormous and erratic energy to labour agitation, and Ben Butler ended his extraordinary career as the Greenback-Labor candidate for president in 1884. These welling springs of optimism, idealism, conscious achievement, and determination to carry forward the revolution thus begun beat fiercely upon established institutions, modes of thought, and hopes for an easy peace.

At the heart of the Reconstruction crisis was a momentous question about the character of national existence. It was framed most often with reference to the vexed question of loyalty. What did it mean to be a loyal American? Was it enough to give formal allegiance to the Constitution, or did it mean acceptance of a once despised but now triumphant political doctrine? In February, 1865 a respected Republican Senator, Jacob Collamer of Vermont, asked when Congress ought to admit the Southern states back into full membership of the Union, and answered that "It is not enough that they should stop their hostility and are repentant. They should present fruits meet for repentance. They should furnish us by their actions some evidence that the condition of loyalty and obedience is their true condition again."[24] This typical Republican comment confused the loyalty of individuals with the loyalty of states, substituted a vague concept of a change of heart for precise and legal tests, and left unspecified the conditions of real loyalty. But if there was no such "loyalty," how could the nation ever be reunited and safe from its enemies? If the Southerners of 1865 had been ready, like the Germans of 1945, to repudiate their leaders and their past, it might have been possible to solve the problem in political terms; as they were not, all that could be done was to ask for "guarantees" of Southern good behaviour and to treat their formal professions of loyalty as insufficient.

A new concept of national existence demanded a new construction of the Union. Once it had been defended as an expedient; then it had gathered symbolical power; now it must have an ideological core. It must be dedicated to a belief in equal rights, and the faithless could not be considered as true Americans. It seemed self-evident that anything less would be a betrayal of those who had died, and this was not the mere rhetoric of politicians but the profound reaction of millions who had been touched by the agonies of war. The restoration of the Southern states was not enough without a reconstruction of Southern minds. On the one hand was an unshakable confidence in the justice and morality of the Northern cause, and on the other a deep-seated and popular conservatism sustained by traditional modes of life. Reconstruction was an ideological struggle, and the crisis must be understood in emotional terms and not merely as a record of personal rivalries, conflicting interests, and political manoeuvres. This was the true crisis of Reconstruction.

NOTES

1. *The Nation*, IV, 414.

2. Message to Congress, 4 Jul. 1861, Richardson, ed., *Messages and Papers*, VI, 20 ff.

3. Lincoln to Greeley, 22 Aug. 1862. Lincoln had read a draft of the Emancipation Proclamation to the Cabinet on 22 Jul. 1862. Roy P. Basler, ed., *The Collected Works of Abraham Lincoln*, V, 336–7; David Donald, ed., *Inside Lincoln's Cabinet: The Civil War Diaries of Salmon P. Chase*, 99.

4. C. G. 39.1.297. For Senator Stewart see p. 117.

5. *"The Times" on the American War. A Historical Study by L. S. [Leslie Stephen]*, (London 1865) , 19.

6. *The Nation*, IV, 520, 26 Oct. 1867.

7. Carl Schurz, *Eulogy on Charles Sumner* (Boston, 1875) , p. 50.

8. *World*, 5 April 1872. "In the revolution we have gone through, the Declaration of Independence has been substituted for The Constitution; in other words the political equality of man has been substituted for the equality of sovereign states."

9. C. G. 39.1.254.

10. From remarks upon the death of Senator Foot. C. G. 39.1. 1923.

11. Ibid.

12. C. G. 38.2.165.

13. C. G. 39.1.114.

14. C. G. 40.3.672.

15. J. T. Trowbridge, *South* (New York, 1866) , 86.

16. In January 1865, when speaking in support of the Thirteenth Amendment, Thaddeus Stevens said, "Those who believe that a righteous Providence punishes nations for national sins believe that this terrible plague is brought upon us for our oppression of a harmless race of men inflicted without cause and without excuse

for ages. I accept this belief.... We are about to ascertain the national will by another vote to amend the Constitution. If the gentlemen opposite will yield to the voice of God and humanity and vote for it, I verily believe the sword of the destroying angel will be stayed and this people reunited." C. G. 38.2.124.

17. *World,* 6 Mar. 1865.

18. C. G. 38.2.167.

19. C. G. 38.2.215

20. Senator Morrill. C. G. 39.1.570.

21. C. G. 39.2.525.

22. C. G. 38.2, Jan. 1865.

23. G. W. Julian, *Political Recollections* (Chicago, 1884), 322.

24. C. G. 38.2.591, 4 Feb. 1865.

John A. Thompson[*]

American Progressive Publicists and the First World War, 1914-1917

John Thompson's essay explores ideas in American history. At the same time it exemplifies the current British interest in the impact of the Progressive Movement during the early decades of the twentieth century. Several features of Thompson's work are readily apparent. First of all, he has made an in-depth study of the primary sources upon which his conclusions are based. This is a mark which increasingly characterizes the writings of the younger British Americanists. Secondly, Thompson writes with an almost native grasp of the subtleties of the American scene, which tends to obscure the distinction between the indigenous and the foreign commentator. Yet Thompson manages to maintain the distinction at the same time. For example, he points out that Wilsonian idealism "was neither novel or exclusively American; it was similar, in particular, to that of radical liberals in Britain." Nonetheless, for his purposes, such a comment remains secondary to the main purpose of the investigation; thus Thompson quickly adds that American idealism abroad tended "to confirm its natural compatibility with a commitment to domestic

[*]J. A. Thompson is a Fellow of St. Catharine's College and Lecturer in History at University of Cambridge.

reform." Finally, the author searches the paradoxes of the Progressive response to preparedness for war with the restraint and caution appropriate to the study of ideas in history.

The subject of progressive attitudes toward foreign policy, and in particular toward the issue of American intervention in World War I, is in a state of some historiographical confusion. Students approaching the question might be puzzled by the contradictory generalizations of leading authorities. Thus, while Arthur Link has seen progressivism as a source of isolationist, anti-imperialist, and pacific sentiment, Richard Hofstadter, basing his conclusion in large part on the work of William Leuchtenburg, has declared that, on the contrary, "the main stream of feeling in the ranks of insurgency was neither anti-war nor anti-imperialist."[1]

This apparently direct conflict of views arises in the first place from the fact that Link and Hofstadter have different people in mind. Link is primarily concerned with those progressive Congressmen and Senators, largely from the South and West and for the most part Democrats, who led the opposition to the preparedness legislation of 1915-1916 and provided the chief source of support for the Gore-McLemore resolution in the early spring of 1916. Hofstadter seems to be writing about those Republican insurgents against Taft's leadership, whose constituency had presumably followed Theodore Roosevelt and the Bull Moose Progressive party in 1912—though Leuchtenburg's contention that the majority of progressive members of Congress supported imperialism has since been challenged in the case of progressive Republican senators.[2]

The striking divergence in the attitudes toward foreign policy of those who might be called loosely the followers of Bryan on the one hand and the followers of Roosevelt on the other has been noted by several historians.[3] Indeed, Walter I. Trattner has concluded that "one cannot correctly talk about 'the progressives' and the War. The progressives, rather, were divided in their views on the War and their divisions merely reflected the divisions of the American people as a whole."[4] But while it is clear that progressives were indeed divided on the issues raised by the war, for some supported and others opposed intervention in 1917, the further assertion that these "divisions merely reflected the divisions of the American people as a whole" implies that there was no connection between a person's views on domestic and on foreign policy. The extent to which this contention can be accepted, and the character and extent of divisions among progressives on the issues raised by World War I during the period of neutrality, raise questions worthy of analysis.

Previous studies have suggested that the attitudes toward foreign policy of leading progressive Congressmen, Senators, and national political leaders were often affected by party and electoral considerations.[5] An analysis of the attitudes of prominent publicists of progressivism might, therefore, be a better approach to an inquiry into the relationship between a commitment to domestic reform and views on foreign policy. This analysis is based on a study of about a score of such men, selected in an admittedly rather arbitrary fashion but broadly on the basis of prominence, with some attempt to take account of "the vexatious variety of progressivism."[6] They include those former muckrakers who retained a serious commitment to reform—such as Ray Stannard Baker, Lincoln Steffens, Charles Edward Russell, George Creel, John Spargo, and William English Walling—and editors of leading progressive journals like the *New Republic, Survey, Independent,* and *Harper's Weekly,* as well as the slightly more conservative *American Review of Reviews.* The views of certain freelance writers of fairly popular reform literature (Amos Pinchot and Frederic Howe) , of a couple of leading progressives who were not at this time holders of public office (Gifford Pinchot and Albert Beveridge) , and of two small-town editors prominent in the Progressive party (Chester Rowell and William Allen White) , will also be considered.

It cannot be claimed, of course, that this limited group of men was representative of progressive opinion as a whole. To determine, for instance, what proportion of those who might be called progressives supported preparedness in 1915–1916, it would be necessary to examine not only the position in Congress[7] but also each of the different constituencies from which progressivism drew its strength.[8] Nevertheless, the writings of these publicists do illuminate the various ways in which men concerned with domestic reform responded to the questions posed by events in Europe. They also suggest that attitudes toward foreign policy were sometimes affected in significant respects by a commitment to liberal reform, and that certain preoccupations and assumptions were often shared by progressives who came to differ over the desirability of American intervention.

The attitudes of these publicists regarding the issues raised for American policy by the war were complicated as well as diverse. The various points of view cannot be reduced to a simple dichotomy between pacific isolationists and militant internationalists. How, for example, can those who believed both in the firm maintenance of national rights and honor and in the need to pursue a truly neutral policy in regard to the war be fitted into these classifications? Moreover, some of the more dedicated opponents of preparedness and intervention repeatedly urged a more active diplomacy directed toward bringing the war to an end. Such complexities as these arise from the fact that World War I was not a single or simple issue for Americans and that their attitudes toward it reflected at least three distinct considerations: the degree of sympathy they felt for one or other of the sides in the European conflict, their attitudes toward the phenomenon of the war itself, and their views on the proper role of the United States in world affairs.

* * * *

In common with most Americans, the majority of these publicists sympathized with the Allied cause from the beginning.[9] For the most part, this preference does not seem to have been strictly ideological, but rather to have been based upon emotional and cultural attachments. Thus, as early as August 2, 1914, Baker noted candidly in his journal that "without knowing just why, I should be with Russia, France and England against Austria, Germany and Italy."[10] Of course pro-Allied sympathy was often justified on the grounds that the Western powers were democracies resisting the aggression of autocratic empires, but Amos Pinchot for one was advising the British Foreign Office on how to appeal to American public opinion before he actually discovered this argument.[11] Moreover, the fact that he read it for the first time in George Harvey's *North American Review* is a reminder that it was also advanced by conservative supporters of the Allied cause.

Indeed, progressives might have been expected to be more inclined to neutrality since many of them had long recognized that Imperial Germany, despite her democratic deficiencies, possessed virtues which England notably lacked. As one writer in the *New Republic* observed, "eighteen months ago Germany was to the American state socialist what free America had been to the European liberal in the early nineteenth century—a country where the heart's desire had been enacted into law, a country where labor won comfort and security, where privileges and obligations were held in true correlation."[12] It might be possible to link the more neutral attitude of such men as Beveridge, Rowell, Albert Shaw, and Randolph Bourne to their awareness of the collectivist virtues as well as the undemocratic vices of the German political system,[13] but it should also be noted that the recognition of the merits of German state socialism by such men as Herbert Croly and Howe did little to moderate their hostility to the policy of the German ruling class.[14]

On the whole, it is difficult to relate the different attitudes of these publicists toward the various belligerents with their general political philosophies. Thus Gifford Pinchot and Beveridge, both Bull Moose progressives and admirers of Roosevelt, were, respectively, pro-Ally and pro-German in their sympathies.[15] Among these men the only one who was as vehement a pro-Allied partisan as Gifford Pinchot was Russell, a Socialist. In regard to this issue, then, it does seem reasonable to conclude that not only were progressives divided but also that their divisions in large measure reflected those of the American people as a whole.

* * * *

The attitudes of progressives toward the phenomenon of the war itself, however, do seem to be associated with their commitment to reform in more than one respect. The shock which most of these publicists experienced when the war broke out was, of course, shared by most Americans. But the humanitarian sentiment which provided, at least for these men, one of the important impulses of progressivism, naturally led to intense feelings of sympathy and distress at the appalling suffering which the course of the war involved. Only Beveridge and Gifford Pinchot viewed the military conflict with anything approaching Roosevelt's robust enthusiasm. *Harper's* editor was typical in feeling that "for Germans and French, with a whole complex and delicate civilization in common, to be using huge death engines to mow down men and cities, is so unthinkable that we go about in a daze, hoping to awake from the most horrid of nightmares."[16]

Indeed, an impression that the reversion of Europe to barbarism was a particular blow to reformers whose political philosophy was based on a belief in progress has given rise to the view that the outbreak of the war itself weakened progressivism. According to Henry May, for example, "Perhaps the most important victim of war was practical idealism. . . ."[17] But the war in Europe did not cause these publicists to abandon faith in the possiblity of a better world, even though some of them acknowledged the need to reevaluate their more optimistic prewar assumptions.[18] It certainly did not induce in them, as it might conceivably have done, a pessimistic fatalism—a belief that human nature was not only unredeemed but also unredeemable, that institutional change was futile in the face of original sin. Evil and suffering did not of themselves invalidate progressivism—on the contrary, its existence had always been the spur—so long as belief in the possibility of amelioration was retained. Such belief could be sustained, indeed reinforced, if one viewed the war not as a manifestation of the Old Adam in Man but as a product of the Old Order in Europe.

This was the interpretation adopted by American progressives, and, from the earliest days of the war, several of these publicists devoted much attention to indicating which particular institutions should be held responsible for the catastrophe. The great majority were agreed in regarding the European phenomenon of militarism as a legacy from feudalism, maintained by and serving the interests of a social order deriving from the Middle Ages, and of the hereditary monarchs whose power rested on this structure. Of course one did not have to be very radical within the American political context to criticize an institution which the United States had repudiated in 1776, and the European monarchs were denounced as vehemently by the conservative *Nation* as the Socialist Russell.[19] More distinctively progressive was the increasing emphasis on the rivalries growing out of capitalist imperialism as the fundamental cause of the war, which is to be found in the writings not only of Socialists, like Walling and Russell, but also of men such as Howe, Amos Pinchot, Paul Kellogg, and the editors of the *New Republic*.[20]

From the point of view of progressives, the degree to which capitalism or feudalism was responsible for the war was perhaps less important than the fact that both explanations accorded with the assumptions on which their political attitudes were based. The *Independent* pointed out that "It matters little whether militarism, monarchism, or commercialism is most to blame. . . . The cardinal fact never to be forgotten is this: The war was precipitated by a handful of captains, kings, and cabinet officers. It was not a people's war."[21] And so the establishment of permanent international peace was not only clearly desirable but also possible—and through means to which progressives were already committed. In a note in his journal, Baker explicitly extended to this new problem the principles which had inspired the muckrakers' campaigns for reform in America—the "essence of corrupt politics is control by selfish interests: big business: and the remedies as we see clearly now after years of agitation is [sic] a more direct control by the people—more genuine self-government. The same is true in the Great World: only the trouble there is complicated by the presence of Royalty: the Big Political bosses of the Earth. Remedy is the same: getting back to peoples."[22]

The belief that the road to peace lay through the extension of democracy is, of course, an aspect of what later became known as Wilsonianism. It is not surprising, therefore, that most of these publicists quickly became committed to several of the main principles which were in time to be embodied in the president's peace program—open diplomacy, national self-determination, and, crucially, recognition of the rights of colonial peoples and the extension of the principle of the Open Door to all the underdeveloped areas of the world.[23] This program was neither entirely novel nor exclusively American; it was similar, in particular, to that of radical liberals in Britain.[24] This, however, tends to confirm its natural compatibility with a commitment to domestic reform.

Certainly the most famous, and possibly the most important, feature of Wilson's later peace program was the idea of a League of Nations. Most of these publicists were early supporters of the concept of an international organization which would substitute collective security for national self-defense, permit disarmament, and make the recurrence of a major war impossible.[25] Hamilton Holt, the editor of the *Independent,* was perhaps the nation's most energetic proponent of the project.[26] Support for this idea was not confined to progressives—the president of the League to Enforce Peace, after all, was William Howard Taft. Beveridge, however, was among the earliest and most vehement opponents of the plan.[27] Yet, on the whole, it seems a reasonable assumption that progressives were more prepared than conservatives to accept the limitations on national sovereignty that a league entailed. In addition, certain of these publicists, such as Rowell, Kellogg, and the editors of the *New Republic,* were quick to point out that it was vitally important what kind of international organization was established. Conscious of the danger that a league of nations could become a new Holy Alliance of satisfied powers determined to freeze the status quo, they insisted that it should be based on the political representation of all interests rather than simply the application of legal principles through judicial procedures.[28] This was, perhaps, a distinctively progressive concern. But, above all, progressives were more likely than conservatives to be moved by the humanitarian idealism which inspired the vision of a new world order—of which a league of nations formed only a part.[29]

If the majority of these publicists were deeply concerned with the establishment of a lasting peace, they were also interested in the effects of war on liberal values and social reform. The relationship between progressive ideals and the experience of war seemed to many of these publicists to be an ambivalent one. For, to many Americans, one of the more remarkable features of the course of the war was the relative success of Germany and the comparative impotence of Great Britain. Several of these progressives attributed this to the advantages in terms of military efficiency which Germany was deriving from that state socialism which they had long admired. This, it was argued, not only facilitated the mobilization of the nation's resources but had also fostered patriotic sentiment through its paternalistic concern for the people's welfare.[30] This analysis seemed confirmed by what the *New Republic* described as "the landslide into collectivism" in the belligerent countries.[31] Most progressive commentators were neither unaware nor uncritical of the authoritarian features of war socialism.[32] But they argued that, while the authoritarianism involved should be seen as an unpleasant wartime contingency, the adoption of collectivist and social welfare measures by European countries in the face of a national emergency constituted, in the words of the *Survey*, "an effective indictment of much of the unsocialized proprietary industrial organization with which we are familiar."[33]

*   *   *   *

On the question of the proper role of the United States in world affairs, progressives were, like Americans in general, divided between those who favored the traditional policy of isolation and those who sought more active involvement. But despite such differences, they shared a strong commitment to the idea that American policy should be framed in accordance with moral criteria rather than simply on the basis of national security and conventional notions of national honor and prestige. For men whose reform commitment derived so directly from the American democratic tradition it was natural to link this idealism with assumptions, pervasive in their culture, about the special virtue and responsibility of the United States. Nearly all of these publicists were to some degree in the thrall of the traditional concept of an American mission, which was based on the belief that the American experience was both unique and of universal significance.

But the idea of an American mission is vague and ambiguous, and can be used to justify the need to preserve American virtue from contamination as well as crusades to propagate American ideals directly.[34] The first interpretation sees the United States redeeming the world largely by example; the second is prepared to contemplate the use of power as well. Few of these men, in fact, advocated either thoroughgoing isolationism or direct participation in the war during the period of neutrality, but there were still significant differences between them in the extent to which they favored active involvement in world politics. Since explicit demands for American intervention were very rare before 1917, the debate on this question centered around the issue of preparedness.

Proposals to strengthen America's armed forces gave rise to sharp differences of opinion among these publicists. It is not surprising, considering their awareness of the horrors of the war, that most of them began by taking a skeptical view of the agitation for preparedness.[35] Some, notably Howe, Kellogg, and Amos Pinchot, remained prominent in the American Union against Militarism, the leading anti-preparedness organization of 1915–1917[36] The pacifist convictions of these men seem to have been a blend of traditional Jeffersonian principle and simple humanitarian sentiment. These considerations were not without force for others of these publicists, but most came, with varying degrees of enthusiasm or reluctance, to accept the need for some increase in national armament.[37]

But as significant as their divisions is the fact that progressives were generally agreed upon the terms within which the issue should be debated. Thus the *New Republic*'s support of preparedness should not simply be linked to the nationalist element in Croly's political philosophy[38] without recognizing its repeated insistence that the crucial question was not the amount but the purpose of American power—"preparedness for what?"[39] In October, 1915, the editors declared that "For our part we should regard these super-dreadnoughts as a hideous waste if we did not believe and expect that they can be eventually used by the American government as the instrument of a better understanding among nations, and of the organization of an international system which will diminish the danger and the costs of war."[40] But opponents of preparedness argued that in the very process of building up its armaments, the United States would be losing its authority to show the way to a better world order. "If at this time we begin to arm our young men and build navies, we will have no standing in a peace conference whose object is disarmament," argued Amos Pinchot.[41] And Kellogg repudiated isolationism as firmly as Croly, demanding "an American policy which, unlike either a do-nothing neutrality or a blind national defence, would be affirmative and fired with a vision for mankind."[42]

Therefore, in a sense, the debate over preparedness among progressives was about means, not ends. As Walter Weyl observed: "the true cleavage in American thought and feeling runs perpendicular to the division between those who favor and those who oppose armament. The real issue is the purpose to which the arms are to be put. We may use our armed strength to secure concessions in China or Mexico, to 'punish' small nations, to enter the balance of power of Europe or to aid in the promotion of international peace."[43] With the exception of such unrepentant nationalists as Beveridge and Gifford Pinchot, these publicists were agreed in accepting Weyl's last alternative as the proper aim of American policy. Indeed, the justification of both preparedness and pacifism in terms of the same common purpose eased the transition of some to one position from the other. Both Baker and Holt, for example, had been appalled by the demand for increased armament when it first arose in 1914, but by late 1915 they were prepared to accept it as a means to the promotion of a new international order.[44]

The majority of these publicists, then, felt that United States policy should be primarily directed toward the establishment of a lasting peace. For this was the form that the concept of an American mission had naturally assumed from the outbreak of the European war. A number had seen America's noninvolvement as further proof of the superiority of her ideals and institutions.[45] And even those who attributed it to fortunate historical and geographical circumstances derived, from the Protestant roots of progressivism, a conviction that of those to whom much is given, much is expected.[46] Moreover, to several, the fact that people from all the warring nations were living together in peace and harmony within the United States was an indication that the way to international peace was through the extension to the world of American principles. Thus, though there was in fact no necessary connection between the ethnic diversity of the American population and the federal character of the American polity, by conflating the two ideas several of these publicists saw the United States as an embryonic model for a "United Nations."[47] Apart from the League, the rest of the peace program to which most of these progressives were committed was based on traditional American ideals—democracy, anticolonialism, the open door. This tended to confirm the view, expressed by the *Survey,* which opposed preparedness, that "If ever the phrase 'manifest destiny' had any meaning, it applies here and now to the task of our nation in its obligation to act as a mediator between the nations of the earth and the new order of which we are all the integral factors."[48]

Pacifism, then, did not necessarily imply isolationism, and most of the progressive publicists who opposed increased defense preparations nevertheless believed in America's special responsibility both to promote a settlement of the immediate conflict and to lead the way toward a new world order in which such wars would no longer occur. But those progressives who advocated preparedness based their case on that same responsibility rather than on the requirements of national security. Consequently, preparedness was, for those on both sides of the debate, an option open to the United States, not a necessity of national survival. As such, a consideration of its effects on American society was relevant, particularly for men to whom domestic reform remained a major, in most cases paramount, concern.

Opponents of preparedness, such as Amos Pinchot and Howe, argued that the adoption of "militarism" would not only be a betrayal of the American democratic tradition but would also, by diverting attention from domestic evils, set back the cause of social legislation.[49] Indeed, they viewed the agitation for a larger army and navy as one inspired by "the interests" to serve their own sinister purposes—an interpretation which gained plausibility from the circumstance that, as Amos Pinchot pointed out, "the war party in the United States is also essentially a moneyed, or leisure-class party."[50]

By contrast, a number of those who supported preparedness insisted that it would necessarily involve the advance of many progressive reforms. The experience of the European belligerents had suggested an intimate connection between military efficiency on the one hand, and collectivist organization and social justice on the other. Such men as Russell and White, as well as some of the leading progressive journals, emphasized that only through the strengthening of the government's central direction of the economy could American resources be efficiently mobilized.[51] Moreover, increased defense spending should be financed through direct taxation, and this would help to create a more just distribution of wealth.[52] "By far the most important part of preparedness for war is preparedness for peace as well," the *Independent* observed as it urged the conservation of natural resources, a federal program of education, and the scientific treatment of mendicancy, crime, and poverty.[53] The social welfare aspects of this program were linked to preparedness through the need to arouse a sense of national loyalty among the lower classes. Thus Creel argued that "in no sense is patriotism an instinct. . . . Oppression and injustice check its development or crush it utterly. It cannot live side by side with a stark individualism that preaches the doctrine of every man for himself and devil take the hindmost." To regain the allegiance of those immigrants whose "hyphenism" Roosevelt and others were so vigorously denouncing, the government should introduce long-term loans for prospective farmers, federal employment bureaus, industrial courts, and a national system of health and education.[54] The thesis that preparedness would necessarily involve sweeping social reform was most frequently emphasized by the *New Republic*.[55] Indeed the editors candidly admitted that they saw in preparedness a "Trojan Horse," by means of which the citadel of privilege could be taken by stealth.[56] To Lippmann it was ironical that preparedness should be demanded by conservatives. "I wonder," he wrote in June, 1916, "whether the defense societies have any notion of the consequences of their propaganda."[57]

* * * *

The debate over preparedness among these progressives was in most respects a dress rehearsal for the debate over intervention in the spring of 1917. The same criteria —its effects on the prospects of a just and lasting peace

and on democracy within the United States—were emphasized by both advocates and opponents of intervention.
In the final event, the majority of these publicists supported, or at least acquiesced in, participation in the war.

This represented a notable difference from the position at the time of the *Lusitania* crisis two years earlier
when the great weight of progressive opinion had been
on the side of peace. In seeking to explain this change of
attitude, one must begin by discounting the hypothesis of
increased sympathy with the Allied cause. Those whose partisanship was sufficiently strong to lead, by itself, to a desire for American intervention—Gifford Pinchot, Russell,
and, possibly, Walling—had wanted war in 1915.[58] But
the undoubted pro-Ally sympathies of journals like the *New
Republic, Harper's Weekly,* and the *Independent,* and of
men like Baker and White had not been able at that time
to overcome their natural reluctance to see their country
involved in the terrible conflict.[59] Nor is there much evidence of growing support for the Allied cause between 1915
and 1917. On the contrary, the increasing belligerence of
Allied spokesmen and their commitment to ever more extreme war aims led several progressives to revise their
original assumption that the Allies, as democracies, were
fighting a defensive war, the aim of which was essentially
a restoration of the *status quo ante.*[60] Since it was generally accepted that a new and liberal world order must be
based on the foundation of a just and moderate settlement
of the present conflict, there was growing support for the
view that the best possible outcome would be a stalemate.[61]
The great majority of these publicists had thus warmly
applauded Wilson's call, in his address to the Senate in
January, 1917, for a "peace without victory."[62] Suspicion
of Allied war aims persisted even among those who eventually supported intervention, despite the Russian Revolution in March, 1917.[63]

It is not, then, in terms of an increase in pro-Allied partisanship that the readiness of most of these publicists to support war in 1917, but not in 1915, should be explained. Certain differences between the two situations themselves were of great importance. The fact that the one led to war while the other did not was the decisive point for some. Men like Beveridge, Rowell, and Shaw did not wish for intervention before it occurred, but once the United States was at war they could not contemplate any other attitude than wholehearted support. As Beveridge wrote to Shaw in February, 1917, "Although our government has not from the very first been impartial as between the belligerents and this fact has drawn us into our present sorry situation, all of us must as a single man support our government in the case of hostilities—this is the very essence of nationality."[64]

Several of those whose opposition to intervention stemmed from pacifism rather than neutralism also came to accept war as inescapable. Some even of those who openly opposed full-scale belligerency in the spring of 1917 subsequently contributed public support to the war effort.[65] These men, like the greater number who acquiesced more readily, were undoubtedly influenced by their faith in the leadership of President Wilson. As Link has pointed out, Wilson had obtained in 1916 the support of most active progressives and a number of these publicists had become actively involved in his campaign and had developed close links with the administration.[66] The president had committed himself by this stage to the main principles of his peace program, and men like Baker, Norman Hapgood, Holt, Creel, White, Howe, and Steffens seem to have been for the most part willing to follow his judgment as to how best it could be achieved. They were ready to accept the assurance in his war message that he had exactly the same objectives in mind in leading the United States into the conflict as he had had when he called for a "peace without victory." His own evident reluctance to enter the war, shown by the long delay between the German announcement of unrestricted submarine warfare and the American declaration of war, no doubt helped to confirm many in the belief that there was no real alternative.

And yet, in the light of the distress which almost all of these publicists had felt when the war broke out and the revulsion they had experienced when they realized the full horror of modern warfare, the enthusiasm with which a number welcomed American participation remains surprising. It may perhaps be linked with those second thoughts about the experience of war which can be discerned in progressive periodicals from the latter part of 1915. In October of that year, the *New Republic* observed that "Instead of a thankfulness that we are providentially escaping the storm, one finds on every hand the sense that we are missing something."[67] World War I was, of course, an awesome phenomenon, and it is not surprising that Americans felt in a sense impoverished by experiencing it only at second hand. But it was not so much the physical valor as the heightened social spirit, the cooperativeness and self-sacrifice, evoked by war which appealed to progressive commentators.[68] Thus the *New Republic* insisted that "No moral gain that war brings is impossible to a civilization at peace" and that "the best way for us to save our souls is by resolutely continuing social reconstruction at home."[69]

Yet the fact remained that America needed some substitute for the purge that the war, dreadful as it was, was providing for Europe. Edward T. Devine, associate editor of the *Survey,* commented that "We who hate war . . . have to discover whether . . . by gentler means the good Lord will deliver us from the evils of selfishness, sordidness, slothfulness, pettiness of soul, sectarianism, sectionalism, provincialism, and above all from the conceit of ignorance."[70] On a visit to Minneapolis in June, 1917, Baker was disgusted by the spectacle of "a whole common people rolling carelessly and extravagantly up and down these streets in automobiles, crowding insipid 'movie' shows by the tens of thousands—there are seventy-six such houses in this one city—or else drinking unutterable hogsheads of sickly sweet drinks or eating decorated ice cream at candy shops and drug stores! All overdressed! All overeating! All overspending! If this war had not come, we should all have been rotten!" he concluded. "We need trouble and stress! . . . I thought once it could be done by some voluntary revolt from comfort and property. . . . But it was not enough. The whirlwind had to come! I *hate* war, I love peace and yet at moments I fear lest this war be over too soon—before the people are scourged into an awakening."[71]

It is not only because progressivism was "a phase in the history of the Protestant conscience . . ."[72] that this calling down of curses on the heads of the people should be related to Baker's commitment to reform. For the materialistic, selfish ethos which he denounced was associated for him with political conservatism. Since 1914 these publicists had been conscious of the decreasing receptivity of American public opinion to demands for reform which had been based, fundamentally, on an appeal to the altruism and sense of justice of the American middle class. The elections of 1914 and 1916 had witnessed not only the decline and death of the Bull Moose party but also an apparent waning of popular support for progressivism generally.[73] In April, 1916, Baker had lamented that "it seems as though the nation was never so completely under the control of privileged interests."[74] To the *New Republic*, the significance of the agitation for preparedness was that it arose "at a moment when public opinion was inert and indifferent, the popular conscience unusually callous, and a conservative reaction dominant throughout the country. . . ."[75] It was under the spur of this sense of frustration that some of these publicists muted, though never entirely silenced,

their apprehensions about the illiberal aspects of war—
the authoritarianism, intolerance, and hatred it could
breed. For such men as Baker, Creel, and White, the war,
as a crusade, provided an opportunity to revive the evan-
gelical idealism which was, for them, the essence of progressivism.[76] The editors of the *New Republic* shared this
feeling, but went further in explicitly insisting that the
war should also advance collectivist and social welfare
measures.[77] Although not unconscious of the threat to civil
liberties war would involve,[78] the *New Republic* was confident in April, 1917 that "liberals who can gain public attention will have a chance to put to good use the forced
draught of patriotism. . . . They can bring home to their
fellow-countrymen that a war on behalf of organized international security and the rights of all peoples would be
the basest hypocrisy in case it supplied to foreigners a
quality of security and opportunity to the national industrial organization denied to Americans."[79]

* * * *

The attitudes of progressive publicists to the issues
raised for America policy by World War I were both varied and complicated. Not only were there divisions among
them but also several modified their views during the
years between 1914 and 1917. It is certainly true to some
extent that the origin of the attitudes which lay behind
these differences of opinion and changes of mind must be
sought in influences to which all Americans were subject.
Neither the intensity of their pro-Allied partisanship nor
the degree of their respect for the principles of Washington's Farewell Address (each of which varied greatly from
individual to individual) was directly connected with
their progressive political views. It does seem, however,
that there was an association, both temperamental and
philosophical, between a commitment to domestic reform
and a concern that the war should result in the establishment of a lasting peace. It is certain that progressives had

a special interest in the relationship, which seemed to most of them to be ambivalent, between war and the preparation for war on the one hand and social reform and liberal values on the other.

Moreover, for most of these publicists, these latter concerns, particularly or peculiarly progressive, provided the crucial criteria by which American policy should be judged. To this extent, disagreement between them took place within a generally accepted consensus. But the effects of preparedness or intervention upon the prospects for establishing a new world order or a more socialized democracy at home were open to argument. Men's views on such questions resulted from a balancing of hopes and fears which was in the last resort personal, dependent in each case on an individual's temperamental inclination toward "pragmatism" or dissent, and his sense of priority among various progressive values.[80] While their revulsion from the suffering predisposed most progressives against American participation in the war, their frustration at the conservative inertia of domestic politics appears to have produced, in some cases, a special motive for welcoming it when it came. In the final event, it seemed to most of these publicists that intervention presented opportunities, at home as well as abroad, which outweighed the costs. But their sensitivity to the suffering that war involved meant that the stakes were high and the price of failure to achieve what they hoped would be disillusionment and guilt.

NOTES

1. Arthur S. Link, *Wilson: Confusions and Crises 1915–1916* (Princeton, 1964), 23–30; Richard Hofstadter, *The Age of Reform: From Bryan to F. D. R.* (New York, 1955), 272; William E. Leuchtenburg, "Progressivism and Imperialism: The Progressive Movement and American Foreign Policy, 1896–1916," *Mississippi Valley Historical Review*, XXXIX (Dec. 1952), 483–504.

2. Howard W. Allen, "Republican Reformers and Foreign

Policy, 1913-1917," *Mid-America*, 44 (Oct. 1962), 222-29; Walter A. Sutton, "Progressive Republican Senators and the Submarine Crisis, 1915-1916," *ibid.*, 47 (April 1965), 75-88; Barton J. Bernstein and Franklin A. Leib, "Progressive Republican Senators and American Imperialism, 1898-1916: A Reappraisal," *ibid.*, 50 (July 1968), 163-205.

3. Eric F. Goldman, *Rendezvous with Destiny: A History of Modern American Reform* (revised edition, New York, 1956), 180-95; Walter I. Trattner, "Progressivism and World War I: A Reappraisal," *Mid-America*, 44 (July 1962), 131-45; Allen, "Republican Reformers and Foreign Policy," 222-23; Sutton, "Progressive Republican Senators and the Submarine Crisis," 75-76; Bernstein and Leib, "Progressive Republican Senators and American Imperialism," 163-64.

4. Trattner, "Progressivism and World War I," 133.

5. Bernstein and Leib, "Progressive Republican Senators and American Imperialism," especially 173-74, 188-89; John Milton Cooper, Jr., "Progressivism and American Foreign Policy: A Reconsideration," *Mid-America*, 51 (Oct. 1969), 267-68.

6. Otis L. Graham, Jr., *An Encore for Reform: The Old Progressives and the New Deal* (New York, 1967), 9. There are some for whom this variety vitiates any attempt to generalize about progressives. For instance, John Braeman has argued that the "line of cleavage between ... the 'traditionalists' and 'moderns' is ... fundamental to understanding the progressive movement as a whole"—and particularly, he suggests, the attitudes of progressives toward foreign policy. Yet it would be difficult to classify in these terms such publicists as Ray Stannard Baker, Norman Hapgood, Frederic Howe, William Allen White, or even, as Braeman himself points out, Gifford Pinchot. However, they all shared those "basic attitudes and assumptions" which Braeman sees as common to the reformers of the Progressive era. John Braeman, "Seven Progressives: A Review Article," *Business History Review*, XXXV (Winter 1961), 592.

7. John Milton Cooper, Jr., *The Vanity of Power: American Isolationism and the First World War 1914-1917* (Westport, Conn., 1969), 238, concludes, on the basis of an analysis of Congressional voting, that "The Isolationist coalition rested upon an amalgam of reformist, partisan, sectional, and ethnic interests. The strongest element seems to have been liberalism or progressivism. . . ." The political stance of a Congressman is not so easy to identify as his geographical base, and the relative importance of sectionalism and progressivism seems to be still open to argument.

8. Arthur S. Link presents impressive evidence of the hostility to preparedness of religious spokesmen, farm organizations, the labor movement, and socialist and radical groups. Link, *Wilson: Confusions and Crises*, 26–27.

9. "Hope for Germany," *Harper's Weekly*, LIX (Aug. 22, 1914), 169; "Russia in the Alliance," *Independent*, 79 (Sept. 7, 1914), 324–25; *New Republic*, II (March 3, 1915), 163–64; Emporia *Gazette* (Oct. 23, 1914) ; William English Walling, "British and American Socialists on the War," *New Review*, II (Sept. 1914), 512–18; Charles Edward Russell, "As to Making Peace," *New Review*, III (Jan. 1915), 20–22; John Spargo, "The Case for Russian Victory," *New Review*, III (July 1, 1915), 109–10; Gifford Pinchot to Charles L. Pack, Dec. 19, 1914, Gifford Pinchot Papers (Manuscript Division, Library of Congress).

10. Notebook III, Aug. 2, 1914, pp. 67–70, Ray Stannard Baker Papers (Manuscript Division, Library of Congress).

11. Amos Pinchot to Sir William Tyrell, Feb. 4, 1915, Box 19; Amos Pinchot to Gifford Pinchot, March 22, 1915, Box 20, Amos Pinchot Papers (Manuscript Division, Library of Congress). One for whom this argument seems to have been decisive was William English Walling. See Walling, "British and American Socialists on the War," 512.

12. *New Republic*, IV (Oct. 30, 1915), 343.

13. Albert J. Beveridge, *What is Back of the War* (Indianapolis, 1915), 195–209; Fresno *Republican*, June 3, 1915; "What Germany Has Had to Endure," *American Review of Reviews*, L (Sept. 1914), 265; Randolph Bourne, "American Use for German Ideals," *New Republic*, IV (Sept. 4, 1915), 117–19.

14. Herbert Croly, *The Promise of American Life* (New York, 1909), 250–54; Frederic C. Howe, *Socialized Germany* (New York, 1915), especially 7, 39.

15. In public, Albert J. Beveridge always denied he was pro-German, but his sympathy for Germany and hostility to Britain is apparent in *What is Back of the War* and emerges quite clearly in the private comments he wrote on the way to Europe in December 1914. See Notebook and Diary, Boxes 327, 329, Albert J. Beveridge Papers (Manuscript Division, Library of Congress). For a fuller exposition and analysis of Beveridge's views on the war, see J. A. Thompson, "An Imperialist and the First World War: the Case of Albert J. Beveridge," *Journal of American Studies*, 5 (Aug. 1971), 133–150.

16. "Incredible," *Harper's Weekly*, LIX (Sept. 12, 1914), 241.

17. Henry F. May, *The End of American Innocence: A Study of the First Years of Our Own Time 1912–1917* (New York, 1959), 361.

18. For example, Graham Taylor, "Labor's Internationalism Tested by the War of Nations," *Survey*, XXXII (Sept. 5, 1914), 561; Norman Hapgood, "When Will the War End?" *Harper's Weekly*, LX (June 5, 1915), 532; "Mental Unpreparedness," *New Republic*, IV (Sept. 11, 1915), 143–44; Notebook VII, Sept. 8, 1915, p. 91, Baker Papers.

19. "The Responsibility for War," *Nation*, 99 (Aug. 6, 1914), 151; Charles Edward Russell, "This King and Kaiser Business," *Pearson's Magazine*, XXXIII (Jan. 1915), 33–41. Also, "Whom the Gods Would Destroy," *Independent*, 79 (Aug. 10, 1914), 195; Norman Hapgood, "Religion and Guns," *Harper's Weekly*, LIX (Aug. 29, 1914), 202; "American Doctrines Not Outworn," *American Review of Reviews*, L (Sept. 1914), 268–69.

20. William English Walling, "The Socialist View II: The Real Causes of the War," *Harper's Weekly*, LIX (Oct. 10, 1914), 346–47; Charles Edward Russell, "Will You Have Peace or War?" *Pearson's Magazine*, XXXIII (March 1915), 323–33; Frederic C. Howe, "Responsibility for War," *Public*, XVIII (June 25, 1915), 622–24; Frederic C. Howe, *Why War* (New York, 1916); Amos Pinchot, "American Militarism," *Masses*, VI (Jan. 1915), 8–9; Paul U. Kellogg, "A Bill of Particulars: Items in an International Policy for America," *Nation*, 103 (Aug. 3, 1916), Section Two, 1; Walter Lippmann, *The Stakes of Diplomacy* (New York, 1915), especially 150–71; Walter E. Weyl, *American World Policies* (New York, 1917), especially 75–166; "Financial Imperialism," *New Republic*, VII (June 17, 1916), 161.

21. "For a Conference of Neutral Nations," *Independent*, 87 (July 31, 1916), 143.

22. Notebook V, 3–4, Baker Papers.

23. For example, Hamilton Holt, "The Way to Disarm: A Practical Proposal," *Independent*, 79 (Sept. 28, 1914), 427–29; "What Sort of Terms?" *American Review of Reviews*, L (Oct. 1914), 398; Jane Addams and others, "Towards the Peace that Shall Last," *Survey*, XXXIII (March 6, 1915), Part II; Hapgood, "When Will the War End?" 532–33; Frederic C. Howe, "Reservoirs of Strife: The Distribution of Wealth in Relation to the Invisible Causes of War,"

Survey, XXXIII (March 6, 1915), 614–15; Lippmann, *The Stakes of Diplomacy*, 127–35.

24. Laurence W. Martin, *Peace without Victory: Woodrow Wilson and the British Liberals* (New Haven, 1958), 1–21, 46–131.

25. Holt, "The Way to Disarm: A Practical Proposal," 427–29; Norman Hapgood, "The Great Settlement," *Harper's Weekly*, LIX (Sept. 12, 1914), 249–50; "Work for Moral Leaders," *American Review of Reviews*, L (Nov. 1914), 521; Addams and others, "Towards the Peace that Shall Last"; John Spargo, "Socialism as a Cure for Unemployment," *Annals of the American Academy of Political and Social Science*, LIX (May 1915), 160n; "A League of Peace," *New Republic*, III (June 26, 1915), 190–91; Notebook V, June 12, 1915, pp. 104–13, Baker Papers; White to Dr. F. B. Lawrence, June 30, 1915, William Allen White Papers (Manuscript Division, Library of Congress); Chester Rowell to Benjamin Ide Wheeler, March 21, 1916, Chester Rowell Papers (University of California, Berkeley).

26. Warren F. Kuehl, *Hamilton Holt: Journalist, Internationalist, Educator* (Gainesville, Fla., 1960), 117–33.

27. Beveridge to Albert Shaw, Feb. 13, 1917, Beveridge Papers.

28. Fresno *Republican*, May 5, 1916; Kellogg, "A Bill of Particulars," 1; "A League of Peace," *New Republic*, II (March 20, 1915), 168; "A League of Peace," *New Republic*, III (June 26, 1915), 190–91.

29. Robert Endicott Osgood, *Ideals and Self-Interest in America's Foreign Relations: The Great Transformation of the Twentieth Century* (Chicago, 1953), 240–42.

30. Emporia *Gazette*, April 8, 1915; Charles Edward Russell, "Why England Falls Down," *Pearson's Magazine*, XXXIV (Aug. 1915), 201–19; Paul U. Kellogg, "Statement before U.S. Commission on Industrial Relations, 1915," Paul U. Kellogg Papers (Social Welfare History Archives, University of Minnesota); "If Germany Wins," *New Republic*, IV (Sept. 11, 1915), 142; "Social Justice," *Harper's Weekly*, LXII (Jan. 29, 1916), 99; Frederic C. Howe, "Socialized Germany," *Pearson's Magazine*, XXXV (Jan. 1916), 1–9; Amos Pinchot, "Preparedness," *Public*, XIX (Feb. 4, 1916), 110–13; Notebook VI, 131–33, Baker Papers.

31. "The Landslide into Collectivism," *New Republic*, II (April 10, 1915), 249. See also Beveridge, *What is Back of the War*, 408–28; William Hayes Ward, "Eighty Years Later," *Independent*,

82 (June 28, 1915), 525–26; "A Great Awakening," *Harper's Weekly*, LXI (July 3, 1915), 2–3; Notebook VII, Aug. 1915, pp. 55–57. Baker Papers; "German Collectivism," *American Review of Reviews*, LV (Feb. 1917), 126.

32. Amos Pinchot to Gifford Pinchot, March 22, 1915, Amos Pinchot Papers; "The Landslide into Collectivism," 249–50; "Social Control Presently," *Independent*, 82 (April 26, 1915), 132; "Do We Want Ships?" *Harper's Weekly*, LXI (Aug. 28, 1915), 193; Edward T. Devine, "Social Forces: Through Good Will to Peace," *Survey*, XXXV (Dec. 18, 1915), 337; Spargo, "Socialism as a Cure for Unemployment," 159; Howe, *Socialized Germany*, 207. Walling, long a critic of "state socialism," argued that its compatibility with "militarism" was simply a further aspect of its menace. "Is not the recommending of state-socialism as a means of achieving militaristic efficiency a strange position for a pacifist like Mr. Howe?" he asked. William English Walling, "The German Paradise," *Masses*, VIII (June 1916), 20. See also William English Walling, "Nationalism and State Socialism," *Publications of the American Sociological Society* (10 vols., Chicago, 1916), X, 82–92.

33. Devine, "Social Forces: Through Good Will to Peace," 337. See also Norman Hapgood, "Fighting and Freedom," *Harper's Weekly*, LX (June 12, 1915), 562; "Socialism," *Independent*, 88 (Nov. 27, 1916), 341; "Republican Reconstruction," *New Republic*, IX (Dec. 16, 1916), 173; Charles Edward Russell, "No More Foes Without—And None Within," *Pearson's Magazine*, XXXIII (June 1915), 692–93; Amos Pinchot, "Preparedness," 112.

34. Osgood, *Ideals and Self-Interest*, 86–88, 240–42; Trattner, "Progressivism and World War I," 143.

35. George Creel, "The Ghastly Swindle," *Harper's Weekly*, LIX (Aug. 29, 1914), 196–97; George Creel, "Our 'Visionary' President: An Interpretation of Woodrow Wilson," *Century*, 89 (Dec. 1914), 192–200; Ray Stannard Baker, "The Last Phase of the Great War: The German Invasion of America—A.D. 1915–16," *American Magazine*, LXXIX (Jan. 1915), 49, 66–70, 72; Norman Hapgood, "In London," *Harper's Weekly*, LIX (Aug. 22, 1914), 176; "The Armament Flurry," *Independent*, 80 (Dec. 14, 1914), 392–93; Ella Winter and Granville Hicks, eds., *The Letters of Lincoln Steffens*. Vol. I: *1889–1919* (New York, 1938), 374–75; John Spargo, "The Monroe Doctrine—Its Democratization," *Intercollegiate Socialist*, V (Feb.-March 1917), 8.

36. Not all antipreparedness leaders, however, were progres-

sives. Oswald Garrison Villard, for instance, an old-fashioned Jeffersonian, had been before the war an uncompromising opponent of progressive reforms and agitation. See, for example, "Justice to Public Service Corporations," *Nation*, 98 (March 26, 1914), 319–20; "Universities in a Democracy," *ibid.* (June 25, 1914), 744–45; "The Vanishing Progressives," *ibid.*, 99 (Aug. 6, 1914), 153–54. These unsigned editorials are attributed to Villard in Daniel C. Haskell, *The Nation: Index of Titles and Contributors, 1865–1917* (New York, 1951).

37. George Creel, "Sound Methods of Preparedness," *Hearst's Magazine* (April 1916), 261, 311–13; Notebook V, June 12, 1915, pp. 104–13, Baker Papers; "Defense," *Harper's Weekly*, LXI (Nov. 27, 1915), 505; "Preparation for National Defense," *Independent*, 84 (Nov. 15, 1915), 250; *New Republic*, I (Dec. 19, 1914), 3; "Peace and Defense," *American Review of Reviews*, LII (July 1915), 3; "The Duty to Be Efficient," *ibid.*, (Sept. 1915), 259; Charles Edward Russell, "In the Shadow of the Great War," San Francisco *Bulletin*, Oct. 30, 1915; Fresno *Republican*, Feb. 14, April 10, 1916; White to Theodore Roosevelt, Oct. 28, 1915, White Papers.

38. Leuchtenburg, "Progressivism and Imperialism," 501–03.

39. " 'Preparedness' for What?" *New Republic*, III (June 26, 1915), 188–90; *ibid.*, IV (Oct. 9, 1915), 245; *ibid.* (Oct. 23, 1915), 293–94; "Why Do We Arm?" *ibid.* (Oct. 30, 1915), 323–24; "Evasions by Mr. Wilson," *ibid.*, V (Nov. 13, 1915), 29–30; *ibid.* (Nov. 27, 1915), 79–80.

40. Ibid., IV (Oct. 23, 1915), 294.

41. Amos Pinchot to Frederick M. Kerby, Nov. 30, 1914, Amos Pinchot Papers.

42. Kellogg, "A Bill of Particulars," 1.

43. Weyl, *American World Policies*, 5–6.

44. Notebook IV, Nov.-Dec. 1914, pp. 11–12, 14, 70–72, 56–57, Notebook V, June 1915, pp. 104–13, Baker Papers; "The Armament Flurry," 392; "Three Roads and One," *Independent*, 81 (Nov. 22, 1915), 292–93.

45. Emporia *Gazette*, Aug. 29, 1914; Creel, "Our 'Visionary' President," 195.

46. Fresno *Republican*, Nov. 26, 1914; Notebook V, March 1915, pp. 1–3, 14–15, Baker Papers.

47. Holt, "The Way to Disarm: A Practical Proposal," 427. See

also *Survey*, XXXIII (March 6, 1915), 631–32; "Hostages to Peace," *New Republic*, III (May 15, 1915), 29; Randolph S. Bourne, "Trans-National America," *Atlantic Monthly*, CXVIII (July 1916), 86–97.

48. Edward T. Devine, "Ourselves and Europe III. Home-Rule," *Survey*, XXXVII (Dec. 6, 1916), 217.

49. Amos Pinchot, "Conscription," *Harper's Weekly*, LIX (Nov. 14, 1914), 463; Frederic C. Howe, "Democracy or Imperialism —the Alternative That Confronts Us," *Annals of the American Academy of Political and Social Science*, LXVI (July 1916), 250–58.

50. Amos Pinchot to Samuel Seabury, Sept. 16, 1916, Box 25, Amos Pinchot Papers. White observed that "the Navy League and all of the big business bunch that are trying to use our national weakness as grist for the hopper of bonds and interest, are doing more harm to the real cause of reasonable and adequate defense than all the Pacifists in the country." White to Annie L. Diggs, Oct. 12, 1915, White Papers.

51. Charles Edward Russell, "Some Obscured Lessons of the War," *Pearson's Magazine*, XXXIII (Feb. 1915), 171; *Emporia Gazette*, Dec. 7, 1915; Howard D. Wheeler, "The Hole in Our Pocket," *Harper's Weekly*, LIX (Dec. 26, 1914), 610–11; *New Republic*, V (Nov. 6, 1915), 3–4; "Government According to Law," *ibid.*, 4–6.

52. *New Republic*, IV (Oct. 30, 1915), 319; "Defense," *Harper's Weekly*, LXI (Nov. 27, 1915), 505; Notebook VIII, Jan. 1916, p. 109, Baker Papers. Opponents of preparedness saw no inconsistency in supporting this proposal, which was to culminate in the agitation of the American Committee on War Finance (largely organized by Amos Pinchot) after the United States entered the war. See Howe to Villard, Oct. 1, 1915, Oswald Garrison Villard Papers (Harvard University).

53. "A Fundamental Preparedness," *Independent*, 83 (July 12, 1915), 41.

54. George Creel, "The Preparedness with a Punch," *Hearst's Magazine* (March 1916), 190, 228–30; George Creel, "The Hopes of the Hyphenated," *Century*, 91 (Jan. 1916), 350–63. See also Norman Hapgood, "The Swiss Army Lesson," *Harper's Weekly*, LXI (July 17, 1915), 56; Russell, "Why England Falls Down," 219; White to Roosevelt, Aug. 27, 1915, White Papers.

55. "The Plattsburg Idea," *New Republic*, IV (Oct. 9, 1915), 248–50; "The Newer Nationalism," *ibid.*, V (Jan. 26, 1916), 319–21;

ibid., VII (May 27, 1916), 75; Malcolm W. Davis, "Labor and the Call to Arms," *ibid.* (June 10, 1916), 137–39; *ibid.* (July 8, 1916), 236.

56. "Preparedness—A Trojan Horse," *ibid.*, V (Nov. 6, 1915), 6–7.

57. Walter Lippmann, "The Issues of 1916," *ibid.*, VII (June 3, 1916), 108.

58. Gifford Pinchot to Horace Plunkett, May 19, 1915, Gifford Pinchot Papers; Charles Edward Russell to the Newspaper Enterprise Association, Diary, May 9, 1915, Charles Edward Russell Papers (Manuscript Division, Library of Congress); Walling to Mrs. Walling [April ?], 1917, William English Walling Papers (University of Wisconsin).

59. "Not Our War," *New Republic*, III (June 5, 1915), 108–09; Norman Hapgood, "America and the War," *Harper's Weekly*, LX (June 5, 1915), 529; "A Task for the Thirty-Five Neutrals," *Independent*, 82 (May 24, 1915), 308–09; Notebook VII, 11–12, Baker Papers; Emporia *Gazette*, May 10, 1915.

60. Norman Hapgood, "The Prussian Menace," *Harper's Weekly*, LIX (Sept. 19, 1914), 274; "Peace without Vengeance," *Independent*, 79 (Sept. 21, 1914), 396; "Chesterton—Viereck," *New Republic*, I (Jan. 23, 1915), 8.

61. "War at Any Price," *New Republic*, V (Nov. 27, 1915), 84–85; "What are You Fighting for?" *Independent*, 84 (Nov. 29, 1915), 332–34; "Peace Efforts," *Harper's Weekly*, LXI (Dec. 11, 1915), 553.

62. "America Speaks," *New Republic*, IX (Jan. 27, 1917), 340–42; "The Declaration of Interdependence," *Independent*, 89 (Feb. 5, 1917), 202; "The President on World Peace," *American Review of Reviews*, LV (March 1917), 246; Notebook XIII, 131–33, 136–37, 139–40, Baker Papers.

63. Herbert Croly to Edward M. House, May 9, 1917, Edward M. House Papers (Yale University Library); Paul U. Kellogg, "Swords and Ploughshares," *Survey*, XXXVIII (Aug. 4, 1917), 406; "Grounds of Lasting Peace," *American Review of Reviews*, LVI (Sept. 1917), 229; Russell to Woodrow Wilson, Nov. 7, 1917, George Creel Papers (Manuscript Division, Library of Congress); "For a Holy War," *Independent*, 92 (Dec. 15, 1917), 497–98; Walter E. Weyl, *The End of the War* (New York, 1918), especially 98–138.

64. Beveridge to Shaw, Feb. 13, 1917, Beveridge Papers. See also Fresno *Republican*, Feb. 3, March 19, April 3, April 29, 1917; "Is-

sues for All Citizens to Judge," *American Review of Reviews*, LV (March 1917), 227; "Presenting a Solid Front," *ibid.* (May 1917), 452–53.

65. This applies to John Spargo, Kellogg, and Amos Pinchot, though their later commitment to the war differed greatly, ranging from the wholehearted to the token. John Spargo, "Reminiscences," 241–42 (Oral History Research Office, Columbia University, 1957); New York *Times*, Sept. 3, 1917; Paul U. Kellogg, "The Fighting Issues: A Statement by the Editor of the Survey," *Survey*, XXXVII (Feb. 17, 1917), 572–77; Kellogg, "Swords and Ploughshares," 406; Amos Pinchot, "Keep Out of War," *Public*, XX (March 16, 1917), 251; Amos Pinchot to Louis F. Post, Oct. 2, 1917, Box 34, Amos Pinchot Papers.

66. Arthur S. Link, *Wilson: Campaigns for Progressivism and Peace 1916–1917* (Princeton, 1965), 124–30.

67. "The Reality of Peace," *New Republic*, IV (Oct. 30, 1915), 322.

68. Notebook VII, Aug. 1915, pp. 55–57, Baker Papers; "Moral Reactions of the War," *Independent*, 84 (Oct. 4, 1915), 6; Graham Taylor, "World Salvage," *Survey*, XXXV (Jan. 29, 1916), 525–26; Emporia *Gazette*, April 7, 1917.

69. "The Reality of Peace," 323, 322.

70. Edward T. Devine, "Ourselves and Europe I," *Survey*, XXXVII (Nov. 4, 1916), 100.

71. Notebook XIII, 147–48, Baker Papers.

72. Hofstadter, *The Age of Reform*, 152.

73. "The Standpat Victory," *Harper's Weekly*, LIX (Nov. 21, 1914), 481; *New Republic*, I (Nov. 7, 1914), 3; "The Progressive Party—an Obituary," *ibid.*, VII (June 17, 1916), 159–61; "The Elections of 1914," *Independent*, 80 (Nov. 16, 1914), 221–22; Winter and Hicks, eds., *Letters*, I, 348; White to James Garfield, Nov. 18, 1914, White to Victor Murdock, June 19, 1916, White Papers; Rowell to Theodore Roosevelt, Dec. 6, 1914, Rowell Papers; Fresno *Republican*, June 12, 1916; Randolph S. Bourne, "This Older Generation," *Atlantic Monthly*, CXVI (Sept. 1915), 391; Walter Weyl, "The Average Voter," *Century*, 90 (Oct. 1915), 901–07.

74. Notebook IX, 69–70, Baker Papers.

75. "The Problem of the Progressive Voter," *New Republic*, VII (July 22, 1916), 290.

76. In 1910, White had traced the origins of the progressive movement to the Spanish-American War, when "The spirit of sacrifice overcame the spirit of commercialism.... If we could learn to sacrifice our own interest for those of a weaker people, we would learn the lesson needed to solve the great problem of democracy—to check our national greed and to make business honest." William Allen White, *The Old Order Changeth: A View of American Democracy* (New York, 1910), 29–30.

77. Charles Hirschfeld has emphasized the prominence of this line of argument, particularly in the *New Republic*, but without associating it with the recognition that the achievement of such reforms in ordinary peacetime conditions seemed remote. Charles Hirschfeld, "Nationalist Progressivism and World War I," *Mid-America*, 45 (July 1963), 139–56.

78. *New Republic*, X (April 14, 1917), 307.

79. "Public Opinion and the War," *ibid.* (April 21, 1917), 336.

80. It is not possible to account for the different positions these publicists adopted in the spring of 1917 simply in terms of the different schools into which some historians have divided progressives. Allowing for the difficulty of categorizing these men along the lines Braeman suggests, Baker, George Creel, and White were surely no more "modern" in their outlook than Randolph S. Bourne and Kellogg. Cooper's distinction between "nationalists," "isolationists," and "liberal internationalists" is easier to apply, but with the excepton of nationalists like Beveridge, Gifford Pinchot, and Shaw, most, including opponents of intervention, seem to have been closer to the liberal internationalist than the isolationist position. See Braeman, "Seven Progressives," 592; Cooper, "Progressivism and American Foreign Policy: A Reconsideration," 260–77.

American Profiles

*Esmond Wright**

Lincoln Before His Election

In this brief account of Lincoln before he came to the presidency, Esmond Wright skillfully narrates the story of the one American who never fails to fascinate the non-American historian. One of the values of this interpretative essay is the manner in which Wright conveys something of the essence of Lincoln: a leader of paradoxical postures largely because he is seen first as a person of paradoxical convictions. By concentrating on Lincoln as a man of his times in the context of those times, we are reminded by this British authority of the necessity of reading history not backwards but forward. A second value in Wright's approach also becomes clear. By considering the formative influences and events in Lincoln's life before he assumed "the glorious burden" of the presidential office, Wright avoids the temptation to echo Stanton's words (which he quotes) that Lincoln "belongs to the ages." The whole sketch benefits from Wright's appreciation of the holes in the fabric of the Lincoln legend. Yet he cares not to repress his admiration for him and the work he was to accomplish, seeming to agree with Sandburg who spoke of Lincoln as "hard as rock and soft as drifting fog."

*Esmond Wright is Director of the Institute of United States Studies and Professor of American History at the University of London.

The United States is quite as addicted to holy days as Catholic Europe or the Islamic world, and among them three are preeminent; July 4, the day on which, it is believed (inaccurately as it happens), the Founding Fathers signed the Declaration of Independence; February 22, Washington's birthday; and February 12, the birthday of Abraham Lincoln. Of these the last has come to hold a special place in the calendar, as Lincoln has come to hold a special, perhaps the central, place in American hagiology.

The reasons are many. One, the rags to riches theme, from log cabin to White House; born to an illiterate and wandering frontiersman and with hardly any formal schooling, a failure at forty, he was at fifty the president of the United States at the most critical moment in its history. Two, the transition from awkward and hesitant Westerner, ill-versed in Eastern politeness and in person ugly and ungainly, to skilful and dexterous politician, the symbol of success in war and the leader of a reunited country. Three, the president in the midst of war who yet stayed civilian-minded, who, even when he studied military manuals to prepare himself for active command, remained the humanitarian, prompt to pardon offenders, forgiving towards deserters, and gentle towards the bereaved; the war leader and elect of the nation had never found it easy even to discipline his own children. Four, the liberator, plagued by the slavery question, who was able to emancipate the slaves from January 1863, and to whom the war then became a campaign to safeguard a covenant. And fifth, beyond and including all these, the folksy man himself with his tall tales and rough humour, the brooding figure addicted to melancholy and acquainted with grief; the human figure, bothered by a shrewish and complaining wife, who in his high office was untouched by pride or pomp, to whom assassination in the hour of his triumph brought the final apotheosis of martyrdom. He was shot on a Good Friday, sacrificed, it seemed, for the redemp-

tion of the Union he loved. "Now he belongs to the ages,"
said Stanton—rarely in life an admirer. And the ages have
seized on his story to make it the most significant personal
saga in American history, and to see in Lincoln the stereotype not only of the democratic opportunities offered by
the New World but also of its conscience and humanity.
In the Lincoln story it has been hard to avoid the use of
the term "Saviour."

> Lincoln, six feet one in his stocking feet,
> The lank man, knotty and tough as a hickory rail,
> Whose hands were always too big for white-kid gloves,
> Whose wit was a coonskin sack of dry, tall tales,
> Whose weathered face was homely as a plowed
>   field—. . . .
> Honesty rare as a man without self-pity,
> Kindness as large and plain as a prairie-wind,
> And a self-confidence like an iron bar.

Or as the school-children of Illinois honor him each
February 12, turning towards Springfield as if to a Mecca
as they chant—

> A blend of mirth and sadness,
> Smiles and tears,
> A quaint Knight-errant of the pioneers,
> A homely hero born a star in sod,
> A peasant prince, a masterpiece of God.

Historical research is usually prompt to destroy mythology—even if few among contemporary American historians aspire, these days, to be called "debunkers." The
Lincoln legend has, however, proved to be well–founded.
It is impossible not to admire his personal qualities—his
modesty, humour, patience, and compassion—his uncanny
skill as a war-leader through the agony of a civil war, or

his faith in the Union. The legends that have been destroyed by recent research are mainly those assiduously fostered by William Herndon, Lincoln's law partner—in particular, the tale of Lincoln's jilting of Mary Todd at the church door, and how she later married him for spite. It cannot be claimed that it was a happy marriage, but the reason now seems clearly to have been Mrs. Lincoln's mental instability, which increased in the war years. About the greatness of the man himself, after the war began, there has been little controversy. Queries do remain, however, about his role in the years before Beauregard's guns opened up on Sumter. Moreover, the legend has itself contrived to minimise some striking features of his early life; it has certainly obscured the extent both of his political ambition and of his political dexterity; and it has in particular obscured his long hesitations on the slavery question. He who earned the title of "the great Emancipator" came to emancipation very late, and with marked reluctance.

In the family migration from Kentucky to Indiana and finally to Illinois, Lincoln had been a jack-of-all-trades —farm-labourer, rail splitter, flat-boatman on the Mississippi, storekeeper, postmaster, assistant surveyor of roads. He held no job for long, but he came to know people and to be known by them. He was phenomenally strong and striking, however ungainly—well over six feet in height, a wrestler, a captain in the Black Hawk War, and a good teller of tales, many of them robust. Not until his election from Sangamon County to the Illinois State Legislature (on the second attempt) in 1834, did he begin the study of law. And as his later partner, William Herndon, tells us, he rarely spent long reading law books. The fact was that from the first, despite the poor schooling, the droll manners, and the lack of grace, he had political ambitions.

Not only ambitions but skill, and some success. His prominence in state politics—he served four terms in the state legislature—derived largely from the fact that he helped to have the state capital moved to the county seat, Springfield. This was politics—then as now—that his county could appreciate; it mattered more than policies or principles.

Where principles were concerned, what was striking about Lincoln in Illinois politics in the 1830s—the heyday of Jacksonian Democracy—was that he was, after all, not a Democrat but a Whig. Raised on the frontier, he was yet no agrarian. He cast his first vote in 1832 for Henry Clay; he preferred "the American system"—the programme of internal improvements, stable currency, and high tariffs —to the programme of equality and reform; he held the Jacksonians to be traitors to Jefferson's ideals. The poor boy was in the rich man's party; he was ultimately to marry into it; and his wife, a Todd from the Lexington Bluegrass, was never to allow him to forget the social gulf between them. In all the discussions of Lincoln as a product of American democracy, a noticeable feature is his determination to rise by his own boot-straps and to become not only successful, but dignified. He was embarrassed in 1860 by the propaganda about his origins, and by the rail-splitter image. Prone to tell a folksy tale, he did not really welcome replies in kind. As Seward was to learn, he could keep his own counsel. "He was not a social man," says Herndon—"too reflective, too abstracted"—"a reticent, secretive, shut-mouth man." Behind the rough exterior he was never a Jacksonian. Despite the Turner thesis, the frontier has in fact produced as many natural aristocrats as it has produced conformists.

Lincoln's single term in the national Congress (1847–9), generally undistinguished, had about it again many of the characteristics of the cautious politician. He was Illinois' only Whig representative, having defeated a formidable backwoods preacher, Peter Cartwright. In his campaign, Lincoln had not opposed the Mexican War, but when his party denounced the war as both Democratic and unjust, Lincoln strongly supported their charges. In the course of doing so he asserted the right of any people, or of a "majority of any portion of such people," to "shake off the existing government, and form a new one"—a viewpoint impossible to reconcile with his stand in 1861. His criticism of the Mexican War and his loyalty to his party lost him the support of his state: he was to many a "second Benedict Arnold," speaking for the East, where the war was unpopular, and disregarding the West, where it was popular. Although his party won the 1848 election, they did not carry his district. Lincoln resumed his law practice—"I was losing interest in politics," he wrote later.

The lack of interest remained until the passing of the Kansas-Nebraska Act in 1854, and the repeal of the Missouri Compromise that it carried with it. This, the work of Senator Stephen Douglas of Illinois, made it possible for the settlers in Kansas and Nebraska, before being granted statehood, to vote for the introduction of slavery. It re-opened the slavery controversy, and brought Lincoln back into politics.

The slavery issue was not only the most perplexing of American—and human—issues. It posed particular problems to the Middle Western states, as it did to the territories, at a time when American society, already very mobile, was becoming polyglot. In the decade 1850–60 the population of Illinois doubled (from 851,470 to 1,711,951) and its foreign-born population trebled (by 1860 it was over 300,000). Nativism was already a feature of the Eastern states—quite as marked a feature, oddly, as the moral concern over the wickedness of slavery—and a dangerously popular Know-Nothing party developed. For this Lincoln had no sympathy.

> I am not a Know-nothing. How could I be? How can anyone who abhors the oppression of Negroes be in favor of degrading classes of white people? Our

progress in degeneracy appears to me to be pretty rapid. As a nation we began by declaring that "all men are created equal." We now practically read it "all men are created equal except Negroes." When the Know-nothings get control, it will read "all men are created equal, except Negroes and foreigners and Catholics." When it comes to this, I shall prefer emigrating to some country where they make no pretense of loving liberty,—to Russia, for instance, where despotism can be taken pure, and without the base alloy of Hypocracy [sic].

But slavery was a much less straightforward matter. Always compassionate and tolerant, Lincoln detested the institution of slavery; equally he deplored the campaigns of the abolitionists who fought slavery by extraconstitutional means, just as he deplored the riots of those who sought to deprive the abolitionists of the right to speak their minds. It was at Alton, Illinois, that Elijah Lovejoy had been murdered. The abolitionists, especially their leader in the West, Theodore Dwight Weld, were far more a problem in the 1840s and 1850s than the pro-slavery advocates—Weld indeed a more important figure, it now seems, than Garrison.

And Lincoln faithfully reflected in these years the viewpoint of his section. The tale that on his second visit to New Orleans, when he was just twenty-one, he saw a mulatto girl being sold on the block, and that "the iron entered his soul," causing him to vow to "hit slavery hard" —this is now suspect among Lincoln scholars. In fact, during his formative years he appears not to have been particularly concerned about slavery. He lived in an area where slaves were rare; his family hailed from Virginia, and if this did not make him pro-Southern at least he seems to have shared the contemporary Southern belief that slavery would gradually disappear. He did nothing when in the state legislature to interfere with the severe laws that were in force against free Negroes or runaway

slaves; he did not denounce—as so many did—the Fugitive Slave Law, despite the obvious hardships to free
Negroes—"I confess I hate to see the poor creatures
hunted down . . . but I bite my lips and keep quiet."
When the Illinois legislature denounced abolitionists, and
came down on the proslavery side, Lincoln refused, it is
true, to support the majority: but he afterwards justified
his position by the unexceptionable statement that "the
institution of slavery is founded on injustice and bad
policy but . . . the promulgation of abolition doctrines
tends to increase rather than abate its evils." As a good
lawyer Lincoln respected the Constitution; slavery where
it existed must be left alone, and allowed to die a natural
death—if it would. It is not surprising but often forgotten
that such moderation, at a time when tempers ran high,
brought him no distinction—and some obloquy. To Wendell Phillips he was "that slavehound from Illinois." However inaccurate this was, Lincoln was certainly no crusader.

When Douglas brought forward his proposals to open
new territory to slavery, he split the Democratic Party and
lost the support of much Northern opinion. It was thought
—probably unfairly—that he was seeking to win Southern
support for his own presidential ambitions; it was thought
—with more justification—that he was planning a railway
route through the Kansas-Nebraska territory; it is certain
that he was not excited about slavery, and that he was mis-
led by his own certainty that neither Kansas nor Nebraska
would be suited to a slave economy anyway. As he put it
in the Lincoln-Douglas debates, "I care more for the great
principle of self-government, the right of the people to
rule, than I do for all the Negroes in Christendom."

Superficially, Douglas was right, as his triumph over
Lincoln in the Senatorial contest in 1858 revealed: but
Lincoln's political flair here proved deeper and shrewder
than Douglas's. Between 1854 and 1856 Lincoln moved
from the Whig to the newly-founded Republican Party.

He did so cautiously; in 1855 he sought unsuccessfully the Whig nomination for the Senate. Although the new party was built on a series of often quite contradictory programmes and issues—the tariff, internal improvements, prohibitionism—Lincoln steered clear of all of these in Illinois. When Douglas was making it plain that he was not pro-slavery, but was ready to permit slavery in the territories, Lincoln was making it equally plain that he was not an abolitionist, but that he was opposed to slavery in the territories. Douglas's stand could only win support in the South, and on the Southern border—and tepid support at that. Lincoln's could win approval everywhere outside the South. And in his opposition to the extension of slavery to the territories, Lincoln was always firm and consistent. A thread of certainty was appearing; and a strong thread it was, for it was Lincoln's refusal to sunder it that caused the Civil War.

He was slow to condemn slavery as such. He did so now and then, but never formally until 1854, and always accompanying his condemnations by a frank avowal that he did not know what to do about it—"if all earthly power were given me, I should not know what to do as to the existing institution." There was, then, distaste for the institution, a firm front against its further extension and a frank avowal of uncertainty how to curb it without offending the South—or the law of the land. But there was something more than this, greatly appealing to Illinois, and that was the theme that the Western states, like the territories, were for white men—free men but white men. Alongside every sentence in every speech condemning the wickedness of slavery and stressing the superior merits of a free to a slave society, there is the equal emphasis that the Negro must not be given political or social equality. The Negro was the equal of the white: but he must not be given citizenship. The Republican Party in the North-west inherited both free-soil sentiments and, in some degree, nativism; if not as cold-blooded about slavery as Douglas, it did not want Negroes, free or slave, in its borders. Its theme-song in Missouri, as advocated by Frank Blair on the masthead of his *Daily Missouri Democrat,* was "White Men for Missouri and Missouri for White Men."

Lincoln's greatest achievement as a politician before the election of 1860—his skills did not stop then—lay in the dexterity with which he used this issue, bred by the section in which he was raised, to reconcile many conflicting groups and win them over to his side. It was not that Lincoln took a moral line, although he sometimes did so—and this was noted in New England, where moral lines were more traditional, and easier, than elsewhere. Hence he was noted with favour "back East." It was not that Lincoln supported abolitionism—he did not, although many abolitionists noted with favour only his condemnations of "the peculiar institution." Nor was it that he opposed the extension of slavery to the territories out of a mere trust in political compromise itself—as Clay had done in 1850. He had found an issue that touched all these and transcended them, and won him fame in the North-west. He expressed it in his speech at Peoria in 1854 when he spoke of the future of the territories:

> We want them for homes of free white people. This they cannot be, to any considerable extent, if slavery shall be planted within them. Slave States are places for poor white people to remove from, not remove to. New free States are the places for poor people to go to, and better their condition. For this use the nation needs these Territories.

The argument—he used it repeatedly in the next six years—was an argument not for equality—of black and white—but for freedom—for whites. It was the fear of poorer whites, almost all of them immigrants into the West and many of them of foreign origin, that they might

now have to compete in hitherto-free states with the labour of slaves, that brought them, in the North-west, into
the Republican Party. It was not difficult for the Republican Party to build around this theme those other planks
—free homesteads, a railway to the Pacific, a protective
tariff—that were in the end to make of it the party of
progress, expansion, and the full dinner pail. The pioneer
of the 1850s was, after all, often the father of the entrepreneur of the 1890s. If Lincoln's father was an illiterate
nomad, Lincoln's son was Ambassador to the Court of St.
James and president of the Pullman Car Company. The
generation that lived in the sod-house—like that which
fought the Indian—was very short; but if short in actual
span of years it too has been long in legends.

It was easy for Douglas, in the debate of 1858, to point
to the flaws in Lincoln's case—to accuse him of being,
in his "house-divided" speech, a sectional leader only,
whose viewpoint assumed "a war of section"; to task him
with favouring equality for Negroes; and to make the
charge that he adapted his speeches to suit the varied
attitudes of the state. He was, said Douglas, "jet black"
in the North, "a decent mulatto" in the center and "almost white" in the South. And the charge was true: in Chicago it was "all men are created equal"; in the South, "the
superior position must go to the white race." Lincoln was
still a moderate—opposed to abolition, opposed to the
repeal of the Fugitive Slave Laws, opposed to Negro
citizenship and to social and political equality of white
and black. The free Negro, H. Ford Douglass, thought
his programme no better than that of Stephen Douglas.
But in all his dexterity, Lincoln never abandoned the
central argument: that slavery must not be permitted to
expand. If the Dred Scott decision of the Supreme Court
in 1857 were permitted to stand—that slavery could not
be excluded from the territories—where could slavery be
halted? "Popular sovereignty" could not be reconciled

with the Dred Scott decision. The Democratic Party had become a "conspiracy . . . for the sole purpose of nationalising slavery." Douglas, in the debates, was the realist, and was right to think that it was idle to thrash out an issue that geography itself would settle. Douglas won the election—since Senators were then chosen by the legislature, and there the apportionment of seats gave the Democrats control. But Lincoln won more popular votes than Douglas, and it was clear now to the nation, as to Illinois, that he saw further and touched deeper chords.

The 1858 debates gave Lincoln a national platform. The compromise programme of Illinois that brought some satisfaction to all the groups in the variegated Republican Party—but not complete satisfaction to any—became the platform of 1860. In the "house divided" references, Lincoln had touched on the moral issue, although he was careful not to develop it too far. He touched it again in the debates with Douglas at Galesburg and at Quincy— slavery was "a moral, social, and political wrong." But it was still *festina lente*. And Lincoln sought the presidential nomination in 1860 as he had sought previous success— by speeches and correspondence emphasising moderation, by managing party business, by being active and being seen to be active. Herndon was right to say, "He was always calculating and planning ahead. His ambition was a little engine that knew no rest." Throughout 1859 he campaigned, as the leading Western Republican, in Ohio and Indiana, Iowa, and Wisconsin. When he delivered the Cooper Institute speech in New York in February, 1860 —the speech and the photograph that in retrospect he thought gave him the Republican nomination—he held to the same note: denial of abolitionism; distaste for John Brown's radicalism; sympathy for the South—but no support for any proposed extension of slavery to the territories of the United States. This was for Lincoln the central precept, ordained by the Founding Fathers.

When he was nominated as the choice of Illinois Republicans at the Republican Convention in 1860—a convention that met, helpfully, in the "Wigwam" in Chicago (a lumber shack built to hold 10,000 and which 40,000 sought to enter) —his efforts were crowned with success. The Democrats had already held their Convention, in Charleston, S.C., and had broken up in disorder. The Southerners wanted positive protection for slaveholding and nominated Breckinridge of Kentucky. The "regular" Democrats nominated Douglas. There were likely to be at least two Democratic Parties; there might be more. Whoever won the Republican nomination was therefore almost certain of victory. This put a premium on moderation, especially if the key states—Illinois, Indiana, Pennsylvania—were to be won. Seward of New York was too biting and too radical, and the redoubtable editor of the *New York Tribune*, Horace Greeley, opposed him. This seemed no time for talk of "the irrepressible conflict" and "the higher law." Chase of Ohio could not control his own state; he was precise, aloof, and abstemious.

Even so, the nomination of Lincoln—like his whole career—demanded skilful mechanics. There is a considerable and rival literature on the question of the division of credit for the dexterities of the "Wigwam" between O. H. Browning, Joseph Medill, and Charles Ray of the *Chicago Tribune*, and Jesse Fell (great-grandfather of Adlai Stevenson). Probably the credit should really go to his campaign manager, stout Judge David Davis, an old friend of the Illinois circuit, with his headquarters in the Tremont House. One of Davis's happiest devices was to print and issue bogus tickets for Lincoln supporters, who, there ahead of time, got into the Convention—and kept Seward's men out. Another was to place stentor-voiced supporters at key points—one of them was reputed to be able to shout across Lake Michigan. And with effect, for when Lincoln was nominated, one witness said that "A thousand steam whistles, ten acres of hotel gongs, a tribe of Comanches, headed by a choice vanguard from pandemonium might have mingled in the scene unnoticed."

Lincoln had instructed Davis to make no bargains. This was honoured as scrupulously as such adages normally are—and are expected to be. "Lincoln ain't here," said Davis, "and don't know what we have to meet so we will go ahead as if we hadn't heard from him, and he must ratify it." The promises were made, and Lincoln's later Cabinet revealed the extent of them. "They have gambled me all round, bought and sold me a hundred times." But this too is normal; and it is normal in democratic politics genuinely to deplore the means even as one esteems the end.

With 465 delegates present and 233 votes necessary for victory, on the first ballot Seward had 173½, Lincoln 102, Cameron of Pennsylvania 50½, Chase 49, Bates 48, and the remainder scattered. On the second ballot, Cameron's name was withdrawn to Lincoln's advantage (Cameron was to become his Secretary of War): Seward had 184½, Lincoln 181, Chase 42½, Bates 45. When, on the third ballot, four Ohio voters transferred to Lincoln, a landslide followed.

In the ensuing months, the landslide spread through the continent. As the South talked of secession—not original talk, it is true, in South or North—if the "Black Republican" were elected, Lincoln sat in Springfield. He made very few speeches, although he talked a great deal to political leaders and delegations. He did little, however, to placate the South. And on Nov. 6, 1860, he was chosen President by a large electoral majority (Lincoln 180, Breckinridge of Kentucky 72, Bell 39, Douglas 12) — but with only 40 percent of the popular vote (Lincoln, 1,866,452; Douglas, 1,376,957; Breckinridge, 849,781; Bell, 588,879). In ten Southern states not a single popular vote was cast for him; he failed to carry his own county in Illinois. But he carried every free state in the North except New Jersey. Moderation paid; the White House awaited him. His silence did not; South Carolina seceded from the Union.

Through the anxious four months between election and inauguration, the silence continued. And Buchanan, the retiring president, took no action. While state after state withdrew, and a Southern Confederacy was formed, Lincoln made his plans in Springfield, but made no statements of policy. He would move, as always, slowly. For what was now emerging was the second theme; as the president-elect, he had an oath to keep, requiring the perpetuation of the Union, for the Union was perpetual. This to Lincoln as lawyer, politician, and citizen was now the first priority. Nothing must be done by him—or by any man or combination of men—that would risk the break-up of the Union. "If I could save the Union by emancipating all the slaves I would do so; if I could save it by emancipating none I would do it; if I could save it by emancipating some and not others, I would do that too." This carried with it respect for the Constitution and the rights guaranteed by it—including slavery where it existed. As late as 1861 he was ready to amend the Constitution to guarantee slavery in the states, and generals who announced emancipation in their commands were promptly rebuked.

Equally, he had won his election on a political platform that for him was quite as binding as his presidential oath. His refusal to consider the territorial extension of slavery wrecked the Crittendon compromise proposals. "Stand firm," he told Lyman Trumball. "The tug has to come, and better now than at any time hereafter." "Hold firm," he told Elihu Washburne, "as with a chain of steel." The consistent thread was now visible through all the stress and pressures put on him.

Lincoln was without training in executive office, and

not, thus far, quick in action. Advice and requests poured
in, of all kinds—from wives seeking promotion for their
husbands; from Southern belles ("For God sake, Dear Sir
give us women some assurance that you will protect us,
for we are the greatest Slaves in the South") ; from supporters seeking "a little of the needful"; from Pinkerton,
the detective, enclosing a private cipher code (in which
apparently the code-word for the Secretary of War was
"pea-nuts" and for the President himself plain "nuts") ;
from enemies telling him to give up—or to shoot himself.

Lincoln left Springfield for Washington on February
11, 1861. Because of reports of likely attempts at assassination he entered the city secretly, at night. His speeches
en route had done nothing to placate the South. General
Winfield Scott had been ordered to be ready to "hold or
retake" the forts in the South as circumstances might require. But the Inaugural Address was conciliatory. Lincoln
once again disclaimed any intention of interfering with
slavery in the states; all Federal laws must be observed
—including the laws compelling the return of fugitive
slaves; the Union, however, must and would be preserved.
But there was no way in which the oath to maintain the
Constitution and preserve the Union could be squared
with secession. "In your hands, my dissatisfied fellow-
countrymen, and not in mine, is the momentous issue of
civil war. You have no oath registered in heaven to destroy the Government; while I shall have the most solemn
one to 'preserve, protect and defend' it."

Lincoln won his election not by moral greatness, or
by compassion for white or black, but by political skills
of a high order. He was to reveal greatness in the years
ahead, moral as well as political. Earnest he was, with
remarkable insight into the essence of the controversy;
and firm he was to show himself. But little of this was
evident in 1860, least of all to his cabinet. The ill-dressed
and awkward figure, with a high nasal inflexion in his

voice, was—to Seward as to the country—an unknown quantity, even perhaps a "Simple Susan." He had shown uncanny skill in compromising on many questions. He had also shown that there were for him some issues on which there could be no compromise, and no surrender. "Hard as a rock and soft as drifting fog" is Sandburg's phrase.

The issues raised by Fort Sumter, an undermanned federal fort commanding the narrows leading to Charleston harbour and held by Federal troops, whose supplies were running short, were his first test as President—the first of many. But that is another story.

*David Nunnerley**

JFK: Assassination, Martyrdom, Impact

The British people have chosen to erect memorials to only three American presidents: Abraham Lincoln, Franklin Roosevelt, and John Fitzgerald Kennedy. In his evaluation of the influence of JFK on Britain, David Nunnerley provides ample evidence for Kennedy's inclusion in this trinity. Several reasons are at once apparent—charisma, vision, openness—the hope held out to so many people. Familiar enough to a Kennedy generation of Americans, one gets some idea of the worldwide scope of his image and appeal from Nunnerley's summing-up. If his account seems a trifle dewy-eyed, British respect for Kennedy rested not on sentiment but on mutual regard and advantage nonetheless, considerations invoking memories of "the special relationship." Further, Nunnerley's final assessment of JFK serves to remind us of the worth of foreign perspectives on Americans and their history. By telling us that late in the twentieth century it was still possible to experience the American sense of mission—Jefferson's "last, best hope" in the words and actions of one man, we have perhaps the importance of John Fitzgerald Kennedy for our times.

*David Nunnerley is Lecturer in Politics at the University of Kent.

Dr. Johnson once remarked, "It matters not how a man dies, but how he lives. The act of dying is not of importance, it lasts so short a time." Yet surely few people do not remember where they were on Friday, November 22, 1963, when the world first heard of the assassination of John F. Kennedy. Who, indeed, will ever forget how the president's widow, having been witness on that day to the lowest level of human cruelty, maintained in the ensuing days the highest level of human nobility: how, throughout the burial rites, her slim, upright figure wavered not an inch in dignity, not an inch in grief? Few people do not recall the tensions and emotions intermingled as they laid President Kennedy to rest in Arlington National Cemetery: the lighting of the eternal flame by his brave widow; the young son saluting his father's memory; the silence of the grieving city broken only by the mournful tolling of a single bell and the monotonous roll of drums.

Literally millions of people were to be wholly involved in the death and burial of President Kennedy to an extent unthinkable before the age of electronic communications. Through television, the magnitude of the tragedy involved and overwhelmed us all in a way that would have been inconceivable but a few years before. Three previous American presidents had been assassinated but none, not even Lincoln's, had evoked such an immediate sense of grief and despair that the world felt with Kennedy's murder. "I can recall no single blow in my lifetime," Lord Boothby was to write, "which has struck us all with such stunning force as the assassination of President Kennedy."[1]

"Great Britain," Mr. David Bruce remarked at the time, "has never before mourned a foreigner as it has President Kennedy." The traditionally undemonstrative British people unashamedly displayed their own grief and horror. We felt that we had lost not just a leader but a friend. "We have lost our champion," lamented the *Daily*

Mirror (November 23, 1963). We discovered that he had
been more familiar to us than we had previously known
or been prepared to admit. We had perhaps taken him
too much for granted, for he had been the one Western
politician of his era who had restored politics to its former position as a respectable and honourable profession.
A television tribute given by the Prime Minister aptly sum-
marised the grief experienced by the British people.
"There are times when the mind and heart stand still,"
declared Sir Alec Douglas-Home; "one such is now."

In varying degrees, all of us felt such a standstill. "To
the whole of humanity struggling in the world of darkness," remarked Macmillan, in a deeply moving personal
tribute, "it seemed a sudden and cruel extinction of a
shining light." Our anguish was universal, but it was also
very individual. Millions of ordinary people suffered a
personal loss. Countless thousands from all over the country were to file through the American Embassy in Grosvenor Square to sign the books of condolence. A requiem
mass for the dead president filled Westminster Cathedral
beyond capacity. The extremity of our dismay was perhaps the true measure of the grandeur of his achievement
and our response to his murder will forever be a monument to the affection in which he was held in Britain.
But why was it that, in common with the rest of the world,
we felt such a desolation of spirit at the news of his death
and such a sense of utter despair about the future which,
for as long as he lived, had seemed so bright with promise?
Was it not perhaps that we were simply being carried
away by our emotions in the face of a stark human tragedy
—the gunning down of a young president in the presence
of his beautiful wife?

The personal tragedy was certainly the one that
struck hardest. Here was a man only forty-six years of
age, boyish in looks, young in heart, eager and vigorous
in spirit. He had presented himself to the British public

as an attractive, vital, and friendly personality, the embodiment of youth, pulsating with fresh ideas and the political courage to espouse them. In British eyes, he had brought to international politics the excitement and the integrity of youth. He was of course no child: he was only fourteen months younger than Harold Wilson, and no one talked of Wilson's youthfulness! Yet Kennedy looked very young (to many, ridiculously young). He was tanned, handsome, and rich, with a personal magnetism and a photogenic family. He united in one commanding person the idealism of some of the younger generation with the itch for success of the rest. The torch had been passed to a new generation of leaders and now it had been extinguished so cruelly soon, so unnatural seemed the deprivation. "It is the realisation that the future held the promise of great accomplishments for Joe," John F. Kennedy had written in an appreciation of his late brother, entitled *As We Remember Joe*, "that made his death so particularly hard for those who knew him. His worldly success was so assured and inevitable that his death seems to cut into the natural order of things." Millions of people felt the same sense of loss about John F. Kennedy's own passing. His worldly success had seemed so assured and inevitable that his death had tragically cut into the natural order of things. He had so much life and promise ahead of him until it was all so dastardly ended that day in Dallas.

Beyond the personal tragedy, the British nation shared the American anguish in a peculiarly special and poignant way. There was the great loss derived from the knowledge that, at least since 1940, Britain has increasingly been dependent upon American power and its exercise. "The President of the United States," wrote David Butler, "is the President of Britain. However closely the British guard their indepedence, however scrupulously the President respects it, he still makes decisions that are more important to their fate than any made by the Prime Minister." Everything a president does carries world-wide significance. "When he creaks, they groan," Sidney Hyman wrote, "When he wobbles, they feel unhinged." It was thus that, in the first shock reaction to Kennedy's assassination, we had a brief glimpse of the possibility that the scale in the international balance of power might be significantly, even dangerously, tipped. Understandably we were fearful of what the future might bring, our apprehension heightened by our lack of knowledge of the vice-president, who seemingly had neither experience nor great interest in foreign affairs. Yet it was Lyndon Johnson who was to be the real hero during those traumatic days. He held the American nation together when they had yet to accept the death of Kennedy, let alone the succession.

Successful as Johnson was in taking over the reins of power, he was nevertheless unable to replace Kennedy in our affections. For Britain, the personal sentiments, biases, and prejudices of a president often assume overriding importance, and, unlike his two immediate predecessors, Johnson had no close personal links with Britain. Thus did Nicholas Carroll write, "For the British Government, the death of President Kennedy is an unqualified disaster."[2] "There has not been an American President for many years," observed Michael Hilton, "who had a more realistic, and at the same time sympathetic, appreciation of the value of the Anglo-American relationship."[3]

It is perhaps remarkable how the British people felt that they could join in the activities of President Kennedy in a way that was simply not possible with a president of the United States thirty years before. Difficult as it is to explain, we felt Kennedy, like his predecessor, to be *our* president. We shared in the jokes and gossip about the White House. We took a fascinated interest in the vivacious First Lady who, in the hour of America's greatest need, gave them majesty. We delighted in the enchantingly informal pictures of the president at play with his children, attesting proof that every man, no matter how great and powerful, belongs to the one big family that is the human race. We shared not only the triumphs but also the misfortunes of the Kennedy family: their anguish was ours at the death in August, 1963, of their baby son, Patrick, born with a respiratory disorder which proved too much for his tiny heart. To an unprecedented extent, we immersed ourselves in the details, great and small, of the White House under President Kennedy. Whatever we thought of his politics, President Kennedy became part of our own national history.

But it is surely right to ask whether our instinctive judgement that here was a great man was not perhaps somewhat superficial? Only a very few people are in a position to gain their impressions of a man's character and worth at first-hand. Was it, therefore, not difficult—perhaps impossible—for the majority of the British people to distinguish between myth and reality? Did not the nature of Kennedy's death influence both our assessments of his achievements and more, our expectations of future successes? Was not the halo fixed upon President Kennedy the day he died? During those few agonising days, the Kennedy legend was put before the television cameras and firmly established by them. "His life, not his death, created his greatness," argued Sorensen. "In November, 1963, some saw it for the first time. Others realised that they had too casually accepted it. Others mourned that they had not previously admitted it to themselves. But the greatness was there and it may well loom even larger as the passage of years lends perspective."[4]

To be true, he was a man on the verge of greatness, but how could he establish his greatness in less than three years? Despite his youth, he was given no chance to write the full history of his times. Was it not, therefore, an ironic twist of fate that posterity should relegate his greatness to legend, his martyrdom making a myth of the mortal man? The legend was so absurdly built up in the weeks following his death, the myth so absurdly portrayed, that, as the passage of years has lent perspective, so history, not cynically but inevitably, has come to challenge it. Hallowed in 1963, the Kennedy name no longer carries a mystique of majesty about it. Indeed, with Jackie Kennedy's marriage to Aristotle Onassis, with Edward Kennedy's involvement in the tragic accident at Chappaquiddick in 1969, and more recently his meddling in the Ulster Crisis, the Kennedy legend no longer goes unquestioned in Britain. But this is not necessarily something to be lamented. Only as the Kennedy name emerges from the slough of public forgetfulness, which tends to follow the death of all great men, will President Kennedy cease to be considered a yesterday's hero (or villain for some) and instead become a properly proportioned figure in history, who at least in Britain made a lasting impact upon our politics.

America's involvement in the Vietnam War has been the most important single element in the tragic estrangement between the United States and its allies and, had he lived, President Kennedy might have handled it better than his successor. It is almost inconceivable that he would have made the miscalculations made by Johnson. But no one can ever be sure. "It will indeed never be possible to measure the consequences of the loss," commented *The Sunday Times* (November 24, 1963). "Great statesmen are rare at any time: great statesmen with the gift of hope are even rarer. . . . No one will ever know what opportunities might not have arisen if he had still been there to bring them to life." In certain instances, however, what people believe might have happened can be as important in terms of public opinion on an issue as what actually happens. For the American nation, the Vietnam War is one such instance. To be true, it was in Vietnam that the Communists were to call the bluff of a major promise of President Kennedy's given in his Inaugural Address: "Let every nation know, whether it wishes us well or ill, that we shall pay any price, bear any burden, meet any hardship, support any friend, oppose any foe to assure the survival and the success of liberty."

Vietnam was in fact the price paid for magnificent rhetoric but impossible policy. It was not a question of whether America was right to escalate the war but whether, physically and psychologically, she was able. And at a high price—the alienation from government of many segments of American society—we now know the answer: America simply cannot play St. George to so many dragons. Nevertheless, for most people, in America, in Britain, and around the world, the Vietnam War and its consequences are neither automatically nor obviously associated with President Kennedy. There were two thousand American troops in Vietnam when he took office and only sixteen thousand troops there by the time of his death. In the public's estimation, the Vietnam War is identified with Johnson and, to an increasing extent, with Nixon. Thus, looking back on those thousand days, which so many were to remember as a Golden Age, holding the promise of a bright and exciting future, they were to be less the beginning than possibly the end of an age. Certainly with Kennedy's death so also passed the age of American innocence. Men rejected their politics and turned to violence to achieve their ends; they questioned the usefulness of their institutions and challenged the very foundations of American society. The war created huge and bitter divisions in society which neither Johnson nor Nixon, both of whom, despite their efforts, remain basically "unloved" and enigmatic characters, have been able to heal. Had he lived, President Kennedy perhaps could have led his country through their convulsions to a better and more stable order. Again, however much people fervently believe this, we cannot be sure. But of one thing we can be confident: there can have been few more cruel illustrations than the tragedy at Dallas of the great danger in relying on anything so fragile as human flesh. Yet even then, as the passage of years has lent perspective, so increasingly Americans have come to view the Kennedy presidency with disappointment and disillusionment. He had promised them so much. He had pledged himself to get the country moving again. But by 1963 the United States, for many Americans, had moved neither very fast nor for that matter very far. It was in foreign affairs, more than in domestic affairs, that the presidency of John F. Kennedy was to leave its mark: and, in certain respects, he was to be better remembered, held in higher regard, and make a more lasting impact in Britain than in his own country.

The British people have thought it fitting to erect monuments in London to only three American presidents: Abraham Lincoln, Franklin D. Roosevelt and John F. Kennedy. In Kennedy's case, they have also raised a memorial to him on the hallowed ground of Runnymede, opened by the Queen in May, 1965, and established a scholarship scheme that will forever bear his name. Remarkable as it was that Kennedy, in British eyes, should be placed in the same category as two of America's greatest ever Presidents: it was an honour made even more noteworthy by the fact that his presidency lasted but a brief three years. How was it then that this young man, who held office for such a short period, should have so captured the imagination of the supposedly undemonstrative British people? What was it that this son of an unpopular American ambassador to Britain did and stood for that made his achievements so paramount in our memories?

It was extraordinary how popular Kennedy proved to be in Britain where, as recently as 1969, by a significant margin, the British people (as reflected in a Gallup Poll) voted him the Man of the Decade.[5] "Beyond doubt," concluded *The Sunday Times* (November 24, 1963), "President Kennedy was the man the British people would have chosen if they had had the right to choose. Astonishing as it is to remember, President Kennedy won in 1960 by a tiny margin. [His victory over Nixon had in fact been the narrowest since 1888.] He would always have won here by a landslide against any opponent." The British sense of judgement was attuned to his judgement. The slogans of the New Frontier did not have time to leave as deep an imprint in Britain as those of Roosevelt's New Deal. But they influenced men as widely different as Harold Wilson and Edward Heath. President Kennedy's desire to move forward in social and economic affairs all but mirrored our own almost obsessive needs. As Lord Boothby was to summarise his impact, "Kennedy was the living embodiment of what we have all been longing for and have desperately missed . . . Youth, Energy, Courage and —above all—Hope."[6]

Kennedy's personality roused impatience and hope of change and fresh aspirations in British politics. An unassuming manner and Edwardian elegance are no longer sufficient to meet the needs and aspirations of the British electorate. In place of the "gifted amateur," who had for centuries assumed a patrician rule, we now demand total commitment and professionalism from our politicians. More than this, we look for a man who can offer the same kind of charismatic leadership as Kennedy did. Kennedy's style had been essentially a British style, in that his oratory was the kind to which the British people felt they could respond. But it made a lasting impact in Britain through the President's skilful combination of personal magnetism and "telly-genetics." Thus did the younger generation of British politician try hard (though without much success) to capture the same kind of image which

Kennedy had, of somebody belonging very much to the modern world.

Kennedy's example was to herald a new era in the style and manner of politics in various Western countries. It greatly enhanced the fortunes of Willy Brandt, now Chancellor of West Germany, and paved the way for Pierre Trudeau, whose pitted skin and battered boyishness combined to make him touted as Canada's JFK. But of other Western political leaders, it was the British Labour Party policy-makers who were probably most visibly influenced in their attitude to America, and their approach to politics, by the personality of President Kennedy. And no single politician was more affected than Harold Wilson, who observed Kennedy with an admiration which developed rapidly into a form of hero-worship. A visit to the White House had long been considered by many a British politician as a must. Now the younger politicians went further: they imitated Kennedy's style, analysed his campaign techniques and permitted their publicists to portray them as "another Kennedy." Thus was Wilson's visit to the United States in the spring of 1963 put across by his public relations team as the visit of a Kennedy man, espousing Kennedy ideas, and discussing the future of the world, and especially the Anglo-American relationship, in modern, purposive terms.

President Kennedy fascinated Wilson as no politician had fascinated him since Stafford Cripps. The "new broom"—energetic, vital, dynamic, technocratic—set for Wilson, and for many in Britain, in even sharper relief the kind of old-school tie incompetence, represented by Macmillan and Home, which he so despised. The new administration of President Kennedy, Wilson, then Shadow Chancellor, told the Commons on February 7, 1961, "are looking to new frontiers, while this tired, discredited, caste-ridden Government, boasting of nothing but a cer-

tain amount of Edwardian elegance, allows Britain to lag
behind."

A devoted student of Kennedy methods, Wilson was
to model his campaign in the 1964 British General Election very much on Kennedy's 1960 campaign. As Kennedy
had done with such effect so Wilson presented himself
as the man to get his country moving again. He campaigned to free the country from the "grouse moor conception" of leadership, continually emphasising the theme
of purpose, "social purpose, economic purpose, purpose
in foreign affairs." He may have been derided by Douglas-
Home as a "slick salesman of synthetic science," but who
can deny that such a campaign reaped great dividends?

In government, Wilson was a faithful follower of
Kennedy's style of decision-making. He insisted on pulling
an issue out of the bureaucratic rut in time and defended
his own freedom of innovation and right of decision.
Later he was to speak of the importance of getting in on
emerging questions "by holding meetings of all relevant
Ministers at an early stage before the problem gets out
of hand. That's one of the techniques the world owes to
Kennedy."[7] Like Kennedy, Wilson was to bring into the
discussions only those ministers whom he considered had
a useful contribution to make, though in so doing he was
on more than one occasion to upset some of his cabinet
colleagues.

Wilson further emulated Kennedy in attaching great
importance to his dynamic First Hundred Days in office,
which (as it had for Kennedy) was to produce unfortu-
nate consequences. Neither Nixon, nor for that matter
Heath, can be blamed for not having even attempted to
match the youthful exhilaration of Kennedy and Wilson,
for the examples of both men suggest that overconfidence
can produce costly mistakes. For Kennedy, this was reflected in the considerable disenchantment in him produced by the Bay of Pigs fiasco. When he came to power,

he had represented the finest idealism of American youth
and his eloquent Inaugural Address had been all but a
clarion-call to the youth in Britain and around the world.
He had been represented in the three months between
the inauguration and the Cuban invasion as the last hope
for the West, a brilliant and exciting hope, conveying the
impression of a mature, responsible and, above all, intelligent American foreign policy. Now, through his own emphasis on the importance of his first hundred days, by this
one failure, he seemed to reveal himself as but a continu-
ation of past policy. Fortunately for Kennedy, (though
the experience was not to be repeated in the case of Wilson), there remained enough reserve of good-will in Britain for him to overcome this temporary set-back. "You
really have got off very lightly," Richard Crossman told
Arthur Schlesinger of Britain's reaction to the Bay of Pigs.
"If this had taken place under Eisenhower, there would
have been mass meetings in Trafalgar Square. Dulles
would have been burned in effigy and the Labour Party
would have damned you in the most unequivocal terms.
But because enough faith still remains in Kennedy, there
has been very little popular outcry, and the Labour Party
resolutions have been the very minimum. But one more
mistake like this and you will really be through."[8] There
were to be no further mistakes of that magnitude and, indeed, if Cuba was to be the occasion for Kennedy's greatest blunder, it also figured prominently in his greatest
single triumph. His handling of the missile crisis, his
calm determination and absence of display, were to be
universally recognised in Britain as the most responsible
management of a crisis in the thermonuclear age. "To
the world," reported *The Guardian* (November 23, 1963),
"he will be remembered as the President who helped to
bring the thaw in the cold war."

President Kennedy's efforts to get a more meaningful
East/West détente were but to confirm the British judge-

ment that he was a man to whom leadership came naturally. He had perhaps the ideal mental equipment for the nuclear age: an imaginative appreciation of power and a blend of caution, judgement and intuitive wisdom with which he wielded it. He was ruled by reason, common sense, and by what was politically feasible. He possessed courage, moral and physical, extraordinary speed of thought and clarity of decision, high ideals and vision, a keen sense of history, and acute sensitivity to the problems of others, friend and foe alike. Above all, to operate these qualities, he possessed a personal dynamism and seemingly unquenchable energy. At this critical juncture in international politics, the world needed a leader with just such a synthesis of these qualities.

The presidency is a unique institution. It places enormous and incredibly diverse responsibilities upon a single individual. It gives him inadequate authority as an outright gift but permits him to acquire whatever power he is capable of winning by leadership, combativeness, guile, and sheer stubbornness from the people, the Congress, the states, and a lumbering bureaucracy. In these times, the same qualities have to be extended to exercise presidential leadership of the Western world, and this Kennedy perceived better than most. However difficult, on occasion, it proved to be, Kennedy tried always to work honestly with his allies. All the time, he treated them with respect and in turn he earned their respect.

Britain will, however, remember Kennedy not for what he did alone, but also for what he stood for and what he started. The energies which he released, the standards which he laid down, the goals which he established, the hopes which he raised, and the purposes which he inspired are the same energies, standards, goals, hopes, and purposes that will influence future British generations. He stood for excellence in an era of relative indifference, hope in an era of frustration and mortal danger, conciliation above confrontation. He gave men confidence in the future and in each other, lifting them beyond their capabilities. Last, but by no means least, he restored to the world pride and dignity in itself and gave a vision of the possibility of men living in peace and harmony with one another. Our loss was so great, said Macmillan, "because he seemed, in his own person, to embody all the hopes and aspirations of this new world that is struggling to emerge —to rise, phoenix-like, from the ashes of the old." Thus did the British people grieve as though they had lost a friend, even a brother.

Our dismay and despair were the greater for by November, 1963 everything seemed to be moving in the right direction for Kennedy. Already, in under three years, he had presided over a new era in East/West relations, and a new era in alliance relations. His presidency was just beginning to come into its own, and our loss, and the world's loss, was what might have been during his second term. For, at Amherst College, Massachusetts, in October, 1963, he had offered to Britain, and to the world, his vision of the American promise: "I look forward to a great future for America, a future in which our country will match its military strength with our moral restraint, its wealth with our wisdom, its power with our purpose ... I look forward to an America which commands respect throughout the world not only for its strength but for its civilisation as well."

America, under President Kennedy, was beginning to command such respect for its civilisation. In his own person, he had represented what Britain liked best about America: he had restored decency to patriotism and had revived some of the romance about America. He had left us with a lasting impression of an America as it ought to be, as the Founding Fathers had conceived it—brave, energetic, gay, civilised, challenging, and, above all, young. His greatness was thus assured in Britain not by what he was alone but by what we wanted him to be: not by what he did alone but for what he promised to the young who have felt themselves, ever since, to be without a leader.

NOTES

1. Lord Boothby, *The News of the World* (24 November 1963).

2. Nicholas Carroll, "A Shift in East-West Relations," *The Sunday Times* (24 November 1963).

3. Michael Hilton, "Effect on World Scene," *The Daily Telegraph* (23 November 1963).

4. Theodore Sorensen, *Kennedy* (Hodder & Stoughton, 1965), p. 758.

5. The actual figures of the poll conducted at the end of 1969 were, from a sample of 1000: Kennedy, 146 votes; second was Churchill, with a vote of only 67; third was Dr. Christian Barnard with 48 votes.

6. Lord Boothby, *The News of the World* (24 November 1963).

7. Quoted in Arthur Schlesinger Jr., *A Thousand Days* (Andre Deutsch, 1965), p. 594.

8. Quoted Ibid., pp. 264–5.

Anglo-American
Comparative Analysis

A. E. Campbell*

The Nature of the Anglo-American Rapprochement

A. E. Campbell was among the first of the British Americanists to analyze the Anglo-American rapprochement through a conscious comparison of the principles and policies of the two countries. His book, *Great Britain and the United States, 1895–1903*, deals with what were the crucial years in the formation of the functional entente of the two leading English-speaking nations as it came into being with the onset of the twentieth century. In the last chapter of the book, "The Nature of the Rapprochement," Campbell brings together the diverse elements of policy in both Britain and the United States. As he shows, there was constant interaction—both of challenge and response and of give and take—in relations between the two powers. Perhaps more important, this interaction is explained in terms of ideas entertained in each country at the time, not alone about themselves and about each other, but about the other nations of the world, too. Do Campbell's British background and training lend an Old World air to his treatment, not likely in an American-

---

*Alexander E. Campbell is Professor of American History at the University of Birmingham.

born historian? By intertwining threads of British and American history, this discussion exemplifies some of the possibilities of comparative analysis.

When Britain and the United States came into conflict at the end of the nineteenth century, it was as a result of new demands, of larger ambitions, on the part of the United States. Those demands, however, were related, as such demands usually are, to accepted American traditions. The United States had developed in relative isolation from Europe, isolation which had come to be taken for granted. That America developed behind the guns of the British fleet is a commonplace of present day historiography. It was by no means so obvious to the Americans of fifty years ago, though Alfred Mahan, Brooks Adams, and a handful of others were beginning to take the point. As George Kennan has reminded their descendants,

> those Americans had forgotten a great deal that had been known to their forefathers of a hundred years before. They had become so accustomed to their security that they had forgotten that it had any foundations at all outside our continent. They mistook our sheltered position behind the British fleet and British Continental diplomacy for the results of superior American wisdom and virtue in refraining from interfering in the sordid differences of the Old World. And they were oblivious to the first portents of the changes that were destined to shatter that pattern of security in the course of the ensuing half-century.[1]

The shift in viewpoint has, however, been overdone. American security till the 1890s *was* based at least as much on her policy of remaining aloof from events outside her own continent as on British protection. The first, indeed, was a necessary precondition of the second. True, the United States before the Civil War could not have protected the continent against a serious European attempt at encroachment. But then, between the Spanish loss of her South American colonies and the growth of the new colonialism at the end of the century there was no serious European attempt to establish political dominion in the Western Hemisphere. The characteristic event of those years is Russia, not only willing but eager to get rid of Alaska, selling it to the United States in 1867 for some seven million dollars, a ridiculous sum whose size can be judged by comparison with the fifteen odd million dollars paid by Great Britain at about the same time in settlement of the *Alabama* claims. Throughout most of the century the British fleet protected the United States at a time when she needed little protection. No wonder the Americans of 1898 thought they were the architects of their own security.

When, at the end of the century, conditions changed, the British fleet was of little use to the United States, and was quickly seen to be of little use by the generation that fell under the spell of Mahan. That was not because in some new and rash enthusiasm the European powers were casting greedy eyes on the Americas, and the British fleet was inadequate to protect them, but because the United States herself could not long avoid being caught up in the wave of imperialist fantasy which surged over Europe. The same causes which might have made the British fleet useful prevented the United States from continuing in her placid acceptance of its presence. Nothing is more futile than to attempt to understand the Spanish-American War in terms of any rational calculation of self-interest. Americans were swept off their feet in a wave of unreasoning emotion against which the few voices that attempted to stem it resembled nothing so much as the woman with the mop immortalized by Sydney Smith.

During the Spanish-American War, British policy and still more the support of British opinion won for Britain a considerable harvest of uncritical American gratitude. Yet the British attitude was possible, and was effective, for two reasons neither of which was long to continue.

The first was that the war was begun, and chiefly fought, in a region contiguous to the United States and subject to much the same strategic considerations as if it had been on the continent itself. (Chichester's gesture in Manila harbour has gained by its dramatic quality an importance it did not possess.) The second and more important reason was that the Americans themselves carried over into their new expansiveness traditional attitudes and preconceptions. For years the foundation stone of American foreign policy, both as reiterated in orotund oratory and as expressed in practice, had been just the virtuous abstention from the sordid quarrels of Europe noted by Kennan. The extent of their new ambitions was only slowly realized. The language of Congress and the executive in the discussion which preceded the Spanish-American War owes, for the most part, far more to such well-established American ideals as concern for liberty and self-government than to any enlarged notion of the American part in world politics. Nor was this hypocritical. If we can now look back and see in that discussion a classic example of self-deception by a whole people, if historians point out now, as the Spaniards pointed out then, that Spanish concessions were more than adequate to meet the demands Americans thought they were making, the important thing for the present argument is just that self-deception. Others were deceived, too.

A tradition to which such constant reference was made had obviously considerable vitality. In the Far East, the first area of American interest,

> up to 1898 — indeed to 1900 — the American policy of respect for the territorial integrity of the Far Eastern nations had the effect of a purely self-denying ordinance. It did not enjoin on the United States the obligation of defending this territorial integrity from others. The U.S. was then able to keep free of serious involvement in the politics of Eastern Asia.[2]

Even long after 1900 American intervention in world affairs was often ineffective because half-hearted. The new ideas of expansion, economic imperialism, strategic interests on the other side of the globe, the importance of sea power, fought a long battle with the older conception of the United States as a nation apart, fortifying on the North American continent a shining citadel for free men, a nation with only the most secondary interests abroad. Both survive today; but there can be no doubt how much the second has modified the first.

The two conceptions did not, of course, necessarily come into direct conflict. Sometimes, as during the Spanish-American War, they mingled and strengthened each other. It was plainly in the Western Hemisphere that they conflicted least. There the idea of manifest destiny, that the future of the United States necessarily included domination over North America, or even the Americas, had been a commonplace for a generation. It had often been suggested, in many tones of voice, that it was only a matter of time before Canada was acquired. When the United States began to extend her claims, Britain, having been at some pains to keep other European powers out of the Western Hemisphere, was now the power with which she came most obviously and forcibly into conflict. The British position was challenged and strongly, not to say rudely, challenged. As the three occasions of conflict—Venezuela, Panama, Alaska—were all in the Americas, so there was very little doubt or self-criticism in the American challenge. The expressions of American politicians and public opinion on those issues (and sometimes those of responsible statesmen, too) were marked by the loudest kind of self-assertion. British resistance would have been, whatever its outcome, more protracted and effective than that of Spain. The British government and public hardly considered it.

What, then, was the British attitude towards the new

pretensions of the United States? First, surprise that any conflict should have arisen, a refusal to believe that after at least thirty years during which the United States and Britain had had no cause for disagreement of major importance to either, any could now arise. A habit of regarding the Western Hemisphere as an area which could be ignored had developed and was not lightly broken. Since Canning's day Britain had accepted, and had helped to make others accept, the idea that the *status quo* there should not be disturbed. When in the 1890s she came into conflict with the United States, it was natural to suppose that there must be some mistake. No one in Britain could suppose for a moment that there had been any change in British policy, that Britain was making any new demands. Her resources were fully engaged elsewhere. Therefore, if there had been no cause for disagreement with the United States before, there could be no valid cause now.

Yet it might be supposed that British consciousness of British virtue would lead to the obvious conclusion that the United States must be making some new and revolutionary claim, some outrageous aggression. That was not so. There was an assumption of goodwill, a readiness to believe that there must have been some mistake, which is not to be found in British dealings with the European powers. A number of elements can be analysed in this attitude. First is the simple fact that the United States was the newest factor in the equation, and that men's habits of thought change slowly. Britain had been concerned for centuries to match the shifts in power and prestige of European states by new stratagems of her own. The points at issue might range from the Channel to China but the underlying preconception remained the same. The growth of imperialism enlarged the scope of European competition and stretched British resources further than before, but the tendency was to see it as an extension of the old problem. Increasingly difficulties which, whatever their setting, had their origin in Europe, were fully engaging British attention and energy. The British were the less ready to debate the exact significance of new American pretensions because it was highly inconvenient for them to do so. The newest, the least known, factor in the equation was the easiest to cancel out. A concession to the United States was the least possible concession, the least revolutionary, the one that involved least analysis and least reorganization of Britain's world position. Such an attitude, useful as it was, meant that most British statesmen were underestimating the effect of the rise of the United States. It was not only a new phenomenon, but by far the most important in generations, for Britain as for other countries, and they were slow to take proper account of it. In part, this was no more than the conservatism induced by the conduct of foreign policy; and it was doubly excusable at that time. British statesmen might have been more ready to make fundamental assessments of policy had their attention not been directed elsewhere. But more important, American expositions of American policy made underestimation of its importance easy. British analysts could follow American in carrying over into the new era the mental conventions of the old.

In minimizing the importance of American ambitions, the British could point to the fact that, initially, American claims were confined to the Western Hemisphere. Americans themselves went to a good deal of trouble to insist that their aggressions were not new, but no more than a logical extension of traditional claims, an extension which nature itself would limit. It was easy to maintain that the Monroe Doctrine, offensive as its immediate expression might be to Britain, was really a limitation on the activities of the United States. This argument was used on both sides of the Atlantic. As Andrew Carnegie protested, Britain could not "fairly grudge her race here one continent when she has freedom to roam over three."³ From this it was only a short step to the idea that if the United States could be induced to take charge of the Americas, it would be a positive advantage for Britain. Once allow other European powers to become involved there, and the results for Britain would be unpredictable but probably expensive. An enhanced determination by the United States to prevent that was welcome even if it reacted on Britain. If Americans themselves were so slow to admit their new pretensions, so eager to identify them with the old, British acceptance of their arguments is understandable.

Anglo-American relations did not, of course, deal in abstractions like these. The disputes were real and immediate, but their confinement to the Western Hemisphere had other consequences. It had long been established British policy that the Western Hemisphere was not an area open to European expansion. When Canning initiated it he had trade chiefly in mind; the policy now paid a different dividend. Europe had, on the whole, accepted the injunction laid down in the Monroe Doctrine. Though Germany was now suspected of cherishing designs on Brazil—the British press was generous in warnings to our American cousins that they must keep an eye on the Kaiser⁴—there was in the event no European activity in the Americas. The United States would have opposed attempted expansion by any other power quite as vigorously as she opposed Great Britain; but American antipathy was to any involvement of Europe in the Western Hemisphere, and not merely to expansion. The same Monroe Doctrine which was invoked against Great Britain forbade the United States to get support from Britain's rivals. The same American traditions which until the Spanish-American War were against adventures outside the Americas led the United States to play a lone hand in diplomacy. When the expansionists had won their first success, this tradition of operating alone remained, and decreased both the immediate effectiveness and the larger impact of American foreign policy.

Outside the Americas the refusal to enter into joint action was undoubtedly a weakness in American policy, since it often implied a reluctance to act at all. Long after 1900, and even in those regions such as the Far East in which the United States claimed consideration, American policy could be discounted, and was, by the European powers. This inevitable weakness was hardly felt when the arena was Venezuela or Panama. There, indeed, the United States actually gained from having no commitments elsewhere or to any other power, gained, in short, from concentration of strength. The tradition of isolation did, however, mean that a conflict with the United States could be treated as a thing apart, unaffected by European politics except in so far as these modified the resources Britain could spare. Not because of the unimportance of the matter in dispute, but because of American determination to avoid commitments, a concession made to the United States involved no weakening of the British power position in Europe.

These considerations did not prevent real friction between the two countries. They came into play at a later stage, when a crisis had arisen, and helped to moderate its effects. Surprise that there could be any dispute—always about matters which most Englishmen had hardly heard of—was inevitably followed by annoyance at the brusquerie of the United States and a firm resolution to defend an old position against unwarranted American expansion. American braggadocio caused great irritation, and outspoken assertions that the United States must have her way, however unimportant the issues and whatever the cost in offence, were treated firmly. "It is not the custom of this country," snapped *The Times* on one occasion, "to conclude treaties of surrender with any nation—even with those whose friendship we value most—and that is a custom from which we have no mind to depart."[5] Even this, however, was not quite the reaction that was felt towards the activity of other nations. It was modified by the unwillingness already noted to suppose that there could be any real ground of difference, and for that and other reasons it was easily assuaged. In fact, Great Britain signed what *were* virtually treaties of surrender on a number of occasions, but a very small amount of diplomatic camouflage apparently sufficed to conceal the fact.

The idiosyncrasies of United States diplomacy helped, in a way, in achieving this result. The very brusquerie which did so much to annoy made it difficult, somehow, to take Americans quite seriously. When an American president decided to settle himself a dispute between two independent states, one of them a great power, or the American Senate spoke as if it had the right, of its own action, to abrogate a valid treaty with a great power, the magnitude of the affront to the established standards of diplomatic conduct distracted attention from the real question at issue. The first reaction was resentment—how dare the president or the Senate adopt this tone with Great Britain?—but it called up its own antidote of amusement. No man or body of men so innocent of the ways of the world, so ignorant of the proper way to behave, could be regarded as a serious menace to Britain or as cherishing any deep designs against her. The very different British reaction to the Kruger telegram is paradoxical. His breach of diplomatic manners did not lessen the Kaiser's offence. In part at least the explanation is that the Kruger telegram was out of character. The Germans did not normally behave like that. They knew better, and must be presumed to have some deep and hostile reason for breaking the rule—even if it was the Kaiser's doing. With Cleveland it was not the manner that startled, so much as the evidence that the United States felt strongly about Venezuela—not that he was rude, but that there was anything to be rude about.

The important characteristic of American diplomacy, of which brusquerie was no more than a symptom, was its obvious lack of calculation, its rash spontaneity. That was noted and held unto the United States for virtue, though its most obvious implication was enormous confidence. Americans themselves paid so little regard to the effect of any action of theirs on the international scene, that it was natural for men of other nations to ignore those effects, too. There was a concentration in their diplomacy on the immediate and ostensible object that was unique. When the United States undertook to settle the boundary dispute between British Guiana and Venezuela, most Americans thought of themselves as dealing even-handed justice and protecting a small state from oppression. Their action was devoid of any desire either to score a diplomatic victory at the expense of Britain, or to obtain advantages for themselves in South America, though it had both these results. When the United States decided to take Cuba—for whatever reason—very little regard was paid to the larger implications of a war with Spain. Americans really wanted Cuba, or the control of the Panama Canal, or a given boundary in Alaska; and they were able to convince themselves that it was mere justice that they should have these things.

An attitude so direct had both advantages and disadvantages for a country in conflict with the United States. In the American discussion of, say, the canal issue, there was necessarily plenty of reference to American interests —and even strategic interests—but extraordinarily little calculation. Once established that American interests demanded an American canal, the next stage in the argument was that no country of goodwill would oppose the demand. Opponents of the United States were not ill-advised or merely furthering their own interests, but malevolent —since the demands of the United States were reasonable —and their opposition proved that the initial demands had been justified. This made Americans extraordinarily tenacious in dispute and impervious to compromise, but it meant also that they were not engaged in the constant battle for compensation and prestige which was the essence of European diplomacy. The American insistence on a canal treaty of American dictation had nothing in common with, for instance, the British demand for Weihaiwei because other powers had just acquired ports. American diplomacy in those days competed with none, and Britain was relieved of the need to compete. Both these characteristics of American foreign policy can be found long before the 1890s. They were survivals from an earlier age. The objects of American policy changed more rapidly than habitual methods conducting it.

These arguments suggest that the instinctive British feeling, that the United States was unique and could be treated differently from any other country, was sound. But they were not the arguments used at the time. The British attitude had other roots. A great part of the explanation of British willingness to withdraw came from a sense of kinship with Americans felt towards the people of no other country. When *The Economist*, though grumbling that the upshot of the Venezuela crisis was something of a defeat for Britain, nevertheless continued that "we may congratulate ourselves on the avoidance, though at some cost, of a quarrel which our own people regarded with disgust as a kind of civil war,"[6] it was voicing no more than the general opinion. The British took a pride in the achievements of the United States, in its growing strength and wealth and population, as one takes pride in the achievements of one's descendants, and gave the credit to the Anglo-Saxon stock which had first settled the country. America was an English-speaking nation, flourishing by

British virtues, owning British institutions, a daughter country in whose self-assertiveness even there was cause of a sort for satisfaction, though the immediate victim might be Britain herself.

The notion of identity of race was central in British thinking about America. The United States was regarded as an Anglo-Saxon country, and little attention was paid to the other diverse strains which went to make up its population. The United States, in fact, was treated as a branch of the British Empire which, owing to a regrettable misunderstanding, had broken away and achieved political independence in the past. This fact naturally seemed of smaller and smaller importance at a time when the imperial trend was towards increasing political autonomy. The links holding the Empire together were far from merely political. Canada controlled her own internal affairs. In external affairs she was a considerable nuisance. The problem of giving what support they could to the (often unreasonable) demands of Canada, at a time when imperial feeling was very strong, without earning the hostility of the United States, was one which bedevilled British statesmen all through these years. Yet despite all that, imperial ties were strong enough to bring Canada unasked into the Boer War. It was natural to regard the United States as another example, though perhaps a deviation from the classic pattern, of the British tendency to spread over the globe, something not to be opposed but to be applauded.

Only this view can explain both the endless references to "our American cousins" and "the trans-Atlantic branch of our race" which can be quoted from the writings of the time, and the readiness with which qualities infuriating in anyone else were explained and excused in Americans. Were Americans brusque and discourteous in speech? Plain blunt-spoken Englishmen had never had the subtle—and by implication double-dealing—suavity of French and

Italians. Were Americans aggressive and domineering? They were only displaying the same drive and energy that had made Britain great. Always the question that was never adequately faced was why this expansive energy should be unexceptionable in Americans, and not in, say, Russians. The answer was not that they were good democrats, but that they were British. The acceptance of kinship was not, indeed, new. One can find references to "Brother Jonathan" in the British Press much earlier than the 1890s. But such phrases were then used in scorn as often as in friendship. What was new was the assumption, implicit in the use of phrases like "the trans-Atlantic branch of our race," that ties of race created ties of sympathy, and that civilization itself depended on the strength of the ties.

As the United States was rose-tinted, so also was the relationship between the two countries. Salisbury's speech at the Guildhall announcing the satisfactory conclusion of the Venezuelan dispute was a masterly example of how to display a defeat, not as a victory—victory over the United States was never what British opinion wanted—but as an honourable compromise, a triumph for Anglo-Saxon common sense and fair play. Salisbury, of course, had the most obvious reasons for trying to give this impression, but the readiness with which it was accepted—had indeed been accepted in essence many months before—is remarkable and characteristic.[7]

The British sense of kinship with Americans owed, indeed, surprisingly little to any similarity of political tradition or theory. At few times have ideological considerations been less effective in the determination of European foreign policies than at this. The division between the liberal and the autocratic powers of Europe which had had some reality following the Napoleonic War had almost disappeared. Britain found it no easier to come to terms with the Third Republic than with Imperial Germany or Russia, and owned a tenuous tradition of friendship with Austria-Hungary. Among the powers of Europe at least, no differences of ideology important enough to modify the calculations of shifting alignments were to be found. The fear of revolutionary doctrines had died down with revolutionary enthusiasm; the increasing competition among the states of Europe, competition outside the continent, meant that one found allies where one could. In comparison with the "lesser breeds without the law" whom they were concerned to exploit or to civilize, the differences among themselves diminished in importance. The world was divided into states which came within the operation of the public law of Europe, the powers and the small nations which existed among them, and the rest.

The pattern of British thinking was most clearly shown at the time of the Spanish-American War. There was in Britain as elsewhere in Europe a good deal of sympathy for Spain, sympathy for gallantry in decline. In Europe the feeling went further, and there was a strong sentiment for intervention on behalf of Spain. The difficulty of forming a European concert, and the danger of acting without one, together with the known temper of the United States, were strong arguments against action, and even the Germans confined themselves to fishing in troubled waters. The British position was a crucial one, if only by virtue of sea power, and it is plain that both British official policy and the bulk of British opinion were friendly to the United States. There was calculation in this, of course, but also much uncritical enthusiasm for Anglo-Saxon advance. Latins were inefficient colonizers—far better to let the United States take over Cuba and the Philippines. Indeed the two elements went together—the calculation assumed the advance. If Spain lost the Philippines, Britain was anxious for the United States to keep them, as the least awkward of possible owners, but also on the assumption that American involvement in the Far East would be profitable to Britain.

It is doubtful if this feeling of kinship was reciprocated to any great extent. The American population was
already largely of origin other than British, a fact the British press was apt to ignore. The assumption in Britain
of sympathy between her and the United States caused
a good deal of irritation there even among those who were
not of German or Irish stock. As for these latter, they were
always ready to see the hand of Britain in American policy,
and their loud objections were a constant source of em-
barrassment to the executive. British statesmen were aware
of the extraordinary sensitivity of the United States to
anything that might be considered interference in her domestic affairs, or to any suggestion that she was tied to
Britain. They were apt to regard this sensitivity as spring-
ing more from the Revolution and republicanism than
from the real differences between the two countries—and
indeed these elements were also present, important in the
anglophobia of a man like Henry Cabot Lodge. They saw
it as a kind of neurosis rather than anything more, anything that need shake their sense of kinship. Nevertheless,
they remembered well the uproar caused by Sir Lionel
Sackville West's innocent incursion into American politics
when minister in Washington, and were not disposed to
underestimate American sensitivity. "They are deeply interested in it here," wrote Henry White of the prospect
of McKinley's reelection in 1900, "and quite understand
that they must not let this feeling be known."[8] Chamberlain's speeches almost certainly did more harm than good
—his speech at Leicester on November 30, 1899, produced
a storm of American dissent—but even Chamberlain usually confined himself to generalities and was careful not
to assume too much.

These are valid reservations, but the British feeling
was not absurd. There was a real concord between the two
countries; the reservations imply only that in the United

States it did not have the same narrowly racial base. Americans could not avoid sharing the ideas current in Europe. There was plenty of race sentiment in the United States, but the history of the country and the composition of its population made the expression of that sentiment so various and complex that it was ineffective in directing policy.

The hostility to Britain of Irish and German Americans was of limited effectiveness. The dominant groups in the United States were still of English or Scots-Irish stock, and, though prepared on occasion to adopt a defiant American policy in opposition to Britain, still felt more sympathy for her than for any other country. The non-English stock in America, when most politically effective, made its effect by acting as a racial opposition, and principally in state or local politics. Just as the Irish vote in England could on occasion bring parliamentary business to a standstill but could not direct it to any more constructive end, so the racial minorities in America were limited. They could elect Senators, they could hamper executive policy, but, if only because the constitutional role of the Senate is to prevent activity, not to further it, they could do little more. They either remained detached minorities with comparatively little effect on policy or merged in the general population.

When the latter alternative happened, it was remarkable how fully they adopted the whole outlook of the earlier settlers. As Nathan Glazer has pointed out,

> everywhere the first-comers were Anglo-Saxons ... the economic prosperity attendant on the superior technique of the immigrants did not give them the power to mold the cultural and political life of the state. Again and again it can be seen how the first few thousand settlers in an area had far more weight in this respect than hundreds of thousands who came later. They set up the school system; the legal system; they

wrote the state constitution; they had the most political experience; they had the prestige which led the later coming majority—or at least their children— to conform to *their* standards, rather than vice versa.[9]

Insofar, in fact, as Americans were primarily Americans, and not displaced Germans or Irish, they accepted the attitudes and prejudices of the dominant Anglo-Saxon stock.

These attitudes and prejudices, however, were themselves far from simple; and they were not, as American diplomacy shows, so wholly well-disposed towards Great Britain as were those of the British towards America. Pride of race among Americans of British ancestry there was, and a growing suspicion of newcomers of other stocks. The Progressive movement expressed a good deal of resentment against the immigrants from Southern and Eastern Europe whose ready obedience to party machines was ruining American politics. The demand for immigration control was already under way. The lamp had hardly been lifted beside the golden door before men were urging that its welcome was too indiscriminate. Yet in the most Anglo-Saxon of Americans, pride of race struggled with an inherited, republican distrust of Britain as the old—and the perfidious because the related—enemy, a distrust which was not so much a prejudice as an article of faith, and to which they clung the more because they could not use against Britain the weapons which were so effective against the rest of Europe. In an extreme example like Henry Cabot Lodge, cultured, conservative, arrogant, this struggle fatally warped his political judgment.

American sympathy for Britain, then, could not have a simple racial basis. Successful political leaders threaded their way through a complex of emotions, their own and their followers'. A consideration of the views of Theodore Roosevelt may throw some light on the problem; he was the most successful and one of the most articulate, if not quite a typical specimen of the group. Roosevelt was a remarkable figure, open to the gibes of cartoonists and humorists even in his day, and his ideas were not general; but he would never have gained his huge popularity had they not made a large appeal, and in a cruder and less original form they were widely shared.

It was one source of Roosevelt's strength and one of the best qualities about him that, where individuals were concerned, he had remarkably little racial feeling. He could meet a Japanese, a Samoan, an Indian, and assess them as men; and many of his judgments of events were modified by his friendship with some representative of the nationality concerned. Nevertheless, he could not avoid the general characteristic of his time of judging races and nations as a whole. He could not help regarding some races as inferior to others. Thus most of the brown, black, and yellow races he found inferior, with perhaps a mental reservation in favor of the Japanese; but their day was not yet. The Germans he approved, for their efficiency, their masterful qualities, their militarism, and their energy. (The British, he thought, were not sufficiently aware of the potential of the Germans.) The Russians, too, he respected. They were handicapped by backwardness, they were barbarians, but tough, thrusting barbarians who might yet have to be opposed by force. The Latin races on the whole he despised as effete and cruel through fear and weakness. With these views Roosevelt combined, though in a complex form, most of those ideas that have commonly gone with racism—respect for the fighting man, a primitive code of chivalry, emphasis on the family as a unit (with its tendency to nepotism), and so on.

Two elements can be isolated from Roosevelt's philosophy as relevant to this study, the first shared with Britain, the second unique to the United States. The first was the general extension of biological thinking and biological analogies into political thought until even many who were

unconscious of the influence came under it. It was a commonplace that nations like species competed for survival,
that by a kind of political evolution a race held a dominant position till its natural vigour faded or its power to
adapt to new circumstances declined, when some new
power would drive it out and take its place. The weakest
would go to the wall, on this theory, not because of ma-
levolence on the part of the strong, but because it was in
the natural order of things for the strong to prey on the
weak.

The natural order was ethical as well. It would be
immoral as well as impracticable to interfere with the process, since it was to result in the survival of the physically
and mentally fitter race on which the whole progress of
mankind depended. "This dependence of progress on the
survival of the fitter race," said Professor Karl Pearson
speaking for many others, "terribly black as it may seem
to some of you, gives the struggle for existence its redeeming features; it is the fiery crucible out of which comes
the finer metal."[10] The struggle for existence was assumed. It was taken as a fact. What was needed was to
prove it moral. Neither *Machtpolitik* nor doctrines of race
conflict strictly depended on Darwin's work or involved
the idea of natural selection. But the theories of the rac-
ists gave a moral basis—of a kind—to national conflicts,
and affected the choice of an opponent which they did
so much to make necessary.

The idea that strife was necessary to the health of nations probably flourished more strongly in Britain than
anywhere in Europe except Germany. It did not, however,
exclude a strong sense of trusteeship towards peoples so
backward as to be outside immediate competition. This
is not the place to discuss at length the complex of ideas
summed up in the phrase "the white man's burden" or
its connection with social Darwinism; both were strong
in Britain. The political tradition of the United States

modified greatly there any sense of a duty to lift less fortunate peoples towards the light, though Americans could not altogether avoid ideas so current in the Western world. But to the notion of a necessary struggle among advancing aggressive nations they were particularly prone. Nor were the two ideas unconnected. Incompetence in colonial government was one of the first symptoms of decadence. The well-being of dependencies could be invoked as a reason for removing them from weaker rulers.

While these ideas might be held to foster sabre-rattling in diplomacy, each nation striving to assure itself and others of its virility, nothing in them demanded that tests of strength should be sought. The emphasis was on disposing of the weak rather than on challenging the strong. Spain was feeble; better for all if the United States took over her tasks—to condense the half-spoken argument. Arguments like this could readily lead to a kind of accommodation among the powers. The idea of a preventive war was at a discount. Britain, like the United States, was obviously strong, a force for the furtherance of civilization. In the circumstances the United States, like Britain, came strongly to feel that there was a kind of larger alliance, overriding differences in policy, between nations so plainly bound to the same task of furthering the advance of man, and sharing so many of the same qualities. The obvious solution to conflict was a division of the spoils.

So far Britain and the United States could agree. They differed in that no American conscious of the diverse origin of his people could hold the narrow racial view of Anglo-American affinity taken in Britain. By a minor adaptation, however, racism could be incorporated into the American philosophy. A distinction could be drawn between the individual and the group, and in the United States, with its tradition of welcoming men of all stocks and forging them into a new nation, the distinction was an easy one. That there was excellent stuff in individual Spaniards

or Frenchmen, that they had something to give to the new
race, need not as yet be denied—the theory of the "melt-
ing pot" had not yet been effectively challenged—even
while it was maintained that as a group on their native
soil they were decadent. Yet if not race, there was need
for some other cohesive principle to hold the new nation
together. No country was better fitted to provide it than
the United States, the outstanding example of a state
founded on a political theory. The United States was a
nation endowed with both the vigour and the opportunity
to propagate those principles of liberty and equality established by the Founding Fathers.

The Boer War provided an excellent test. There arose
in the United States a considerable outcry against what
appeared to many an open aggression by Great Britain
for the crassest material gain against two innocuous small
republics battling for existence. Not only was there considerable racial sympathy among German Americans for
the Boers, but the magic of the word "republic" (together
with the discrepancy in size between the contestants and
the gallantry of the Boers) blinded many Americans to the
real questions at issue. As at the time of the Venezuela crisis, they tended to assume virtue in a republic and vice
in a monarchy, especially that against which they had won
their own independence. Nevertheless, the United States
government firmly refused to take any action, however
formal, in favour of the Boers. It would have been difficult for them to do anything effective, but the studied
friendliness to Great Britain of Roosevelt and Hay went
far beyond the strict demands of neutrality. A considerable
body of opinion could be found in the States to uphold
the view that, monarchy or no monarchy, the Anglo-Saxon
tradition of political freedom and social equality flourished in Britain as in the United States and could not survive in the racist republic of Oom Paul. Roosevelt himself, who felt a strong emotional sympathy for the Boers,

hardy open-air individualists good with horse and rifle such as he admired, felt bound to admit that they were a small and backward group, and that the advance of civilization in South Africa demanded a British victory.[11]

This suggests that similarities of ideology which were then of secondary importance in Europe were of the first importance in the United States. British emphasis was on qualities of the race which peculiarly fitted it for rule. American emphasis was on the possession of those sacred principles which marked the highest point yet reached by mankind—to make no less modest claim. Americans not only recognized the real similarity of institutions and political outlook between the two countries, but were even prepared to deduce from them alignments of economic interest. At a time when the United States tariff was steadily rising, Britain and the United States were held to share a unique concern for free trade in other parts of the world. Principle was not absent from the British position. The possession of a civilizing mission, after all, involves having something to impart and the British, without conscious hypocrisy often though they were accused of it, regarded themselves as spreading the blessings of Christianity, parliamentary democracy, and British fair play. But principle played a still larger part in American imperialism. Because it had to overcome a living tradition of isolation it was more articulate, more theoretical, than the British variety. Anglo-American sympathies, where they existed, were based, in Britain on a sense of racial community, in America on a sense of ideological community.

The difference is not a minor one of emphasis. It is fundamental and of wide importance. Clearly the American analysis was more rational and more in accord with the facts. The two countries *did* share important political principles and practices. Racial community was a far more dubious basis for concord. It would have been stronger if "Anglo-Saxon" had been used merely as a shorthand description of a whole complex of qualities essentially cultural which Britain and the United States had in common. Sometimes the word was used in just this way—the British attitude was not entirely unreasonable—but the choice of a racial term, loosely used, to sum up cultural attributes is suspicious. The American analysis of Anglo-American relations could be checked against the facts. It was relevant to political action. The British analysis could not be used in the same way. It was one thing to argue that countries with the same political beliefs have something important in common, and that they should cooperate in spreading their advantages. It was quite another to deduce some mystic sympathy from a common origin, a sympathy whose major characteristic was that it need never, and could never, be tested.

The important difference between Britain and the United States, then, lay not so much in what they said about each other, as in the political philosophy on which their opinion about each other was based. In the United States similarities with Britain were emphasized, and differences from Britain minimized, under the influence of a new concept that was generally applied. For some influential political leaders a traditional hostility to Britain was modified, for others a sympathy for Britain which had other origins was strengthened, by racial thinking. But British activities—and sometimes American—could be tested by Americans against the principles to which both countries laid claim. In Britain, on the other hand, racial thinking supported an attitude to the United States which could have no other foundation, and which differed in kind, from that to any other country.

The distinction made in Britain between the United States and other countries is striking. It was not reciprocated in America, but it owed what realism it had to a more fundamental peculiarity of American foreign policy. The American approach to foreign policy may have been rational, but it was also unique. However imperfectly, it treated the domestic politics of other states as relevant in the discussion of American policy towards them. In this it differed from the general practice of the great powers at that time. The American sense of mission had not weakened, even if the image of America was losing its effectiveness in the radical mythology of Europe. Americans still did not think of themselves as like other peoples, as members of a nation state like other nation states. How was this possible? The answer is in the stage which American emergence from isolation had reached.

It is not too fanciful to draw a parallel between this period of American foreign policy and Jackson's tenure in the development of the American presidency. Jackson was dictatorial by temperament, a man who liked to exercise power. He was extraordinarily conscious of the dignity and importance of his office. As a result he was extraordinarily sensitive to anything that might be considered an affront to the presidency, and met any challenge with exaggerated vigour. These traits might have damaged American government far more than they did. If Jackson had given them free rein, his activities would certainly have roused more opposition; but they were held in check by his Jeffersonian distrust of government, all government. Jackson resented limits set to his power, but the limits he set for himself were narrow. American foreign policy in the 1890s might be described as Jacksonian. There is the same confidence of power. There is the same enlarged sense of dignity. There is the same sensitivity to anything that might be considered an affront, however unimportant. And there is the same sort of check on all these traits, a distrust of international relations and a reluctance to engage in them.

The phenomenon was a temporary one, and necessarily temporary. Paradoxically, the limits set by tradition to the exercise of American power enabled Americans to exaggerate that power, and to ignore the context in which it would have to be exercised. It was already supposed that the United States would shortly play an important part in world affairs, but she was not yet playing that part. It was therefore still possible to maintain old notions of the nature of foreign policy which could not survive the test of practice. (They have proved remarkably durable, but they have steadily been forced to give way.) Isolation had bred enormous confidence, which survived after the end of isolation. American ideas were incompatible with the exercise of power, but not with a sense of power. This was hardly understood in Britain. American aggressiveness was ascribed to other causes, and judged by other standards. The judgment was faulty, but it made for good relations.

It is not difficult to expose inconsistencies in British thinking about the United States. The inconsistencies were there, and any attempt to summarize British opinion is more apt to reveal them than to account for them. Britain was undoubtedly taking the brunt of the new American energy and interest in foreign affairs. It might have been that it was worthwhile to put up with this in the expectation of future gain, to encourage the United States to foreign adventure in the belief that a strong America with a strong foreign policy could only be of advantage to Britain. This belief was indeed present in British thought. But American activity in the Western Hemisphere provided little basis for it. There was no need to postulate hostility to Britain to order to reach the conclusion that American interests might conflict with British elsewhere than in the Americas. The assumption that they would not do so was logically unsound. Another British argument did nothing to strengthen it. For British opinion tended, when convenient, to minimize the importance of American activity by regarding it as limited in area and not related to any consistent world policy. Britain need not take American activity in the Western Hemisphere too seriously, since it would go no further. Not weakness, of course, but the American political tradition would prevent it. On this hypothesis any benefit to Britain from American policy was unlikely to be great.

The second argument was the better of the two. The United States gained half her strength in Venezuela or Alaska from the fact that she could neither be threatened nor be bribed in other parts of the world. More, the very ideas which made the United States strong on her own ground weakened her elsewhere. (Theodore Roosevelt may have introduced some real understanding of the implications of *Weltpolitik*, but he was a political accident.) American policy during the Boer War was friendly, and the friendliness was of considerable benefit to Britain; but it was entirely negative, it consisted in avoiding effective sympathy for the Boers and in looking after British interests in Pretoria. Since it was clear that there was no likelihood of American intervention, it was not necessary to bid very high for American support, and British treatment of American shipping, though reparation was made later, was severe. American policy in China has been recognized as feeble, the "open–door" note notwithstanding. It is true that any American policy in the Far East was likely to profit Britain, and what logical content there was in British policy towards the United States had this as its origin. But on their own assumptions the British might have seen that American policy would have very little effect.

There is a third point. If American activity, when the two countries clashed, was not based on anti-British feeling—and the British Press insisted that it was not—then presumably it would be very difficult for any British action to make that policy pro-British. Either American interests would lead the United States to pursue a policy favourable to Britain, in which case there was no need to buy the favour, or to one unfavourable to Britain, in which case nothing could be done. This is over-simplifying the logic, but there is no evidence that this line of reasoning occurred to anyone but Salisbury. In general, a determination not to conflict with the United States was concealed behind an assumption that no conflict would arise.

The simplest explanation of British policy is that Britain gave way to the United States at the end of the century merely because she could do nothing else, because the demands of imperialism had stretched her resources too far to meet a new challenge. It is probably impossible to say whether external circumstances or special elements were more important in Britain's American policy, but certainly those elements were very important. It is impossible to imagine the Englishmen of Palmerston's day, for instance, whatever the circumstances, reacting in the same way to the activities of the United States. Palmerston foresaw American expansion, but he did not suppose that it would necessarily benefit Britain, and he thought it should be opposed as far as possible. The prospect he foresaw gave him no pleasure. A generation later his successors thought otherwise. It has been a chief object of this study to argue that they did so irrationally.

Their irrationality was less in the assessment of policy than in the deductions they made from it. The policy of the United States might be judged hostile; it was not judged *naturally* hostile, the hostility did not conform to a larger pattern, it was not what one would have expected. This appeal to nature is implicit rather than explicit in writing about foreign policy in the late nineteenth century. The appeal to nature had slipped out of the language of political thought, and to reintroduce it is strictly an anachronism. Its use seems legitimate, however, to illuminate an attitude of mind which was of great importance. The language of international Darwinism, with its reference to the race struggle, was, after all, employing a "natural" metaphor. But more than that, even when "natural" language has no footing in current political discussion, some activities are apt to appeal to the emotions as natural, and others as not. The extent to which these emotions are rational ones may vary, but they are effective even when they are extraordinarily difficult to justify.

Generalization from so limited a study must be tentative; but it may be worth suggesting that although irrational emotions confuse judgments of policy, they change, no less than does policy, in response to changes of power. The changes of power may be relative, between the two states concerned, or absolute, affecting the place of both in a larger power structure. They modify national attitudes far more than changes of policy do.

If there is any truth in this suggestion, the development of Anglo-American relations may have been somewhat as follows. The power relations between the two countries fall, broadly speaking, into three periods. The first is that in which the United States was both small and distant, something that could be ignored in the consideration of power politics. The second is that in which the two countries were roughly comparable in power. The third, of course, is that in which the United States is very much more powerful—though it is perhaps permissible to envisage a time when the growth of other states will make power differences between Britain and the United States less dominant in the relations between them.

The first period is that in which the dominant image of the United States—in the rest of Europe as well as in Britain—was that of the embodiment of a radical political theory. This role is one that can be played inoffensively only by a small state, and safely only by a state remote as well as small. A shift in power beginning about the time of the Civil War—after which the United States began to move towards the status of a great power—made its impact on the British consciousness towards the end of

the century. It became less easy to think of the United
States as the harmless embodiment of a political theory
when that country was already outstripping Britain in
population and industry. The prevalence at that time of
Darwinian theories of race and the race struggle dominated the new image. Those theories themselves hardly survived for more than twenty years, but the image they had
helped to induce survived rather longer. When it began
to break down, it did so because of a further growth in
American power which made inappropriate an image developed in response to a situation of rough equality. To
this latest shift we are still slowly adjusting, as we cling
to our old power pretensions. The change may take another generation to complete.

Anglo-American relations in the late nineteenth century, then, display the elaboration of an unusually effective
myth. (The word myth here indicates not an idea which
is merely false, but one which, whatever its content of
truth, is sufficiently persuasive to influence men's judgment of reality, and so their political behaviour.) In one
respect, however, this myth is somewhat unusual. The normal function of a myth is the justification of larger claims
than reality allows. It is essentially a moral weapon. Men
try to defend old privileges in a changing society, or to
justify the demand for new ones, by describing their role
in society in terms which, bearing some relation to reality,
do not conform to it. This myth is different in that, so
far from justifying a sense of grievance, it minimized it,
allowing a larger measure of concession than would have
been possible without it.

The contradiction is a real one, but its resolution may
lie in the peculiar nature and the extraordinary rigidity
of the nation state. Myths concerned with the place of
man in society are dealing with a fluid medium. Claims
can be enlarged or diminished in an infinite series of
small gradations. But the relations of nation states are

well–defined and closely interlocking. There can be no enlargement of the claims of one which does not strain the whole complex structure. Nor is this rigidity incidental. Debate about the moral nature of man and the proper structure of society is unending, and it frequently involves debate about the nature of the state. But such debates have almost always been internal to the state. It was in its international relations that the state earliest acquired rigid definition, as the protector and the collective voice of the people who composed it, a definition as yet effectively unchallenged, and certainly unchallenged at the end of last century.

When, in these circumstances, two nation states came into conflict, the only possible use of a political myth was in minimizing the claims of one. That was its use in Anglo-American relations; but to be effective the myth had to have larger reference than the nation state, and had to appeal to the race. The concession of British interests was made in a context which could represent it as the furtherance of Anglo-Saxon interests. The climate of opinion which fostered imperialism, which strained British resources and brought Britain and the United States into conflict, also bred the theories of human progress and the sense of kinship which prevented withdrawal from appearing defeat.

NOTES

1. G. F. Kennan, *American Diplomacy, 1900–1950* (London, 1952), p. 5.

2. Griswold, *Far Eastern Policy of the United States*, p. 7.

3. "The Venezuelan Question" in the *North American Review*, CLXII, February 1896, p. 142.

4. A favourite line with *The Spectator*. To select one article from many, see "The Meaning of the Venezuelan Settlement" in LXXVII, 14 November, 1896, p. 665.

5. Leading article, 19 December, 1900, p. 9e.

6.   "The New Horizon" in LIV, 14 November 1896, p. 1488.

7.   Salisbury's speech was fully reported in *The Times*, 10 November, 1896, p. 4*e*, and discussed in all the reviews.

6.   "The New Horizon" in LIV, 14 November, 1896, p. 1488.

9.   Nathan Glazer, "America's Ethnic Pattern" in *Perspectives*, IX, Autumn 1954 (reprinted from *Commentary*, April 1953) , pp. 141-2.

10.   *National Life from the Standpoint of Science* (London, 1901) , p. 24.

11.   Morison, ed., *Roosevelt Letters*, II, to J. St L. Strachey, 27 January 1900 no. 1460) ; to C. A. Spring Rice, same date (no. 1461) ; to F. C. Selous, 7 February 1900 (no. 1496) ; to A. J. Sage, 9 March 1900 (no. 1550) ; III, to A. H. Lee, 18 March 1901 (no. 1958). H. H. Bowen, "American Public Opinion of the War" in the *Nineteenth Century*, XLVII, May 1900; and E. J. Hodgson, "An American View of the Boer War" in loc. cit., XLVIII, August 1900. Both these emphasize pro-British opinion. For American policy, see J. H. Ferguson, *American Diplomacy and the Boer War* (Philadelphia, 1939) .

Philip S. Bagwell
and G. E. Mingay

Britain and America:
Social Progress 1850-1939

Britain and America: A Study of Economic Change 1850–1939 by
Bagwell and Mingay is an explicit effort to write Anglo-American
history by means of comparative analysis. Clearly some aspects of
common history lend themselves to a more positive use of this method
than others. In attempting to underline areas of Anglo-American
similarity, the sharp edges of difference manage to protrude nonetheless. The authors' account of "social progress" in the two nations
from 1850 down to 1939 is a good example of the effective use of
comparison despite difficulties inherent in the materials. The selection begins with a discussion of background pertinent to Britain and
America in which there is an instructive paralleling of conditions in
the two industrial societies. But in treating the problems and remedies the authors resort to a clear-cut division, reviewing the British
scene independently of the American. True, the reader will discover
some instances of cultural flow, e.g., the fact that the new tax on
increases in land values in Lloyd George's war budget was an idea

*Philip S. Bagwell is Professor of Commerce at the Polytechnic
of Central London; G. E. Mingay is Professor of Agrarian History,
University of Kent.

borrowed from *Progress and Poverty* by the American reformer, Henry George. But since the two social phenomena were distinct, the discussion tends to confirm the division. The ill effects of this division are partially offset by the conclusion of the chapter, a summary coordinating the likenesses and admitting the differences in social progress attained in the two countries. One salutary result of this selection is to remind the American reader that other advanced industrial societies faced problems not unlike those in the United States, and that solutions were often kindred.

THE BACKGROUND

In social matters as in economic, America and Britain were closely inter-linked in the nineteenth century. There was a fertile exchange of ideas, and reformers found in the other country inspiration and evidence to support their particular views.[1] American democracy was held up as a model to the unenfranchised mass of Britons, while social reforms in Britain had, and still have, some impact in America. It was of course on the sparsely populated and undeveloped western border of Indiana that Robert Owen experimented with his famous settlement of New Harmony, and it was London with its splendour and squalor, its striking contrasts between the dignified and spacious West End and the overcrowded slums of the East End, that provided American observers with so much to criticize and condemn.[2]

The social problems and progress of the two countries were bound to be influenced, of course, by the characteristics of the respective societies. In Britain class consciousness, based on differences in wealth, education, and occupation, permeated society and even existed as a divisive force within the working classes themselves. Class barriers very slowly yielded ground before the onslaught of equalitarian ideas, reforms in the franchise and in education, and the gradual creation of the "national minimum"; but it would not be too much to say that even as late as the 1930s, the country's social institutions still reflected the class structure and were still largely geared to the maintenance of class distinctions.

In America class consciousness was not absent, but it assumed a different form. In the early stages of American development the generous abundance of natural resources, the ease of changing occupations and of acquiring property, encouraged a considerable degree of equality. But as occupations became more specialized, and as industry, agriculture, and commerce became more capitalistic, so class divisions became more marked, especially the essential American distinction between the man who made good and became rich, and the failure who remained poor. Such a distinction existed even in colonial times between the wealthy merchant or professional man and the poverty-stricken backwoodsman and farmer, and the process by which this class structure developed in nineteenth-century frontier conditions has been studied in detail by Merle Curti in his analysis of a pioneer Wisconsin settlement.[3]

The open character of American society, and the enormous opportunities the country afforded for the ambitious, energetic, able, and unscrupulous, encouraged the rise of the self-made millionaire land speculator, lumber baron, railroad financier, investment banker, and business tycoon. Conditions of natural abundance, together with the constant influx of immigrants anxious to make good and possessing some degree of skill and powers of innovation, helped to give to Americans the bustling, industrious, restless, and ambitious character commented upon by so many foreign visitors. The American, wrote Michael Chevalier,

> is brought up with the idea that he will have some particular occupation, that he is to be a farmer, artisan, manufacturer, merchant, speculator, lawyer, physician or minister, perhaps all in succession, and that if he is active and intelligent he will make his fortune.... No one else can conform so easily to new

situations and circumstances. . . . In Massachusetts and Connecticut, there is not a labourer who has not invented a machine or a tool. There is not a man of any importance who has not his scheme for a rail-road, a project for a village or a town, or who has not some grand speculation in the drowned lands of the Red River, in the cotton lands of the Yazoo, or in the cornfields of Illinois.[4]

The geographical and occupational mobility of Americans, their flexibility and adaptability, and their unlimited belief in progress created that prejudice in favour of self-reliance, better known, perhaps, as "rugged individualism," that still forms an important characteristic of American society. This is not to say that American society was atomistic; on the contrary, neighbourliness (as instanced by the communal raising of log cabins in areas of new settlement), and conformity to the behaviour and manners of the community, were very much part of the American tradition. Furthermore, American government at all levels played an important part in the development of transport, the extension of settlement, improvement of farming techniques, conservation of resources, protection of industry, and provision of education. In nineteenth-century Britain, too, government intervention in railways, industry, and commerce, and in the fields of working conditions, education, housing, and health, became more widespread and effective, especially in the fifty years before 1914. Nevertheless, "self-help" and self-reliance were widely-praised virtues, and the children's school books, as in America, spread the gospel of hard work, thrift, and sobriety. The post-1834 Poor Law was designed to force the able-bodied labourer to stand on his own feet, the Charity Organisation Society taught the need to distinguish between the deserving and the undeserving, and even at the end of the century social reform, it was urged by liberal philosophers, should go no further than "hindering the hindrances" which prevented people from en-joying the good life.

The working classes' interpretation of "self-help," however, was rather one of improvement through com-bination and co-operation. Trade unions began their long struggle for recognition and power over wages and work-ing conditions; friendly societies, like the unions, pro-vided a degree of protection against the common misfor-tunes of life; co-operative societies of consumers procured supplies of cheap and unadulterated food (producers' co-operatives, however, enjoyed little success) ; working men's clubs and mechanics' institutes provided wholesome enter-tainment and education; temporary co-operative building societies helped to house the poor, while savings banks encouraged a remarkable growth of working-class thrift. There were many too poor or too indifferent to benefit from these movements, but for a large number the rigours of daily life in Victorian England were greatly eased. It is often forgotten that the welfare state, when its modest beginnings appeared in the early twentieth century, was a logical outgrowth of these movements, and was in fact grafted on to the collective self-help which had developed during the previous hundred years.

NATIONAL WEALTH AND
THE STANDARD OF LIVING

Social progress accompanied, and was made possible by, the rise in national wealth and living standards. Dur-ing the nineteenth century and the first four decades of the twentieth century, the workers' share of the growing national income of Britain remained broadly stable at a little over 40 percent. It was only after 1939 that this share increased substantially. Real wages, however, rose mark-edly in the last forty years of the nineteenth century, and the increase between 1860 and 1891 may have been of the order of 60 percent. Thereafter there was a slight decline until the First World War. Then between the wars the basic factors of rising productivity and cheaper food reasserted themselves, and there was an improvement of some 15 percent between the later 1920s and 1938.

The long-term rise in real wages was supplemented of course by improvements in the environment in which people lived—in housing, education, health, security, a shorter working day, and in facilities such as libraries, workhouses, parks, swimming pools, paid holidays, and a widening range of cheap entertainment and leisure activities. Nevertheless, all this should not obscure the fact that there existed a substantial proportion of poverty-stricken slum dwellers, some of whom existed at barely subsistence level. Investigations by Charles Booth in London from 1886 showed that 22 percent of the population of the metropolis could obtain the necessities of life only by constant struggle, and over 8 percent could not even achieve this. In York, Seebohm Rowntree, chocolate manufacturer of that city, found in 1899–1900 very similar results; and in subsequent years surveys of other industrial towns confirmed these revelations. Between the wars a further spate of social investigations found that in widely different towns like Bristol, Liverpool, and York there was still widespread evidence of the effects of low wages and unemployment—slum housing, inadequate diet, squalor, and disease. The hard core of extreme poverty had been reduced, but there was still a large class of extreme poor whom the benefits of industrialization had largely passed by.

In America, as in Britain, the period of falling prices in the later nineteenth century was one of rapidly growing real incomes. Wage rates (at $1.25 or $1.50 a day for an unskilled man) remained nearly stationary, while prices fell considerably between 1865 and 1898. Recently published estimates of the rise in real incomes show a more favourable situation than was once thought to have been the case. Real wages in manufacturing increased by about 50 percent in the period 1860–90, and by about a third between 1890 and 1913.[5] Real wages continued to rise in the 1920s, although by the end of that prosperous decade there existed a great inequality in the distribution of income. In 1929 the wealthiest 5 percent of the population received a third of all disposable income. There was a slow decline from this level in the slump years of the 1930s, but a major fall occurred only with the high taxes and return to full employment of the war years. In 1940 the top 5 percent still had a quarter of disposable income, but in the war years the proportion dropped to 16 percent, from which level it has since risen again.

As in Britain, the rise in real wages in nineteenth-century America was accompanied by improvements in the environment. There was a marked increase in the proportion of expenditure going to consumer durables, stretching from stoves and food grinders to the reed organ and treadle sewing machines, the washing machine, clothes presser, and icebox; while in due course the introduction of electricity and the motor-car reduced rural isolation and created new types of labour-saving machinery and sources of entertainment. Although real wages were rising, it is probable that already in the nineteenth century the distribution of wealth was becoming more uneven. By 1892 there were over 4,000 millionaires, and at the end of the century 10 percent of the families owned some three-quarters of the national wealth.

The great wealth of a minority, and the comfortable circumstances of many, proved the point that America was the land of opportunity for the European immigrant. But of course many of the immigrants merely added to the mass of poverty and unemployment. In 1890, it has been estimated, 11 million of the 12½ million families in the United States had an average annual income of only $380, and at least a quarter of urban workers were unemployed for a part of each year owing to seasonal variations in production and other factors. Severe slumps affected many workers following the three great financial crashes of 1873 (originating in the collapse of Jay Cooke, the great Civil War and railroad financier), 1893 (when nearly 600 banks failed and some 3 million workers lost their jobs), and 1907 (when J. Pierpont Morgan and the federal government between them restored confidence after the collapse of the Knickerbocker Trust).

There was also a great deal of rural distress in the era of falling prices from the end of the Civil War to the later 1890s and again between the wars. Low prices for produce, periodical crop failures, and heavy indebtedness and high interest rates, meant that many farmers experienced hardship and some were forced into bankruptcy. Farming conditions varied greatly, of course, according to region, soil, products, and communications. The worst conditions were found then, as now, among the sharecroppers of the cotton belt and the hill farmers of the Appalachians, and in the semi-arid regions of the high plains.

The growth of large industrial cities spelled poverty of a different kind for many thousands of unskilled workers. Overcrowding in slum tenements, without ready access to fresh air and healthy relaxation, produced squalor and disease, care-worn adults and stunted children. In working-class sections of New York City in the 1890s people were crammed into tenement blocks at nearly 1,000 persons to the acre, and similar examples of gross overcrowding could readily be found in the other large industrial centres. Inadequate housing, diet, and sanitation spread epidemic disease, like that which killed off a tenth of the population of Memphis in 1873. For how many poor immigrants, swallowed up in squalid slums in a harsh and extreme climate, did America provide a premature grave rather than a golden future?

THE PROBLEMS AND THE REMEDIES

The growth of industrialized society in Britain and America in the nineteenth century created many social problems, but the three greatest evils were poverty, ignorance, and bad health and housing. These three core problems were of course interlinked, since inadequate education was a major cause of poverty, and it was the worst-paid who were the worst-housed and the most liable to ill-health and premature death, which again led in turn to poverty.

Britain The problem of poverty was not capable of solution in the conditions of nineteenth-century Britain. Poverty was widespread (affecting some third of the population, if the figures of Booth and Rowntree were typical), and its roots lay in the low and irregular earnings of the poorly educated unskilled labourer, the illness and early death of the breadwinner, and the high proportion of income spent on drink and gambling. The long-term remedies thus lay in the diminishing numbers and higher productivity of the unskilled, better public health and personal health services, and education. The nineteenth-century Poor Law rested on the Act of 1834, the main purpose of which was to discourage the able-bodied from seeking relief, so keeping down the poor rates. The post-1834 workhouse, with its punitive rules and harsh discipline, discouraged all but the desperate from seeking its shelter. However, as time went by conditions in the workhouse were slowly moderated, and large numbers of widows, sick, and aged were relieved in their own homes by weekly doles of money, as they had been for long before 1834.

The evidence of Booth, Rowntree, and others showed quite clearly, however, that there existed a whole mass of poverty completely untouched by either the Poor Law or the numerous charitable organizations of the time. In line with the arguments of the Fabians, a society of middle class intellectual Socialist reformers founded in 1884, state action was increasingly urged to tackle the problem. It so happened that the time was becoming ripe for effective state intervention in the social sphere. Innovations in social policy abroad, particularly in Bismarck's Germany, showed what could be done to provide insurance against unemployment and sickness, create health facilities such as maternity clinics and home visiting by trained nurses, and advance the cause of education. Political and administrative changes in Britain paved the way: the widening franchise gave to social matters a heightened political importance and urgency, a development which was encouraged by the rise of various Socialist movements in the 1880s and the formation of the Labour Party in 1906; while administrative reforms—especially the gradual modernization of the Civil Service and the reorganization of local government (following the landmark of 1888, when the County Councils were created) —provided the necessary machinery and a corps of professional experts such as medical officers of health and schools inspectors. Already the more progressive cities had shown what could be done to overcome the worst slums and inadequacies: in the 1870s Joseph Chamberlain, the radical mayor of Birmingham, endeavored to make his corporation into a model municipality, providing parks, museums, art galleries, sewage farms, slaughter houses, artisans' dwellings, and even a municipal bank.

Money—the essential ingredient—was also forthcoming. In 1894, and again in 1907, death duties were stiffened, and in 1909 Lloyd George raised the income tax to 1s. 2d. in the pound—an unprecedented level in peacetime. "This is a war budget," said Lloyd George, "it is for raising money to wage implacable warfare against poverty and squalidness." Lloyd George's "war budget" also introduced a new super-tax of 6*d*. in the pound on incomes of over £5,000, a steeper scale of death duties, and a new tax on increases in land values. This last was suggested by Henry George, the American writer, in his *Progress and Poverty*, but as a tax it posed too many practical problems and was eventually dropped. The budget brought to a head the antagonism between the Liberal-dominated Commons and the Conservative-dominated Lords, and the subsequent constitutional struggle resulted in the Parliament Act of 1911, which greatly reduced the Lords' power over legislation and removed any power to delay a money bill. The principle of using taxation as a means of redistributing income and of providing social services was thus established. Within a very few years the First World War was to raise greatly the levels of taxation, and they never fell back to their pre-war levels: an enormous rise in the permanently acceptable level of taxation was a vital prerequisite of the welfare state.

The foundations of the modern British system of social security were laid by the Liberal Government of 1906 in legislative measures as well as fiscal reforms. While the Royal Commission on the Poor Law, which had begun work in 1905, was still deliberating, new policies designed to relieve unemployment and poverty were already emerging. In 1908 old-age pensions—7*s*. 6*d*. a week for old couples of limited means—were introduced, and in 1909 employment exchanges, meant to reduce frictional unemployment which arose through lack of contact between master and man, were established. Then in 1911 came the National Insurance Act. This was based upon German models and was grafted onto the existing voluntary schemes of insurance provided for members by friendly societies and trade unions, under which many workers already enjoyed some degree of protection against unemployment and sickness. The act made use of the voluntary organizations for administering the national scheme, a plan which had the merit of economy, and emphasized the insurance aspect while gaining support for the act of the friendly societies and trade unions. The workers, the employer, and the state each contributed 2½d. per week, and the worker was guaranteed 7s. a week during unemployment up to a maximum of fifteen weeks in any year. (When the act was introduced, weekly wages of the unskilled were about 20s. a week, and skilled men's wages were some 30s. or more.)

The unemployment provisions of the Act (Part II) at first applied to only 2¼ million workers in certain trades subject to severe fluctuations in employment: building, shipbuilding, mechanical engineering, ironfounding, vehicle construction, and saw-milling. (Part I of the act, which dealt with insurance against sickness, covered far more people—all those wage earners with income below £160 per annum, and aged between 16 and 70.) Between 1916 and 1920, however, Part II of the act was extended to cover all workers, except those in agriculture, domestic service, and certain occupations with low levels of unemployment. By 1927 fourteen million workers were covered. Between the wars, of course, the persistently high unemployment in the staple industries and elsewhere meant that many workers ran out of insurance benefit. In the depressed areas the strain on the Poor Law and local rates became intense, and in 1934 a new central authority, the Unemployment Assistance Board, administered the funds (originating mainly from the central government) which since 1931 had supplemented the relief provided by the Poor Law. The position then was that a person who became unemployed relied first on insurance benefit, and when that was exhausted, on unemployment assistance, subject to a means test—"the dole."

Unemployment reached its peak of nearly three million in the winter of 1932–3, and some 800,000 depended on the dole, regulated in 1934 by the Unemployment Assistance Board. Meanwhile, in 1929, the Local Government Act had abolished the Boards of Guardians instituted by the Poor Law of 1834, and placed responsibility for poor relief (now renamed "Public Assistance") on the County Councils and County Boroughs for those in poverty who were too young or too old or sick to work. This measure thus created larger areas of administration allowing greater efficiency and economy, and followed the line of the "break-up" of the Poor Law into specialized services as recommended by the Minority Report of the Poor Law Commission of 1905–09. As a reform it delighted the Webbs, the moving Fabian spirits behind the Minority Report—and incidentally it would have delighted Chadwick, the main author of the Act of 1834, who firmly believed in the advantages offered by large units of administration.

Poverty, although relieved, did not disappear, as new social surveys of the 1930s showed. At the current wages for the unskilled of £2 to £2 10s. a week, an employed family man might be worse off than one receiving unemployment assistance. Rowntree's second survey of York, *Poverty and Progress*, showed that while extreme poverty was only half as common as in 1899, nearly a third of the working class of York had too little in wages (or in relief) for the minimum income necessary to sustain a healthy life: this, he calculated, was 53s. for families with three dependent children. Progress there had been, but poverty remained.

Bad housing and bad public health—intertwined evils—had early received attention in nineteenth-century Britain. Chadwick's great Report of 1842, *The Sanitary Condition of the Labouring Population*,[6] drew together the existing evidence of overcrowding, disease, inadequate water supplies, and lack of sanitation, and began a public debate which has gone on to the present day. The Public Health Act of 1848 was a first modest attempt at reform, but the problem was a complex and enduring one beyond

the resources of a society that had still to make fundamental discoveries in the causes and prevention of disease.

Inadequate housing and deplorable sanitary conditions sprang basically from the rapid flow of labour into
large industrial towns, creating hasty development and
overcrowding. It was not until late in the century that
the town authorities had the powers or were sufficiently
aroused to undertake slum clearance, make building regulations, and introduce adequate systems of sewage disposal
and water supply. The large average size of the Victorian
family put pressure on housing and gave rise to overcrowding. Further, a large part of the working population had incomes too low to be able to afford a decent
standard of housing. It simply did not pay to build houses
for families with low and irregular incomes, whose honesty
and habits of temperance and cleanliness were doubtful.
Thus there was always at the bottom of Victorian society
a large group of people who were badly housed, or indeed
not housed at all.

Much of the legislation, such as the Torrens Act of
1869 and the Cross Act of 1875, was merely permissive and
had little effect. Only in 1890 did slum clearance and rebuilding become mandatory on local authorities. While
private reformers experimented with model industrial estates, garden cities, and cheap tenements for the poor,
building and sanitary by-laws made the mass of English
housing conform to minimum standards of space, water
supply, and sanitation. The Public Health Act of 1875
brought every area of the country under the charge of a
Medical Officer of Health, and hospital and general medical practice moved on to modern lines following the work
of Pasteur, Simon Koch, and others. By the late nineteenth century, British towns were in general safe to live
in, and violent uncontrollable epidemics were a thing of
the past. Nonetheless, the towns still contained vast slum

areas, and too often were unhealthily dirty and smoky, and depressingly monotonous and ugly.

The First World War had a great impact on attitudes toward housing and led to the introduction of new policies. Rent controls were introduced during the war to check the inflationary effects of the cessation of house building and the control of rents of smaller houses persisted after the war and down to the present. Subsidies to lower the cost of housing provided for rent by local authorities were introduced in 1919, and were supplemented by subsequent legislation in 1923, 1924, 1930, and since the Second World War. For the most part, however, this legislation failed to help the very poorest classes who, as in Victorian times, continued to be extremely ill-housed. In 1939, despite large-scale slum clearance and rapid building of private housing estates in the 1930s (aided by low interest rates and cheaper methods of construction), large areas of old, sub-standard housing still existed, although the general situation was better than it had been for perhaps two centuries.

English education developed along class lines. The state system, as it grew after 1870, provided a basic elementary education for the working classes; for the children of the middle classes there existed a variety of private schools from the little Dame schools and local grammar schools to the great public schools of national reputation, whose fortunes were revived in the nineteenth century by headmasters such as Arnold of Rugby and Thring of Uppingham.

The building of schools by the government itself came only late in the nineteenth century partly because of the activities of the voluntary societies—the National and British Societies, aided after 1833 by government grants—and partly through the existence of religious and political objections to the principle of state-provided education. In the later nineteenth century there was a growing sense of the inadequacy of the English system. The extension of the franchise and the consequence that "we must now educate our masters," the pressure of trade unions, the growing needs of industry, commerce, professions, and public administration for personnel with a certain minimum of education, the belief that mounting foreign competition, especially that from Germany, was based upon superior education—all contributed to a feeling that reform and expansion were needed.

Thus, from the Act of 1870, a series of measures raised the minimum school-leaving age, and in 1891 abolished fees in state schools. The 1890s saw a rapid growth of technical colleges, and in 1902 the principle of direct state support was formally extended to secondary education, while administrative reorganization placed the responsibility for secondary and higher education upon the county councils created in 1888. The Fisher Act of 1918 marked a further advance by raising the school-leaving age to fourteen, and abolished the part-time system under which children over eleven had been allowed to spend half the day in school and the other half at work.

Between the wars, the agitation of the Labour Party for "secondary education for all" was widely heard. In 1926 the Hadow Committee supported the view that the inadequacy of secondary education was resulting in human wastage and loss to the nation of unexploited talent among the working classes. The government followed up this lead and encouraged local authorities to go further in providing separate secondary schools or classes for children over eleven who had not won places through the "scholarship" system in grammar and technical schools. By 1938 this "Hadow reorganization" encompassed some 60 percent of children of secondary age, and secondary education for all finally became a reality with the great Butler Act of 1944.

America Despite the abundance of natural resources and rapid industrialization, serious social deficiencies, including widespread poverty, existed both in the countryside and in the towns of America. It has been estimated that in 1890 some 11 million of the total of 12½ million families received an average annual income of only $380. The enormous material progress made in industry and agriculture, the rise of great industrial and commercial centres, and the march to success and vast personal wealth of such figures as Carnegie and Rockefeller, created a sense of complacency which obscured the true social facts. Carnegie even denied the very existence of pauperism in America (despite the existence of such a classification in the federal census), and academic exponents of *laissez-faire* philosophies claimed that no evidence of distress or misery had been produced by the pessimists.

Just as these opinions appeared, radical thought and literature, concerned since the Civil War with such varied questions as feminism, temperance, Negro rights, labour claims, land reform, currency, and civil service and city government reform, burst forth into its great period of "Progressivism" (circa 1890–1917). The dominant theme of this period was hatred of corporate wealth and power, and it was marked by "muckraking" attacks on the great corporations such as Standard Oil, the meat-packing industry, and wheat speculation.[7] But a good deal of attention was directed also towards poverty and social conditions.

The first attempt to survey the problem of poverty comprehensively and systematically was made by Robert Hunter in 1904. He deplored the lack of reliable statistics for the problem in the United States, and referred to the pioneer work of Booth and Rowntree in England. However, he was able to draw on a variety of sources to produce the following broad survey of the problem:

> There are probably in fairly prosperous years no less than 10,000,000 persons in poverty; that is to say, un-

derfed, underclothed, and poorly housed. Of these
about 4,000,000 persons are public paupers. Over
2,000,000 working-men are unemployed for four to
six months in the year. About 500,000 male immigrants arrive yearly and seek work in the very districts where unemployment is greatest. Nearly half
of the families in the country are propertyless. Over
1,700,000 little children are forced to become wage-
earners when they should still be in school. About
5,000,000 women find it necessary to work and about
2,000,000 are employed in factories, mills, etc. Probably no less than 1,000,000 workers are injured or
killed each year while doing their work, and about
10,000,000 of the persons now living will, if the present ratio is kept up, die of the preventible disease,
tuberculosis.

The causes of poverty were much the same as Booth
and Rowntree found in England: lowness of wages, unemployment, and irregularity of earnings, death, injury
or sickness of the wage-earner, and misspending of income
on drink and other non-essentials. As in England, poverty
was concentrated among the mass of unskilled workers,
most of whom earned, Hunter believed, less than the $460
a year (or $300 in the South) estimated as the minimum
necessary to support a family of two adults and three
children.[8]

The central problem of reform, as pinpointed by
Hunter and many others, was that of getting effective
legislation passed and enforced against the apathy of the
majority, with their predilection for state rights, and
against also the active opposition of the influential minority of property owners and businessmen. The railroads
each year might kill over 2,500 employees and maim
nearly 40,000 more (the figures for 1900), the anthracite
mines of Pennsylvania might employ children of eight or
nine upwards to work ten hours a day picking slate out
of coal in the "breakers," slum tenements in New York
City might kill off whole families with tuberculosis—but

property rights and profits must be respected. Existing legislation was difficult to enforce, and in any case touched only the fringe of the problem. Hunter estimated that the official poor—the public paupers in receipt of institutional care (often provided as in England, in an old mixed poorhouse), or receiving outdoor relief of meagre doles of money or goods—represented only two-fifths or less of the total in poverty. In New York City the newly created Board of Health passed a series of laws on tenement houses from 1867. But these laws applied only to new buildings, and so ensured that the old buildings, with their lower rents, remained grossly overcrowded and insanitary while making for their owners an annual profit of 40 percent.[9]

Misgovernment of the cities sprang from the view that politics, as also social institutions, should be subservient to business; that politics and administration were fields for those men with insufficient talent to succeed in business; and that, as Lincoln Steffens said, it was thought "natural, inevitable, and—possibly—right that business should be—by bribery, corruption, or—somehow get and be the government."[10] The city "boss" controlled the slum districts where he had large property interests. In return for votes he dispensed patronage, city jobs, reduced court sentences, railroad passes, admission to hospitals. In some cities the policeman did not dare to enter places which he knew violated the law; his superior took orders from the boss, as did the mayor also. The practice of electing important city officials, and the division of powers among mayor, department heads, aldermen, councillors, and magistrates created confusion, irresponsibility, and administrative incompetence. The low salaries paid to municipal officials and civil servants attracted an inferior class of worker and encouraged corruption and the taking of bribes. In this situation the voting power of the mass of poor was nullified, and reformers were seldom elected;

or if elected, they found it almost impossible to achieve progress or to maintain it when achieved.

By the Constitution the reform of social conditions was the province of the states and cities, and this necessarily meant that the growth of effective legislation was gradual and piecemeal, while evasion was made easy. Children could be sent across state boundaries to work (as from New York to New Jersey) and thus escape control in either state, putting-out work could be sent to states which lacked restrictions on home employment, and the greatest field of child employment—farming—was almost entirely unregulated. Lack of federal control meant also that businessmen could threaten to transfer their concerns to other cities or states if labour legislation was passed, while reformers had to meet the power of the city bosses and overcome the apathy of the state legislatures, in which the rural areas were overrepresented.

The progressives were drawn principally from the middle class; as in England, it was mainly the educated and intelligent man and woman of professional status or independent means who developed a strong social conscience. Uncommitted to business or politics, and free of dogma that nothing should stand in the way of profits and property rights, this group of writers, university professors, teachers, ministers, and leisured women had the time and resources to become amateur social investigators, reformers, and propagandists. "Between 1897 and 1914 Progressive societies multiplied rapidly in number and membership. Child Labour Committees, Consumer's Leagues, charities' aid societies, church organizations, and women's clubs appeared in all our industrial cities and states and formed national associations with branches everywhere. They employed professional social workers, secretaries, treasurers and sent trained lobbies to state capitals and to Washington. They sent practical lecturers to address groups all over the country, published their own periodicals, and competed successfully for space in popular journals."[11]

The principal concern of these Progressive societies was the plight of the 2 million children revealed by the census of 1900 as employed in wage-earning occupations. A typical Progressive publication of 1914 castigated the human cost in terms of physical suffering, mental stunting, early deaths and deformity, that this figure implied. It stated that one in every seven children between the ages of ten and fourteen was not at school, and pointed to child employment as a major factor in the existence in America of 6 million illiterates.[12]

In England the history of effective factory legislation had begun with the Act of 1833 which appointed inspectors to enforce the law that no children under nine should be employed in textile mills, and that children under thirteen should work no more than nine hours a day. Subsequent acts in 1844 and 1847 extended the law to women and also governed the use of dangerous machinery, and after 1842 no women or children could be employed underground in coal mines. In 1867 all factories were brought within the pale, and subsequent legislation further widened the scope of the law, provided for workmen's compensation for accidents (ineffectively in 1880, and effectively in the Acts of 1896 and 1906), and eventually brought control to the workshops of the sweated trades—the surviving domestic industries—in the Trade Boards Act of 1909. Even more important than the Factory Acts in restricting child employment were the provisions for compulsory school education in the Education Acts from 1870 onwards.

In America the introduction of effective factory legislation came much later, partly because the factory system itself developed rather later than in England (and in the South very much later), and partly because the size and nature of the problem were not realized until about the beginning of the twentieth century. By then twenty-eight northern states had some kind of child labour laws, but none of these laws was adequate in scope or was fully enforceable. In the early years of the new century, however, Progressive Child Labour Committees made rapid progress. New laws, or amendments to old ones, extended regulations to children employed in non-factory occupations such as newsboys, bootblacks, pedlars, and messengers, and included such measures as compulsory education, a maximum eight-hour day, prohibition of night work. By the time of the First World War, legislation in many states had extended also to women, and covered public health, workmen's compensation, minimum wages, and tenements—and in some states there were special provisions for enforcement.

In the years between the opening of the new century and the First World War the Progressives also made some important gains in the sphere of national legislation. True, much of the legislation was merely nominal and was largely ineffective, such as the first Pure Food and Drug Act of 1906. Under Theodore Roosevelt and Taft, Republican administrations learned to make concessions that kept the Progressives at bay and removed some of their impetus while maintaining intact the privileged position of the large corporations. Some of the concessions, however, were of enormous importance for the future—the eight-hour day for federal employees, establishment of the Bureau of Mines to supervise safety and working conditions, the Children's Bureau, the Labour Department, and last but perhaps most important the income tax, submitted to the voters in 1909 and finally achieved in 1913. Between 1902 and 1913 total federal, state, and local government expenditure on education more than doubled, and education and public welfare together accounted for a fifth of total government spending in 1913.

Some progress thus was made, but much remained to be done. New laws were one thing, enforcement was another. The main causes of poverty—low wages, unemployment, industrial accidents, unhealthy living and working conditions—remained largely untouched. Further, the opposition of businessmen was growing and was becoming organized. Some Progressives gave up the struggle, others turned to socialism or regulation of the trusts. Then the First World War took priority of interests and energies. After the war the movement took another form. Instead of trying to enforce increasingly detailed legislation, the leading states developed new agencies, industrial commissions, whose function was to set up and maintain general standards, originally in the fields of health and safety but in time extending to the whole gamut of factory regulation. Progress was very uneven, however: in 1925 twelve states still allowed children under sixteen to work for over forty-eight hours and up to sixty hours a week, and thirteen states allowed boys of fourteen to work in mines; child labour in agriculture was still largely unregulated. Over the whole country nearly 400,000 children aged ten to thirteen—probably an underestimate—were at work in 1920.[13]

It was the great slump of the 1930s, and the New Deal programme arising out of those years, that gave social reform a new impetus and a changed direction. The sense of economic crisis that followed the Stock Exchange Crash of 1929, the appearance of mass unemployment, the bank failures that destroyed the savings of years, the street beggars and the soup-kitchen lines convinced many Americans that "rugged individualism" was a myth and that the individual workman and his family were helpless in the face of this economic blizzard of unprecedented severity. Hoover's view, echoed by many conservatives, that poverty was due to individual failing, and that "some folk won't work," was no longer tenable. Only massive intervention by the federal government could provide the security that the economic system had so signally failed to provide.

For political and practical reasons the federal intervention was necessarily piecemeal and mainly directed along already established lines. The Fair Labour Standards Act of 1938 set minimum standards for all labour engaged in inter-state commerce or in the production of goods for such commerce, and eventually covered some 13 million workers. The act authorized the introduction of a maximum working week of forty hours and a minimum wage of forty cents an hour, and it also prohibited the employment of children. The measure represented the logical federal capping of earlier measures in the individual states, and followed on the creation of employment exchanges (1933), the regulation of railroad workers' pensions (1934), and control of working conditions of labour engaged on public contracts (1936). Similarly, the Social Security Act of 1935 represented a federal generalization of the limited measures introduced in some states to provide old-age pensions, and the solitary example of unemployment insurance (Wisconsin).

The federal intervention of 1935 was designed to *encourage* state provision of social security, not to enforce it. There were in fact two schemes for providing help for the old. Where the state participated, the federal government met half the cost of paying pensions to needy persons over sixty-five, and enabled workers, through graduated contributions paid partly by themselves and partly by the employers, to participate in pension schemes; under the second scheme, however, all workers earning less than $3,000 a year in 1935 (with the important exception of those in certain large occupations such as agriculture and domestic service), were compelled to join a federally-financed programme under which pensions proportionate to earnings at retirement were paid from 1942 onwards. For security against unemployment, where the individual states had adequate unemployment insurance schemes, 90 percent of a federal payroll tax on employers was handed over to the state to support them. Finally, the states were given annual appropriations to provide relief for dependent children, support maternity and child welfare schemes, and give aid for crippled children, the blind, and for vocational retraining. Further, under the New Deal's work-providing programmes, thousands of miles of roads were built, together with bridges and sewers, many airports, and thousands of public buildings, parks, playgrounds, reservoirs, and power plants. Low-cost housing and slum clearance under the U.S. Housing Authority of 1937 was another offshoot of the attempts to provide jobs, but in this case the opposition of private real-estate interests restricted the new housing to very small proportions.

In contrast to Britain, the development of social reform and welfare legislation came late and piecemeal. In 1939 the measures in force and the actual achievement still varied widely from state to state. In part this diversity sprang from the size and diversity of the economy itself; in part it sprang from the existence of the federal system and the predominant belief in the sanctity of state rights —a sentiment which often provided an excuse and cloak for the maintenance undisturbed of vested interests concerned to preserve private enterprise, low taxes, and a provincial obscurantism on social matters. The rapid growth in the United States of agriculture, industry, and commerce had made the country populous and wealthy, but the dominance in politics and the national consciousness of business and its interests often proved a great obstacle to progress in providing social security and justice.

In the development of education, for example, the influence of business and practical needs were particularly marked. Scientific schools or technical institutions were established in connection with Yale, Harvard, and other colleges as early as the 1840s, while from the 1820s, Mechanics Institutes were opened in the major cities. Elementary education before the Civil War, however, was often weak or nonexistent in parts of the country, particularly in the South, although the New England states required young workers under fourteen or fifteen to spend some three months a year at school. From 1862 the Morrill Land-Grant Act provided the newly-established Western states with means to found agricultural colleges, following the lead set by Michigan in 1857. And in 1890, the second Morrill Act provided Federal grants to enable the new colleges to expand in size and raise their standards. A number of these land-grant agricultural colleges grew into great state universities of international reputation. But the importance attached to agricultural education remained strong, and was seen in Acts of 1914 and 1917 which provided federal aid for farm demonstration work and agricultural education.

After the Civil War, elementary education still suffered, as in England, from poor school attendance, an inadequate supply of school places and of teachers in some areas, and a restricted view on the part of parents and school authorities of the scope and value of education. As the school system developed there was a marked tendency for teaching and curricula to reflect the ideals and interests of the business community.

> New Englanders sought almost from the start to impose the ideals of Eastern cities upon the merchants and farmers of the West. After the Civil War similar intentions dominated urban educators in relation not only to farmers but also to city workers. Standard textbooks, written to a large extent by people associated with city schools and distributed by publishing houses in New York, Boston, and Philadelphia were bound to convey urban mores and business ideas, and it early became a matter of policy for educational agencies to see that contrary ideas were shut out.... Business led the drive in the late nineteenth

century for the training of skilled artisans and mechanics in the public schools and at the public expense. The objective was education for industrial
efficiency.[14]

The trend continued between the wars when the business leaders, supported by the middle classes, sought to
eliminate radical ideas and make "socialism" and "communism" dirty words. Community pressure and direct
intimidation were employed to make recalcitrant teachers
toe the conventional mark. But more important, textbooks
were written in accordance with business ideas, or cor-
rected to get these ideas across. Whole courses, especially
in government and civics, were introduced to preach the
business gospel, while business publications themselves
were used in many schools.[15]

Meanwhile, the numbers in school and college rose,
although the levels of attainment were still often unsatisfactory. While by 1920 the majority of northern states required children leaving school to have reached at least
the sixth grade (nine states specified the eighth grade),
in the South a definite leaving standard (usually the fifth
grade or "proficiency in specified subjects") was laid down
in only seven states. In all, thirty-five states allowed children to go to work without a common school education,
and eleven states discounted the opportunity of further
education by permitting children under sixteen to work
from nine to eleven hours a day. School attendance remained poor: in 1920 the average number of days attended
by each pupil under eighteen years of age was less than
100 in twenty-five states, and the annual expenditure per
pupil attending school was below $50 in fourteen states,
all in the South. In twenty-two states with large rural, Negro, or immigrant populations (fifteen of them in the
South), the proportion of illiterates among persons of ten
years and over was more than 5 percent. The proportion

of total government spending devoted to education was about 18 percent in 1913 and in the 1920s, but fell below this level in the 1930s.

Many Americans believed they were right in placing the creation of wealth before the security and welfare of the under-privileged, and the high living standards of the middle classes seemed to some to justify this view. But there remained, and remains, at the base of American society a large body of people badly educated, very poor by the standards of the affluent part of the nation, and basically insecure—lacking the certainty of adequate relief in time of unemployment, ill-health, accident, and old age. Nevertheless, the New Deal measures did provide the foundation for future progress. And the wealth of the country, and the income and special security taxes, as in England, provide the financial means for the more just society which both countries are still in the process of creating.

CONCLUSION

Social reform and the development of a "welfare state" in Britain came gradually: severely limited early reforms paved the way to the broader measures of later years. There was little or no conscious planning, but rather the adoption of *ad hoc* measures to meet particular problems as they became urgent. The impetus to reform came from a variety of directions—the stirring of the social conscience by middle-class investigators and propagandists like Booth, Rowntree, and the Fabians; the socialist and labour movements, made politically powerful by extension of the franchise and the organization of unskilled workers; the example provided by reform overseas, particularly in Germany; and the appreciation of social inadequacy revealed by the Boer War and the First World War. Progress in reform depended ultimately on the growth of a favourable public opinion, the acceptance of higher levels of taxation (here the First World War had an important influence), rising national wealth, and administrative reforms in the civil service and local government.

The American experience showed many of the same factors, but there were important differences. The stimulus again came from middle-class Progressives and overseas example, in this case the example of Europe, particularly Britain; administrative reform and the income tax were also significant. On the other hand, the movement began later, and without the assistance of an American Booth, Rowntree, or even a Chadwick; the socialist and labour movements were smaller and relatively without influence; wars had a more limited effect. A favourable public opinion was much slower to develop, partly because of the primacy of business interests in American education and politics, and the cherished belief in "rugged individualism." Great and persistent obstacles were placed in the path of reform by corruption in the cities and by the constitutional entrenchment and public reverence for states rights; this meant in effect the preservation of large areas of low standards, and limited and ineffective measures. While Progressive states, such as Wisconsin, led the reform movement, federal intervention, begun in the Progressive era before the First World War, and greatly extended by the New Deal of the 1930s, proved necessary to bring in the laggards, and so meet the problems of the poor and neglected in the wealthiest country in the world.

NOTES

1. Particularly was this so among nonconformist groups in the movement for the emancipation of women, and in educational reform. See F. Thistlethwaite, *America and the Atlantic Community* (New York, 1963), ch. 3–5.

2. See for example, *Palace and Hovel* by Daniel J. Kirwan (A. Allan, ed., 1963), especially ch. 21–5.

3. Curti, Merle, *The Making of an American Community: a case study of democracy in a frontier setting* (Stanford, 1959).

4. Chevalier, M., *Society Manners, and Politics in the United States* (1839; New York, Anchor Books, 1961), pp. 267–70.

5. See Long, Clarence D., *Wages and Earnings in the United States* 1860–1890 (Princeton, 1960), p. 61, and Rees, Albert, *Real Wages in Manufacturing* 1890–1914 (Princeton, 1961), p. 120.

6. Recently re-issued with an introduction by M. W. Flinn (Edinburgh U.P., 1965).

7. See for example Tarbell, Ida M., *History of the Standard Oil Company* (New York, 1904), Sinclair, Upton, *The Jungle* (1906), Norris, Frank, *The Octopus* (1901), and *The Pit* (1903).

8. Hunter, Robert, *Poverty* (1904), pp. 52–3, 327.

9. Ford, James, *Slums and Housing* (Harvard, 1936) I, p. 166.

10. Steffens, Lincoln, *The Autobiography of Lincoln Steffens* (1931), II, p. 606.

11. Cochran, Thomas C. and Miller, William, *The Age of Enterprise* (New York, 1961), pp. 276–7.

12. Markham, E., Lindsey, B. B., and Creel, G., *Children in Bondage* (New York, 1914), p. 306.

13. National Industrial Conference Board, *The Employment of Young Persons in the United States* (New York, 1925), pp. viii, 6, 64.

14. Cochran and Miller, op. cit., pp. 270–1.

15. Ibid., pp. 332, 338.

Suggested Reading

GENERAL

Allen, H. C. *Great Britain and the United States* (New York, 1955)
———. *Conflict and Concord* (New York, 1960)
Beloff, Max. *The United States and the Unity of Europe* (Washington, 1963)
Brock, William R. *The Character of American History* (New York, 1965)
Brogan, D. W. *American Themes* (New York, 1949)
———. *America in the Modern World* (New Brunswick, N.J., 1960)
———. *American Aspects* (New York, 1964)
Jenkins, Roy. *Afternoon on the Potomac* (New Haven, Conn., 1972)
Thistlethwaite, Frank. *America and the Atlantic Community* (New York, 1963)

SPECIAL STUDIES

Allen, H. C. *The Anglo-American Predicament; The British Commonwealth, the United States, and European Unity* (New York, 1960)

_____. *Bush and Backwoods; A Comparison of the Frontier in Australia and the United States* (E. Lansing, Mich., 1959)

Bagwell, Philip S. and Mingay, G. E. *Britain and America: A Study of Economic Change 1850–1939* (London 1970)

Beloff, Max. *Thomas Jefferson and American Democracy* (New York, 1962)

Bellot, H. Hale. *American History and American Historians* (Norman, Okla., 1952)

Bolt, Christine. *The Anti-Slavery Movement and Reconstruction: A Study in Anglo-American Cooperation* (London and New York, 1969)

Boston, Ray. *British Chartists in America* (Manchester, 1971)

Brock, William R. *An American Crisis: Congress and Reconstruction 1865–1867* (New York, 1963)

_____. *Conflict and Transformation, The United States 1841–1877* (Baltimore, 1973)

Brogan, D. W. *The Era of Franklin D. Roosevelt* (New Haven, 1950)

_____. *Abraham Lincoln* (New York, 1963)

Campbell, A. E. *Great Britain and the United States, 1895–1903* (London, 1960)

_____. *America Comes of Age, The Era of Theodore Roosevelt* (London, 1971)

Charnwood, Lord. *Theodore Roosevelt* (Boston, 1923)

Collier, Basil. *The Lion and the Eagle, British and Anglo-American Strategy, 1900–1950* (London, 1972)

Cunliffe, Marcus. *George Washington, Man and Monument* (Boston, 1958)

_____. *The Nation Takes Shape, 1789–1837* (Chicago, 1960)

_____. *Soldiers and Civilians, The Martial Spirit in America, 1775–1865* (Boston, 1968)

Devlin, Lord. *Too Proud to Fight Woodrow Wilson's Neutrality* (London, 1974)

Donoughue, Bernard. *British Politics and the American Revolution: The Path of War, 1773–1775* (London, 1964)

Ellison, Mary. *Support for Secession, Lancashire and the American Civil War* (Chicago, 1972)

———. *The Black Experience American Blacks Since 1865* (London, 1974)

Erickson, Charlotte. *American Industry and the European Immigrant, 1860–1885* (New York, 1957)

———. *Invisible Immigrants* (Coral Gables, Florida, 1972)

Haffendon, Philip S. *New England in the English Nation, 1689–1713* (London, 1974)

Hawgood, John A. *The Tragedy of German-America: the Germans in the United States of America during the Nineteenth Century* (New York and London, 1940)

———. *America's Western Frontier* (New York, 1967)

Jones, Maldwyn A. *American Immigration* (Chicago, 1960)

Lloyd, Alan, *The Scorching of Washington, The War of 1812* (New York, 1975)

MacLeod, Duncan J. *Slavery, Race and the American Revolution* (New York, 1975)

Morgan, David. *Suffragists and Democrats: The Politics of Women Suffrage in America* (E. Lansing, Mich., 1971)

Nicholas, Herbert G. *Britain and the U.S.A.* (Baltimore, 1963)

Nicholas, H. G. *The United States and Britain* (Chicago, 1975)

Nunnerly, David. *President Kennedy and Britain* (London, 1972)

Olson, A. G. *Anglo-American Politics, 1660–1775, The*

Relationship Between Parties in England and Colonial America (London, 1973)

Parish, Peter J. *The American Civil War* (New York, 1975)

Pelling, Henry. *America and the British Left: From Bright to Bevan* (New York, 1957)

Pole, J. R. *Political Representation in England and the Origins of the American Republic* (London, 1966)

————. *Foundations of American Independence, 1763–1815* (Indianapolis, Ind., 1972)

Taylor, Philip. *Expectations Westward: The Mormons and the Immigration of Their British Converts* (Ithaca, N.Y., 1966)

————. *The Distant Magnet* (London, 1971)

Thistlethwaite, Frank. *The Great Experiment* (Cambridge, 1955)

————. *The Anglo-American Connection in the Early Nineteenth Century* (Philadelphia, 1959)

Thompson, Roger. *Women in Stuart England and America: A Comparative Study* (London, 1974)

Vale, Vivian. *Labour in American Politics* (New York, 1971)

Walsh, Margaret. *The Manufacturing Frontier, Pioneer Industry in Ante-bellum Wisconsin, 1830–1860* (Madison, Wisc., 1972)

Wright, Esmond. *The Fabric of Freedom, 1763–1800* (New York, 1961)

————. *Washington and the American Revolution* (New York, 1962)

————. *Benjamin Franklin and American Independence* (London, 1966)